George Barnett Smith

Poets and Novelists

George Barnett Smith

Poets and Novelists

ISBN/EAN: 9783337051211

Printed in Europe, USA, Canada, Australia, Japan

Cover: Foto ©Thomas Meinert / pixelio.de

More available books at **www.hansebooks.com**

POETS AND NOVELISTS

A SERIES OF LITERARY STUDIES

BY

GEORGE BARNETT SMITH

NEW YORK

D. APPLETON & CO., BROADWAY

1876

I INSCRIBE THIS VOLUME

TO

ROBERT BROWNING

IN REMEMBRANCE OF HIS PERSONAL KINDNESS

AND

AS A TRIBUTE TO HIS GENIUS

G. B. S.

LONDON : 1875

PREFACE.

THE following Studies—however defective in other respects—possess some claim to exhaustiveness, and consequently I have ventured to hope that with many persons they may have a permanent value. They have been revised, and in some cases extended, from the leading Reviews and Magazines. Notwithstanding, however, the favourable reception the Essays met with on their original appearance, I might not now have collected them, and endeavoured to give to them 'a local habitation and a name,' but for the fact that I have been repeatedly pressed to do so by numerous individuals—whose tribute (in some cases, at least) I cannot but regard as flattering —who were desirous of possessing them in a volume. I can only trust that the public and the press will now endorse their verdict. The subjects of the papers, however imperfectly treated, are amongst the most attractive which can be named for lovers of books. With regard to the Essay on Thomas Love Peacock, I may be pardoned for claiming that it was the first full and substantial recognition of his genius; since it appeared, an admirable edition of his works has been issued, and I am glad that this really remarkable writer has received a much fuller attention than he enjoyed during his lifetime, and even down to the last two or three years. As for the volume generally, my end will have been answered if it should in any appreciable degree strengthen the taste for our noble English Literature.

G. B. S.

CONTENTS.

LLIAM MAKEPEACE THACKERAY

[EDINBURGH REVIEW]

B

THE pure humourist is one of the rarest of literary characters. His nature is not content with detecting foibles, nor his pen with pointing them out for derision; his purpose is infinitely higher and nobler. The humourist must have emotions, nerves, sensibilities, and that marvellous sympathy with human nature which enables him to change places at will with other members of his species. Humour does not produce the sneer of Voltaire; it rather smiles through the tear of Montaigne. 'True humour,' it has been wisely said, 'springs not more from the head than from the heart; it is not contempt, its essence is love; it issues not in laughter, but in still smiles, which lie far deeper. It is a sort of inverse sublimity; exalting as it were into our affections what is below us, while sublimity draws down into our affections what is above us. It is, in fact, the bloom and perfume, the purest effluence of a deep, fine, and loving nature.' Without humour, society would exist in Ice-

landic snows : wit, like the winter sun, might glint upon
the icebergs, but they would not be plastic in its glance
—calm, lofty, and cold they must remain.   But humour
is the summer heat that generates while it smiles—the
power which touches dead things and revivifies them
with its generous warmth and geniality.   Wit engages
and amuses the individual intellect ; humour knits hearts
together ; is, in truth, in a broad sense, that ' touch of
nature which makes the whole world kin.'   Now the
world may be regarded as being composed of three
classes, viz., those of us who laugh, those *with* whom we
laugh, and those *at* whom we laugh ; and the tenderest
solicitude is experienced by each unit of humanity lest,
through some fortuitous circumstances, he should irre-
trievably find himself a denizen of the last-named class.
To some of the first class is given the power of directing
the laugh of others, and this power is current as wit ;
when to the faculty of originating ridicule is added the
power of concentrating pity or pathos upon the subject,
this may be styled humour.   But the irony must be
subjugated to the feeling.   The heart must love while
the countenance may smile.   It will, then, be perceived,
in view of these distinctions, how the humourist may
assert a claim in all great and essential things superior
to that which can be advanced by the wit.   Humourists

are the salt of the national intellectual life. England, who occasionally claims a questionable superiority in some respects over other nations, may, in the growth of genuine humour, be allowed the pre-eminence, Germany approaching her perhaps in the nearest degree. What other literature, since the days of Elizabeth, can show such a roll of humourists as that which is inscribed with the names (amongst others) of Richardson, Addison, Steele, Prior, Gay, Smollett, Fielding, Sterne, and Goldsmith? Yet after the closing names of this galaxy a dearth was witnessed like that which immediately preceded their advent. It appears as though the soil of literature, having grown to its utmost capacity the product of humour, demanded time for recuperating its powers. During the past thirty or forty years another growth sprang up, and Hood, Lamb, and other inheritors of the marvellous gift have enriched the world with the perfume of their lives and works. Amongst the latest band of humourists, however, there is no name more remarkable or more justly distinguished than that which is now under consideration.

From the operation of various causes, the works of Thackeray have not hitherto enjoyed a circulation commensurate with their intrinsic merits. The sale of the best of his writings in his lifetime fell far short of the popular demand for the works of Scott or Dickens. But their hold on society, and the recognition of their permanent value and excellence, have gone on steadily increasing with each succeeding year, and very recently new and complete editions of them have been issued, which are within the reach of all readers. At this period, then, it may be fitting to consider the life's work of this deepest and purest of modern English satirists.

It was in these pages that the first substantial recognition of the genius of the author of 'Vanity Fair' appeared: a quarter of a century has elapsed since then; but in the short period between that epoch in his career and his death, a series of brilliant works issued rapidly from his pen—a pen facile to charm, to instruct, and to reprove. These works have fully justified the terms of praise in which we referred to his first great fiction. Yet it would be difficult to name a writer of fiction of equal excellence who had so little of the inventive or imaginative faculty. ·Keenness of observation and a nice appreciation of character supplied him with all the materials of his creations. He wrote from the experience of life, and the foibles of mankind which he satirised were those that had fallen under his notice in the vicissitudes of his own career, or might sometimes be traced in the recesses of his own disposition. The key, therefore, to Thackeray's works is to be found in his life; and few literary biographies would be more interesting, if it were written with a just and discriminating pen. We would venture to suggest to his accomplished daughter, who has shown by her own writings that some at least of his gifts have descended to her by inheritance, that she should undertake a task which no one else can fulfil with so natural and delicate a feeling of her father's genius. Probably it might already have been attempted, but for the extreme repugnance of Thackeray himself to allow his own person to be brought before the world, or to suffer the sanctity of private correspondence to be invaded. Nobody wrote more amusing letters; but he wrote them not for the public. As it is, even his birth and descent have not been correctly stated in the current works of the day. His great-grandfather was in the Church, once Master of Harrow, and afterwards an Archdeacon. He had seven sons, one of whom, also named William Makepeace Thackeray, entered the Civil Service of India, became a Member of Council, and sat at the Board with Warren Hastings, some of whose minutes he signed. The son of this gentleman, and the father of our novelist, was Richmond Thackeray, also a Civil servant, who died, in 1816, at the early age of thirty. Thackeray himself was born at Calcutta, in 1811, and

was sent to England when he was seven years old. On
the voyage home the vessel touched at St. Helena, where
the child saw Napoleon Bonaparte. The black servant
who attended him attributed to the ex-Emperor the most
ravenous propensities. ' He eats,' said the sable exagge-
rator, ' three sheep every day, and all the children he can
lay hands on.' The joke figured years afterwards in one
of Thackeray's sketches. This early connection with
India left its mark in his memory, and the pleasant allusions to the great Ramchunder and the Bundelcund Bank
were suggested by the traditions of his own infancy. He
inherited from his father (who died when he was five
years old) a considerable fortune, part of which had
fortunately been settled on his mother, who was re-
married to Major Carmichael Smyth. The remainder
was left at his own disposal, and rendered him an object
of envy and admiration to his less fortunate contemporaries. The boy was sent to the Charter House, where
he remained for some years ; and here again the reader
familiar with his works may trace a multitude of allusions
to his school-days under Dr. Russell, then the master of
that school. About the year 1828 he went up to Trinity
College, Cambridge, where he was the friend and contemporary of Tennyson, Venables, John Mitchell Kem-
ble, Charles and Arthur Buller, John Sterling, R. Monck-

ton Milnes, and of that distinguished set of men, some of whom had preceded him by a year or two, who formed what was called the Society of the Apostles, though he was not himself a member of that society. It must be confessed that at Cambridge Thackeray gave no signs of distinguished ability. He was chiefly known for his inexhaustible drollery, his love of repartee, and for his humourous command of the pencil. But his habits were too desultory for him to enter the lists of academic competition, and, like Arthur Pendennis, he left the University without taking a degree. At the age of twenty-one he entered upon London life ; he visited Weimar, which he afterwards portrayed as the Court of Pumpernickel ; and he was frequently in Paris, where his mother resided since her second marriage. His fortune and position in society seemed to permit him to indulge his tastes and to live as a gentleman at large. But the dream was of short duration. Within a few months he contracted a sleeping partnership which placed his property in the hands of a man who turned out to be insolvent, and the fortune he relied on was lost before he had enjoyed it. The act was one of gross imprudence, no doubt, and he suffered bitterly for it ; but it is not true, as has sometimes been supposed, from his lively description of scenes of folly and vice, that he lost his money by his own per-

sonal extravagance. Thus, then, he found himself, at two
or three and twenty, with very reduced means, for he
had nothing to live on but the allowance his mother and
grandmother were able to make him ; with no profession,
with desultory tastes and habits, and with no definite
prospects in life before him. His first scheme was to
turn artist and to cultivate painting in the Louvre, for he
now resided chiefly with his relatives in Paris. But in
the art of design he was, in truth, no more than an accomplished amateur. The drawings with which he afterwards illustrated his own books are full of expression,
humour, grace, and feeling; but they want the correct-
ness and mastery of the well-trained artist. He turned
then, with more hope, at the age of thirty, to the resources
of the pen. But it is remarkable that all his literary productions of this, his earlier period, were anonymous ; and
his literary efforts, though not wanting in pungency and
an admirable style, were scattered in multifarious publi-
cations, and procured for him but small profit and no
fame. These years, from thirty to seven-and-thirty,
which ought to have been the brightest, were the most
cheerless of his existence. He wrote letters in the
'Times' under the signature of Manlius Pennialinus.
He wrote an article on Lord Brougham in the 'British
and Foreign Review,' which excited attention. But po-

litical writing—even political sarcasm—was not his forte; and when politics ceased to be a joke, they became to him a bore. Amongst other experiments he accepted the editorship of a London daily newspaper, called 'The Constitutional and Public Ledger,' but—like its namesake, which had been started and edited, a few years before, by another man of great literary genius, destined to achieve in after-life a more illustrious career—this journal lingered for ten months and then expired. The foundation of 'Punch' was a work after Thackeray's own heart, and he contributed largely to the earlier numbers. But it was not till 1841 that he really began to make his mark in literature, under the well-known pseudonym of Michael Angelo Titmarsh, a name in which the dream of the artist still haunted the fancy of the humourist. In the midst of his perplexities, with that genuine tenderness of feeling which lay at the bottom of all his sarcasms, Thackeray fell in love, and married a young lady who might have sat for the portrait of his own Amelia, but who was not better endowed than himself with the world's goods, and much less able than himself to battle with adverse fortune. But his domestic life was overclouded by a greater calamity than these, and the malady of his wife threw a permanent shadow over the best affections of his heart, which were thenceforward devoted to his children alone.   Such was the school in which the genius of Thackeray was educated.   It was not imaginative ; it was not spontaneous ; it was the result of a hard and varied experience of life and the world.   It left him somewhat prone to exaggerate the follies and baseness of mankind, but it never froze or extinguished his love and sympathy for justice, tenderness, and truth.   In 1847, when he was six-and-thirty years of age, he braced himself up, for the first time, for a great and continuous literary effort, and he came before the world, which hitherto had known him only as a writer of jests and magazine articles, as the author of 'Vanity Fair.'   His style, which was the result of the most careful and fastidious study, had now attained a high degree of perfection.   In the comparison which was naturally drawn between himself and Dickens, then in the heyday of popularity, it was obvious that in the command of the English language Thackeray was incomparably the master. His style was to the style of Dickens what marble is to clay ; and although he never attained to the successful vogue of his contemporary, in his lifetime, it was evident to the critical eye that the writings of Thackeray had in them that which no time could dim or obliterate.

With this novel, then, so surprising in its frankness and in its knowledge of human nature, commenced a career which could know no repression. A mine of gold had been struck, and the nuggets were cast up freely by the hands of the hard and honest worker. In the writing of books admired by every hater of pretence, and the delivery of lectures which were as new in their style and treatment as his novels, the rest of the life of Thackeray passed away. The last fifteen years of it were years of success, celebrity, and comparative affluence. He had attained a commanding position in literature and in society, though it must be acknowledged that except in a very small circle of intimate friends, he rarely put forth any brilliant social qualities. How he impaled snobbery in 'Punch' and gave a new impetus to serial literature by his editorship of the 'Cornhill Magazine,' are facts too widely disseminated to be dilated upon. A most good-natured editor, conscientious as well as kind, was Thackeray; but the work was not to his taste, and after a short period he relinquished it at a large pecuniary sacrifice. To that terrible person, the owner of a 're-jected contribution,' he was frequently most generous, breaking the literary disappointment with the solace of a bank-note in many instances. But finding it painfully difficult to say 'No' when it became imperative to reject would-be contributors, he fled from the field in despair. To a friend he said on one occasion, 'How can I go into society with comfort? I dined the other day at ——'s, and at the table were four gentlemen whose masterpieces of literary art I had been compelled to decline with thanks.' So he informed his readers for the last time that he would 'not be responsible for rejected communications.' On Christmas Eve, 1863, came the event which touched the heart of Britain with a genuine grief. The not altogether uneventful career of one of the truest and best of men was closed. When it was known that the author of ' Vanity Fair' would charm the world no longer by his truthful pictures of English life, the grief was what we would always have it be when a leader of the people in war, arts, or letters is stricken down in the strife—deep, general, and sincere.

Postponing for the moment a consideration of what we conceive to be the leading characteristics of Thackeray's genius, a certain measure of insight into the author's mind may be gained by a glance at his works— premising that they are not taken in strict chronological order. First, with regard to his more important novels. The key with which he opened the door of fame was undoubtedly ' Vanity Fair.' Though other writings of a less ambitious nature had previously come from his pen, until the production of this book there was no evidence that Thackeray would ever assume the high position in

letters now unanimously awarded to him. But here, at
any rate, was demonstrative proof that a new star had
arisen. And yet, general as was this belief, no intelligible
grounds were for a time assigned for it. The novelist
himself always regarded his first work as his best; though
we think that in this respect he has followed the example
of Milton and other celebrated authors, and chosen as
his favourite that which is not absolutely the best, though
it may be equal to any which succeeded it. Probably
the book was one round whose pages a halo had been
thrown by various personal circumstances. But the
famous yellow covers in which the 'Novel without a
Hero' originally appeared were not at first sought after
with much avidity. Soon, however, it became known
that a new delineator of life was at work in society, and
one whose pen was as keen as the dissecting knife of the
surgeon. An author had sprung up who dared to shame
society by a strong and manly scorn, and by proclaiming
that it ought to loathe itself in dust and ashes. The
world was not unwilling to read the reflection of its
weaknesses and its vices mirrored with so much wit,
originality, and genius. How account otherwise for the
favour which the work subsequently attained, when it
lacked as a novel many of those characteristics for which
novels are most eagerly read? To the initial difficulty

of a story without a hero, the writer had voluntarily added that of a lack of consecutiveness and completeness.   It was probably begun by the author not only without a hero, but without a plot.   We doubt whether any of his novels were written on a plan.   Several of them evidently turned under his pen into something quite different from what he had originally intended.   'The Virginians' completely reversed, for instance, his first conception.   But the novelist had what he considered a greater end in view than mere plot, one which has been well summed up by La Bruyère, who says :—'*Tout l'esprit d'un auteur consiste à bien définir et à bien peindre.*' This sentence concisely expresses the fulfilled genius of Thackeray.   His mode of narrative consists in a series of pictures after the manner of Hogarth, but their popularity sufficiently attested their accuracy.   There is no one character in 'Vanity Fair' which can be deemed perfectly satisfactory—not that the reader always cares for that, preferring sometimes the most thoroughpaced villainy (viewing authorship as a question of art) to the most superlative virtue.   Becky Sharp, the unprincipled governess, has been as unduly detested as Amelia Sedley has been too lavishly praised.   There is nothing in the earlier chapters to prove that Becky Sharp was naturally and entirely unprincipled and unscrupulous, and it was obviously the intention of the author to show that society might justly assume a great portion of the responsibility for the after-development of those qualities. With certain ground to work upon, and given conditions as adjuncts, the influence of society on natures like Becky Sharp's would be to encrust them with selfishness and superinduce complete hypocrisy. If heroine there be in the novel it is this clever adventuress, and except on some half-dozen occasions it is scarcely possible to avoid a pity approaching to contempt for the character of Amelia Sedley, who is intended to personify the good element an author generally casts about to discover when concocting a story. Captain Dobbin is overdrawn, and one is well-nigh tempted to wish that he had a little less virtue and a little more selfishness. While we love him he has a tendency to make us angry. The most masterly touches in the volume are those in which the portraits of the Marquis of Steyne and of Sir Pitt Crawley are sketched. The aristocracy furnish the villains and the most contemptible specimens of the race, whilst the excellent persons come from the ranks of the middle class and the poor—their namby-pambyism, however, now and then reducing their claims to our regard. The author speaks for the most part in his own person, and herein lies one of the principal reasons for the success of

c

the book. We feel the satirist at our elbow; he is not enveloped in thick folds in the distance; as we read his trenchant observations and withering sarcasms we can almost see the glances of scorn or of pity which he would assume when engaged in his task. Well might the world exclaim that this was no novice who thus wrote of its meannesses and its glory, its virtues and its vices. This novel lifted him at once into the position of one of the ablest writers of subjective fiction. It is especially remarkable in connection with 'Vanity Fair' to note the extremely little conversational matter in a tale of this great length; another proof that the strength of the author lay not in the conventional groove of the novelist, but in those other powers of Thackeray—rare observation, an acute penetration of motives, an abhorrence of sham or pretence, and an entirely new and genuine humour.

In 'Pendennis,' the next great work by Thackeray, there is not only some approach to a consecutive plot, but we are inclined to think finer drawing of individual character than in its predecessor. There is not so much brilliancy of writing, but there is a considerable advance in the art of the novelist. With all the graphic touches which took form in the features of Becky Sharp, Amelia Sedley, and Captain Dobbin, there is nothing in the

earlier work to compare with the portraits of George
Warrington, Helen Pendennis, and Laura. The hero,
Arthur, is one who succumbs to the ordinary temptations
of life, and has very little attaching to him of that romance in which a hero is generally expected to be en-
shrined. Because it was so natural the book was not
regarded at first as very successful : nothing could be
truer to the original than the manner in which Arthur
Pendennis is sketched, and his love passages with Miss
Fotheringay, the actress, are naïvely related ; but it was
of course impossible to become inspired with the same
feelings towards him as are excited by the chivalric
heroes of Scott. A man who resorts in the morning to a
bottle of soda-water to correct the exuberant spirits of
the night before is not calculated to awaken much personal adoration. He is too fallible, and the novel-reading
community demands sinless heroes and heroines ere it
consents to raise them to the lofty pedestal accorded to
its greatest favourites. There is no exaggeration in a
single portrait to be found in ' Pendennis ; ' all are true ;
are true to the minutest detail, and the author has simply
acted as the photographer to his clients—he ' nothing
extenuates or sets down aught in malice.' The early
follies of Pendennis, and his University career—which
was chiefly noticeable for splendid suppers and dealings

with money-lenders at a hundred per cent.—are described with no sparing pen. The case is typical of
thousands now, and is no credit to the youth of the
Universities. 'Only wild oats,' the apologists for under-
graduate extravagance remind us; but there is no natural
necessity that this particular University crop should be
sown; many men, worthy men too, are compelled to go
through life without the satisfaction of having ruined their
friends by their follies. The result overtook Pendennis
which righteously succeeds, or ought to succeed, to dissi-
pation and neglect of study. When the degree examinations came, ' many of his own set who had not half his
brains, but a little regularity and constancy of occupation,
took high places in the honours, or passed with decent
credit. And where in the list was Pen the superb, Pen
the wit and dandy, Pen the poet and orator? Ah, where
was Pen the widow's darling and sole pride? Let us
hide our heads and shut up the page. The lists came
out ; and a dreadful rumour rushed through the University that Pendennis of Boniface was plucked.' Yet
though he fled from the University the widow went on
loving him still, just the same, and little Laura hugged to
her heart with a secret passion the image of the young
scapegrace. So inexplicable and so devoted is the
character of woman ! The little orphan paid the debts

of the dashing, clever hero. More sketches of society with its hollowness and pretence follow this revelation, and then we find Arthur in the modern Babylon soon to become the friend of George Warrington, who was destined to be his guide, philosopher, and friend. The brains of our hero now became of service, and in dwelling on his intellectual labour Thackeray details the secret history of a literary hack, together with the story of the establishment of a newspaper for 'the gentlemen of England,' the prospectus of which was written by Captain Shandon in Fleet Prison. Brilliant indeed were the intellectual Bohemians who wrote for that witty and critical journal. There are no more interesting or amusing sketches in the whole of the author's novels than those relating to this paper, and the intimate knowledge displayed in the details of the schemes of rival printers and publishers was a part of the author's own dearly-bought experience. Arthur is strangely consoled in his endeavours to live by the aid of literature by his uncle Major Pendennis, who assures him that ' poetry and genius, and that sort of thing, were devilishly disreputable ' in his time. But success waits on him, and he can afford to smile at the eccentric officer. Were it not for the closing pages of ' Pendennis ' we could almost feel angry with Thackeray for challenging our interest in Arthur. But

the lesson he had to teach compensates for all disappoint-
ments.   No stones are to be unnecessarily thrown at the
erring, and the shadows in Pendennis's life are to teach
others how to avoid similar errors.   The unworthy often
run away with the honours.   The history of Pendennis
closes with fruition for the hero, while the nobler character, George Warrington, suffers loss.   But then the
novelist justly observes :—

' If the best men do not draw the great prizes in life, we
know that it has been so ordained by the Ordainer of the
lottery ; we own, and see daily, how the false and worthless
live and prosper, while the good are called away, and the
dear and young perish untimely.   We perceive in every
man's life maimed happiness, the frequent falling, the boot-
less endeavour, the struggle of right and wrong, in which
the strong often succumb and the swift fail ; we see flowers
of good blooming in foul places, as in the most lofty and
splendid fortunes, flaws of vice and meanness, and stains of
evil, and, knowing how mean the best of us is, let us give a
hand of charity to Arthur Pendennis, with all his faults and
shortcomings, who does not claim to be a hero, but only a
man and a brother.'

Passing by temporarily the lectures on the Humourists
in order to preserve the chain of novels unbroken, we
come to a work which is perhaps the most satisfactory
of all Thackeray's writings, regarding them purely in
the light of literary art.   There are few productions in

the world of fiction which exhibit the finish of ' Esmond,'
for the author has not only drawn his characters with
unusual skill, but delighted the reader with repeated
bursts of natural, unaffected eloquence, in language
sedulously borrowed from the age of Steele and Addison.
As regards style, indeed, 'Esmond' is an incredible
tour-de-force, and is by far the most original of all his
books. For the first time the author transplants us to
that age which afterwards became of such absorbing
interest to him that he could not tear himself away from
it ; so imbued was he altogether with the literature of
the time of Queen Anne and George I. that at last he
seemed to live in it. At his death he had another work
in contemplation whose period was fixed in the eighteenth
century. It is easy even to the uninitiated to discover
that Thackeray wrote this history of Esmond, a colonel
in the service of Her Majesty Queen Anne, thoroughly
con amore. He revelled in his theme and in the associations it brought with it. Genial, witty Dick Steele and
Mr. Joseph Addison are introduced to us, and we see
them, along with Esmond, drinking the Burgundy, which,
says Addison, 'my Lord Halifax sent me.' We are
carried through portions of Marlborough's campaigns,
and the spirit blazes with enthusiasm at the pluck which
wrought such valiant deeds, and brought undying honour

on the British arms. The avarice and ambition of the
brilliant Churchill are forgotten as the plans of his consummate genius are unravelled. Esmond's career with
General Webb is traced with intense interest, and the
scenes become as real to us as they undoubtedly seemed
to the author. The plot of the book is not of the
happiest description, the machinations of the Jacobites
being interwoven largely with the thread of the narrative.
The hero loves in the outset Beatrix Esmond, daughter
of a viscount, and the devotion he exhibits to the idol of
his heart and his imagination is something extraordinary
even in comparison with the loves of other heroes.
Beatrix, however, was unworthy of it: homage she would
receive, true passion she seemed incapable of returning.
Self-willed to a degree, the noble nature of such a man
as Esmond was as a sealed book to her. His gravest
feelings she treated with levity, and at length her conduct with the Pretender broke the spell, and threw down
from its lofty pedestal, once and for ever, the idol he had
set up. Like the marble it was beautiful to the eye; like
the marble it was cold and insensible to the touch.
Finally, Esmond contracts a union with Beatrix's mother,
Lady Castlewood, still handsome and comparatively
young, and who had always cherished the memory of
Esmond as one whom she dearly loved in his youth.

Her affection for him had never waned. The volume closes with their settlement on the banks of the Potomac, in a calm and serene happiness. The autobiographer, in describing their Virginian estate and Transatlantic life, says:—'Our diamonds are turned into ploughs and axes for our plantations, and into negroes, the happiest and merriest, I think, in all this country; and the only jewel by which my wife sets any store, and from which she hath never parted, is that gold button she took from my arm on the day when she visited me in prison, and which she wore ever after, as she told me, on the tenderest heart in the world.' In reading 'Esmond,' so cleverly is the story told, and with such ease and truthfulness, that the reader does not stay to note what a difficult task the novelist has set himself in venturing to deal with a plot more than commonly unattractive. Thackeray, however, is nowhere the slave of a story; and in sometimes deliberately fighting against conventional construction and probability, he has proved by his success in enlisting interest and sympathy that he wielded the pen of a master. The world can forgive its hero for not doing what ninety-nine heroes in a hundred perform, when his history is related with the fidelity and ability which distinguish 'Esmond.' There are more characters carefully and vividly drawn in this book than are to be found in the entire novels of many popular writers; and that pungency of Thackeray's pen which cuts through individualities as sharply and clearly as the diamond cuts through the glass, is here in full operation. It was as superior to its predecessor as the latter was to almost all the novels of the time. In regard to historical portraiture it has never been excelled; to read it once is to be struck with its eloquence and power ; to read it a second time is to be impressed with its fidelity and photographic accuracy.

Thackeray rose to the perfection of his art in fiction in 'The Newcomes;' and it is such books as this which show us what a fine teacher and instructor the novel may become in the hands of genius. In the representation of human nature this story is worthy of Richardson or Fielding. It is the *chef-d'œuvre*, in our opinion, of its author. There is not lacking that infinite sarcasm observable in previous works, but the writer has touched more deeply the springs of human sympathy. Within the whole scope of fiction there is no single character which stands out more nobly for the admiration of readers to all time than that of Colonel Newcome. The painter of that portrait alone might well lay claim to an undying canvas. As faithfully and as naturally as though limned by the hand of Sir Joshua Reynolds himself the features of the old soldier appear before us. Having written 'The Newcomes,' Thackeray may be said to have shaken hands as an equal with the two or three great masters of fiction. If it be the province of the novelist to depict human nature as it is, it must be conceded, at any rate, that there was nothing else left for the author to do to entitle him to the highest honours of his class. Nor is it a little singular too that in the story just mentioned Thackeray has given us the best female character which has proceeded from his fertile brain—Ethel Newcome. She comes to us as the sweet teacher of more goodness and religion than a whole company of preachers. We are inclined to agree with her cousin Clive Newcome that to look into her eyes would be almost too much for such unworthy imperfect creatures as men, and that she is one of that rare class of beings sent into the world occasionally to tell us that Heaven has not altogether forgotten us. What a story of society 'The Newcomes' is! First we have the Newcome family, with Sophia Alethea, whose mission and self-imposed duty it was 'to attend to the interests of the enslaved negro; to awaken the benighted Hottentot to a sense of the truth; to convert Jews, Turks, Infidels, and Papists; to arouse the indifferent and often blasphemous mariner; to guide the washerwoman in the

right way ; to head all the public charities of her sect;
and do a thousand secret kindnesses that none knew of ;
to answer myriads of letters, pension endless ministers,
and supply their teeming wives with continuous baby
linen,'—all which she did 'womanfully' for nigh fourscore
years.   Then we have the Honeymans, with the singular
story of the Rev. Charles Honeyman.   Clive Newcome's
uncles occupy a large portion of the narrative, and Sir
Barnes Newcome appears and contrives to earn our
unmitigated contempt.   Grey Friars looms into view,
with the hero Clive at school within its precincts.   Good
James Binnie is introduced, and honest J. J. Ridley.
Electioneering contests, with all their humour, are portrayed, while the scheming members of society are also
flayed for their snobbery.   From the heartlessness of
vampires and fools—the Floracs, the Kews, &c.—we
are pleased to hurry away and to light upon such passages of sweetness and beauty as this, where the Colonel
on his arrival in England from India is welcomed by his
little niece Ethel :—

' He took a little slim white hand and laid it down on his
brown palm, where it looked all the whiter ; he cleared the
grizzled moustachio from his mouth, and stooping down he
kissed the little white hand with a great deal of grace and
dignity.   There was no point of resemblance, and yet a
something in the girl's look, voice, and movements, which

caused his heart to thrill, and an image out of the past to
rise up and salute him. The eyes which had brightened his
youth (and which he saw in his dreams and thoughts for
faithful years afterwards as though they looked at him out
of heaven) seemed to shine upon him after five-and-thirty
years. He remembered such a fair bending neck and
clustering hair, such a light foot and airy figure, such a slim
hand lying in his own—and now parted from it with a gap
of ten thousand long days between. . . . Parting is death,
at least as far as life is concerned. A passion comes to
an end ; it is carried off in a coffin, or weeping in a post-
chaise ; it drops out of life one way or other, and the earth
clods close over it, and we see it no more. But it has been
part of our souls and it is eternal. Does a mother not love
her dead infant ? a man his lost mistress ? with the fond
wife nestling at his side,—yes, with twenty children smiling
round her knee. No doubt, as the old soldier held the girl's
hand in his, the little talisman led him back to Hades, and
he saw Leonora.'

The book has its love passages—in some cases sad
and miserable. Chapters of pathetic interest abound,
where the world is exhibited at its old tricks of topsy-
turvy—Lady Clara loving Jack Belsize and being beloved madly in return, while her hand is sold to Sir
Barnes Newcome, 'society,' forsooth, blessing the bargain : Clive married to Rosey Mackenzie, whom he
loves in a way, though his real devotion belongs to his
cousin, who is put into the matrimonial auction and
knocked down to an idiotic member of the peerage. As

for the marriages which 'have been arranged,' who has
not heard uttered, as our satirist asks, 'the ancient
words, " I promise to take thee," &c., knowing them to
be untrue; and is there a bishop on the bench that has
not Amen'd the humbug in his lawn sleeves, and called
a blessing over the kneeling pair of perjurers?' Hypocrisy and humbug are succeeded by disaster in the novel.
The grand old Colonel is ruined by the failure of the
celebrated Bundelcund Bank, but when there comes in
his need a cheque from one whom he had helped in days
gone by, the bankrupt Colonel only exclaims, 'I thank
my God Almighty for this!' and passes on the cheque
immediately to another sufferer. The story rapidly progresses. The death of Colonel Newcome is told with a
pathos almost unequalled, and dear old Grey Friars
becomes once more the witness of a scene to be ever
held in remembrance. After this sad incident the novel
speedily ends, with the united happiness of the two children whom the Colonel had most dearly loved. It is
one of the few books which we close with regret when we
have finished them. Genial, generous, and noble in its
sentiments, we seem almost to reach the mind of
Thackeray while perusing it. It gives us full assurance
that his mission was of far wider import than that of a
mere scourger of society. It is evidently written by a

man who loves the world, though he hates its follies. He has scorn for its dissimulation, indignation for its oppression, smiles for its happiness, and tears for its woes.

In continuation of his previous novel 'Esmond,' Thackeray returned to the historical vein in 'The Virginians,' which follows the fortunes of the Esmond family after its migration to America. It was one of his characteristics that the creations of his art acquired so complete a reality that he could not part from them, and they continued, as it were, to live on, and reappeared in his later works long after the fiction which had given birth to them had come to a close. Thus his 'Virginians' grew out of 'Esmond,' and it is one of the pleasantest of his works. The course of true love pursues a devious way, and the weaknesses of one character serve to set in bold relief the heroism of others. The fairer sex have no reason to complain of the treatment they receive at the hands of our author, and in this story two of their species are immortalised in a setting for which we must ever be grateful. But while we are interested in much love we are also admonished by much morality, though the moralising of Thackeray on all occasions is anything but offensive. He has the gift of so exhibiting foibles and idiosyncrasies that there is no need for him to lash himself

into a furious state of indignation, as the manner of some
is; that calm, sneering smile is sufficiently effectual;
heavy, clumsy weapons or bludgeons may make much
demonstration, but it is the light, piercing touch of the
pointed steel which is the most dangerous. Thackeray
manages to find the one vulnerable point in our armour;
he introduces the rapier of his sarcasm, and we are slain.
There is no withstanding his weapon. Surely the world
should be the better for the fearless work which this man
accomplished! Honestly has he besought it to discard
its deceit and selfishness, and who knows but vast results
have followed the teaching of the life-long lesson? Does
he not ask us, brother man! to be more true to ourselves,
to our own nature; to drop the cloak which we perpetu-
ally wear when we step forth into the world? He would
have man walk abroad upright, strong in his own virtue,
and not ashamed to meet his fellows, as though in the
great game of life he was determined to revoke through
every trick in order to seize upon the stakes. And is it
so very inhuman to help a friend or a brother that it has
become so uncommon? Are the heavens always to
appear as brass when the cry for help is raised? Harry
Esmond Warrington ' in his distress asked help from his
relations; his aunt sent him a tract and her blessing;
his uncle had business out of town, and could not, of

course, answer the poor boy's petition. . . . My Lord and Lady Skinflint, when they consult in their bedroom about giving their luckless nephew a helping hand, and determine to refuse, and go down to family prayers and meet their children and domestics, and discourse virtuously before them and then remain together and talk nose to nose—what can they think of one another? and of the poor kinsman falling among thieves and groaning for help unheeded? How can they go on with those virtuous airs? How can they dare look each other in the face?' Brave writer! these are manly words, but the world in great part still practises the selfish principle. It takes a long time to make it understand that a religious tract, though possibly very cheap, is not very filling to the hungry stomach, nor does it go far in clothing the shivering limbs. Cropping up here and there in his sparkling leaves, such are the lessons Thackeray would teach. In novels like 'The Virginians' they are subordinate to the more leading purposes of the story, but human nature has changed little since the period when its scenes were fixed. Graphic pictures of American scenery abound in its pages, and celebrated characters of the reign of George II. appear on the stage. The philosophy of the novel may not be profound, but it is always plain and unmistakable. If there be any failure per-

D

ceptible, it is a failure possessed in common with the greatest writers and dramatists, who, in attempting to depict the men, the morals, and the manners of a preceding age, have never been able entirely to get rid of their own.

The remaining works of fiction produced subsequently to 'The Virginians' are somewhat slight in their construction (with the exception of one to be named), but generally exhibit great power. The exception, as regards length and plot, is 'The Adventures of Philip,' a work worthy almost to take rank with any of those which are more widely known, on account of its extremely realistic pictures of life, and its depth of human interest. In the sketches of those 'who robbed Philip, those who helped him, and those who passed him by,' we come upon varieties of love, passion, and duplicity drawn with wondrous skill. The sad parts of the story are written with indelible ink, and all through that fine nervous sensibility which should distinguish the highest novelists is strikingly apparent. The same remark applies to the beautiful story of the 'Hoggarty Diamond.' Of the memoirs of that extraordinary youth Barry Lyndon, it is scarcely necessary to say more than that they are told with no diminution of vigour; all the later short stories of Thackeray, in fact, are written in English noticeable for its simplicity and purity. The wine is not so tart, does not sparkle quite so much, but it is mellower, and there is greater body in it. What could more conclusively exhibit this than the story the author left unfinished, 'Denis Duval'? Here we have the last lines he ever wrote—lines which triumphantly dispose of the taunt that Thackeray was writing himself out. Of few can it be said that their later works exhibit a strength and genius undimmed by time. Yet Thackeray was one of that rare minority. The period of decadence had not set in with him. He had only just reached the top of the hill, he had taken no steps on his descent. To his powers of perception, and his possession of the critical faculty in no small degree, 'The Roundabout Papers,' the inimitable Paris, Irish, and Eastern Sketches, and his imitations of contemporary authors, bear ample testimony; while 'The Snob Papers,' bur- lesques, and ballads, overflow with comic humour. As regards the authorship of ballads alone, we have no writer of *vers de société* at the present time who could be put into competition with him. 'Please- man X.' is famous; yet even Praed or Father Prout can show nothing better than 'Peg of Limavaddy,' 'At the Church Gate,' and 'Little Billee.' Novel, sketch, ballad, or essay, Thackeray has summed up in great part the lessons he would inculcate in these well-known verses :—

> ' O, Vanity of Vanities !
>   How wayward the decrees of Fate are ;
>   How very weak the very wise,
>   How very small the very great are !

> ' Though thrice a thousand years are past,
>   Since David's son the sad and splendid,
>   The weary King Ecclesiast,
>   Upon his awful tablets penned it,—

> ' Methinks the text is never stale,
>   And life is every day renewing
>   Fresh comments on the old, old tale,
>   Of Folly, Fortune, Glory, Ruin.'

In noticing the various works of Thackeray thus briefly, we have purposely left the lectures on the Four Georges and the English Humourists till the close, as they belong to a new and entirely distinct class of effort. Probably this was the first occasion on which a writer assumed the lecturer and the critic in one. Those who were privileged to hear the author deliver his lectures in person will remember how he took the town by storm, and the same enthusiasm was manifested when Thackeray went to Edinburgh and visited the principal towns in England and America, where the whole of the intellectual classes of the population flocked to hear him. To get the opinions of a famous literary man on his distinguished predecessors delivered *vivâ voce* was naturally attractive, and the imposing form of Titmarsh with his snowy hair has not yet passed out of the recollection of his auditors. We heard him on the age in which he was thoroughly at home. He had made that period in a manner his own by an intimate knowledge of all its leading spirits, and he appeared to strike a chord of self-satisfaction when he said, ' I knew familiarly a lady who had been asked in marriage by Horace Walpole, who had been patted on the head by George I.' This immediately takes him to the time of Johnson, Goldsmith, Steele, Pope, and Swift, and he is happy. He then goes on to talk pleasantly of the times and manners of the Four Georges, not sparing the gall of satire, however, when he deems it necessary to mix it with his ink. As a citizen of the time he thus describes the advent of the First George, and the facts of history but too fully justify the sweeping condemnation :—

' Here we are, all on our knees. Here is the Archbishop of Canterbury prostrating himself to the head of his church, with Kielmansegge and Schulenberg with their ruddled cheeks grinning behind the Defender of the Faith. Here is my Lord Duke of Marlborough kneeling, too, the greatest warrior of all times; he who betrayed King William—betrayed King James I.—betrayed Queen Anne—betrayed

England to the French, the Elector to the Pretender, the Pretender to the Elector; there are my Lords Oxford and Bolingbroke, the latter of whom has just tripped up the heels of the former ; and if a month's more time had been allowed him, would have had King James at Westminster.'

But foolish as the foreign gentleman was, he was astute enough to see through loyalty of this description. The bargain with England was that she wanted a Protestant puppet, and as George was not unwilling, for a consideration, to become one, matters were arranged. Though not without his faults, George I. had, as Thackeray points out, the countervailing virtues of justice, courage, and moderation. In introducing his immediate successor, the essayist sketches a memorable scene. An eager messenger in jack-boots, who had ridden from London, forced his way into a bedroom in Richmond Lodge, where the master was taking a nap after dinner. With a strong German accent and many oaths, the man on the bed, starting up, asked who dared to disturb him? 'I am Sir Robert Walpole,' said the messenger. The awakened sleeper hated Sir Robert. 'I have the honour to announce to your Majesty, that your royal father, King George I., died at Osnaburg, on Saturday last, the 10th instant.' *'Dat is one big lie!'* roared out his Sacred Majesty King George II., but that was how he came to be monarch nevertheless. The

Second George was more wrongheaded than his father, and England was saved during many years of his reign by the strong will of that strange mixture of courage, dissoluteness, statesmanship, and meanness, Sir Robert Walpole, and by the good sense and tact of Queen Caroline. Brave the King undoubtedly was, but in and around his court there was the old sickly air of corruption, fed rather than suppressed by a sycophant clergy. The trenchant words of the great satirist are not a whit too strong in which to describe the godlessness and hypocrisy of the period. And when the sovereign died, some of the divines carried their cant behind the grave, and referred to their master as one too good for earth. They had crawled in the dust before his mistresses for preferment, and having got it, must of course pay for it somehow. Diving beneath the surface of society, Thackeray wisely says, 'It is to the middle class we must look for the safety of England ; the working educated men, away from Lord North's bribery in the senate ; the good clergy not corrupted into parasites by the hope of preferment ; the tradesmen rising into manly opulence ; the painters pursuing their gentle calling ; the men of letters in their quiet studies ; these are the men whom we love and like to read of in the last age.' With these classes pure and sound, kings and puppets may sport with im-

punity ; the kingdom is safe ; it is when the middle
classes are corrupt and worthless that the foundations of
society begin to break up.   Pleasant gossip of the good
but obstinate King George, the third of his name, is
vouchsafed to us, with glimpses of his pure court—would
it had always remained so—within whose precincts many
a battle was won over his opponents by the dogged
monarch.   Then we come to the period of his terrible
malady, and in describing the closing scene of all, the
essayist breaks out into a passage of touching eloquence,
which we transcribe here as being in his most successful
vein :—

'What preacher need moralise on this story ; what words
save the simplest are requisite to tell it ?   It is too terrible
for tears.   The thought of such a misery smites me down in
submission before the Ruler of kings and men, the Monarch
Supreme over empires and republics, the inscrutable Dis-
penser of life, death, happiness, victory.   "O brothers !" I
said to those who heard me first in America—" O, brothers !
speaking the same mother tongue—O comrades ! enemies
no more, let us take a mournful hand together as we stand
by this royal corpse, and call a truce to battle !   Low he
lies to whom the proudest used to kneel once, and who was
cast lower than the poorest ; dead, whom millions prayed for
in vain."   Driven off the throne ; buffeted by rude hands ;
with his children in revolt ; the darling of his old age killed
before him untimely ; our Lear hangs over her breathless
lips and cries : "Cordelia, Cordelia, stay a little !"

" Vex not his ghost—oh ! let him pass—he hates him
    That would upon the rack of this tough world
    Stretch him out longer !"

Hush ! strife and quarrel, over the solemn grave ! Sound,
trumpets, a mournful march. Fall, dark curtain, upon his
pageant, his pride, his grief, his awful tragedy.'

The lectures on the English Humourists, a subject
peculiarly adapted to the bent of Thackeray, commence
with Swift, the genius who had a life-hunt for a bishopric
and missed it. The bitterness of a generation of mankind seemed to be concentrated in that one spirit. We
scarcely understand him now, or if we do, then genius is
miserably weak and vulnerable in some points if strong as
adamant in others. He did not succeed, and it was his
constant habit, we are assured, to keep his birthday as a
day of mourning. Yet there are some aspects in which
we like to regard him. We admire his utter scorn at
times, his contempt for the tinsel, and the power of his
eagle eye to pierce to the heart of things. He could also
crush pretence, at once and effectually. A bumptious
young wit said to him in company, ' You must know, Mr.
Dean, that I set up for a wit !' ' Do you so ?' said the
Dean. ' Take my advice and sit down again.' Thackeray
mistrusts the religion of Swift, and mentions as one of the
strongest reasons for doing so, the fact of his recommend-
ing the dissolute author of ' The Beggar's Opera ' to turn

clergyman, and look out for a seat on the bench. But this master of irony varied so in his moods, that it is impossible to know whether this advice was not simply the result of that intense chagrin which possessed him, rather than of a deliberate recklessness of the good. That Swift suffered, mentally, more than almost any man history takes note of may be accepted, but it was partly due to the workings of an 'evil spirit.' It is justly said of him that 'he goes through life, tearing, like a man possessed of a devil. Like Abudah in the Arabian story, he is always looking out for the Fury, and knows that the night will come and the inevitable hag with it. What a night, my God! it was, what a lonely rage of long agony—what a vulture that tore the heart of that giant ! It is awful to think of the great sufferings of this great man. Through life he always seems alone, somehow. Goethe was so. I can't fancy Shakspeare otherwise. The giants must live apart. The kings can have no company. But this man suffered so ; and deserved so to suffer. One hardly reads anywhere of such a pain.' And this pain went through life—in darkness, rage, and misery he spent his days ; no light broke through the starless night. The end came, and terrible is the story, —the witty, the eloquent, the gifted, the godlike in intellect, the devilish in heart, Swift passed away in a state

not unlike that against which he had prayed in a letter to
Bolingbroke, when he said, 'It is time for me to have
done with the world, and so I would if I could get into a
better before I was called into the best, and not die here
in a rage, like a poisoned rat in a hole.' Excellent talk
follows this sketch—gossip of Congreve and Addison,
with wise critical remarks interspersed by the author, who
may be said to have established a prescriptive right to
the age of which he wrote. Somewhat too much, we are
inclined to think, Thackeray made of Pope, though the
executive ability of the young poet was of the most marvellous description. Poor Dick Steele, that bundle of
failings and weaknesses, has a paper all to himself, and
we rise from its perusal with our love for the kindly,
miserable sinner intensified. It was surface wickedness
with Steele entirely: his heart was tender, and his character simple as a child's. For the genius and character
of Fielding Thackeray had of course the highest admiration. Very few lines need be read before it is apparent
that the modern novelist had studied his predecessor
minutely. He quotes Gibbon's famous saying about
Fielding with intense relish. 'The successors of Charles V.
may disdain their brethren (the Fieldings) of England:
but the romance of "Tom Jones," that exquisite picture
of humour and manners, will outlive the palace of the

Escurial, and the Imperial Eagle of Austria.' But here
our pleasant reminiscences of the English humourists
must end, and some observations of a general nature be
made upon the genius of him who has bequeathed to us
his thoughts and judgments on his illustrious predecessors.

The first characteristic which strikes the reader of
Thackeray is unquestionably his humour. It does not
gleam forth as flashes of lightning, rare and vivid, but is
more like the ever-bubbling fountain, the perennial
spring. It is a kind of permeating force throughout all
his works—works now lashed into sarcasm and anon dissolved in pathos. It is one of the great mistakes regarding
this author that he is satirical and nothing else. No
critic who thus represents him can have either studied
his novels or caught the spirit and purpose of the man.
He is one of the best of English humourists simply because his nature is sensitive at all points. What Carlyle
has said of Jean Paul may be said of him—' In his smile
itself a touching pathos may lie hidden, a pity too deep
for tears. He is a man of feeling, in the noblest sense
of that word; for he loves all living with the heart of a
brother; his soul rushes forth, in sympathy with gladness
and sorrow, with goodness or grandeur, over all creation.
Every gentle and generous affection, every thrill of

mercy, every glow of nobleness, awakens in his bosom a response; nay, strikes his spirit into harmony.' It must ever be so. But when the first satirical papers of Thackeray were published the world had only seen one side of his humour. The 'Snob Papers' and burlesques, and the memoirs of Mr. Yellowplush, gave place in due time to a richer vein in more important works. The sparkling Champagne was followed, as it were, by the deep rich Burgundy. As Dickens was his superior in the faculty of invention, so was the former eclipsed by the greater depth of Thackeray's penetration. Truth to life distinguishes nearly all the characters of Dickens, those at least which belong to the lower classes; but this truth is the obvious truth of caricature rather than of reality: Thackeray takes us below the surface ; we travel through the dark scenes of the human drama with him ; he makes his notes and comments without flattery and with astounding realism, and when we part company from his side we wish human nature were somewhat nobler than it is. But his wit does not preclude him from being fair and just. He is indeed scrupulously so, and to the erring kind and tender. It used to be said occasionally of his works as they appeared, ' Ah, there's the same old sneer '—so ready is the world to follow the course in which its attention is directed. Speaking of the maligners of Society, he says, 'You who have ever listened to village bells, or have walked to church as children on sunny Sabbath mornings; you who have ever seen the parson's wife tending the poor man's bedside; or the town clergyman threading the dirty stairs of noxious alleys upon his sacred business;—do not raise a shout when one of these falls away, or yell with the mob that howls after him.' Surely these are noble words to come from one whose intellectual current was set in the direction of contempt! With all his keen sense of the ridiculous and his scathing powers of invective, there is no one instance where for the sake of the brilliancy of his satire he ever cast a slur upon truly philanthropic labour, or perilled his reputation for the worship of the pure and the good. If ever man's humour were useful to instruct as well as to delight, it is that of Michael Angelo Titmarsh. When he laughs we know he will do it fairly—his eye wanders round all, and neither friend nor foe, if vulnerable, can keep out the arrows of his wit. His position, as a humourist, is certainly that of the equal of most of the wits of whom he has written, and one scarcely inferior to even Swift or Sterne.

A second quality that is observable in him is his fidelity. And to this we do not attach the restricted meaning that the persons of his novels are faithful to nature—though that they incontestably are—but the wide import of being true to the results of life as we see them daily. He does not allow the development of a story to destroy the unities of character, and in this respect he resembles the greatest of all writers. Take an example. At the close of 'The Newcomes,' instead of preserving alive the noble Colonel to witness the happiness of the family in its resuscitated fortunes, Thackeray causes him to die, and that in the humblest manner. With most novelists we could predict a very different ending, but one not so true as Thackeray has had the courage to adopt. Sorrow we may indulge that the death should thus occur, but we must acknowledge that it is more consonant with our daily experience than any other conclusion would have been, however pleasant as matter of fiction. The same thing is noticed in the character of Beatrix Esmond; we are first interested in her; then our faith is gradually shattered; and, finally, we are thoroughly disappointed by the catastrophe. The result is contrary to that which we expected; it is other than would have been given by most writers, but it is none the less true. Take the whole of his creations, let the test of fidelity be applied to each, and it will be found that the writers are very few indeed who have been so thoroughly able to disentangle themselves from the

common method of adapting character to plot, or who
have made their individualities so distinct, and kept
them so to the end.   To place him in comparison with
other authors who are distinguished for their delineation
of character as character—as witnessed at certain points
or stages—is unfair both to him and to them.   Conversations, with one, stamp individualities, and the test of
their fidelity is the absence of contradiction in the outward forms of speech and action whenever the individuals
are introduced : this was the life-painting of Dickens,
for instance.   With Thackeray the case is different.   He
does not depend so much on the conversational or de-
scriptive recognition of character.   He gives us more of
their mind or heart than of their person.   He does not
tell us what they look like, but what they are ; and
through all his novels they answer to the bent and the
natural instincts we have been led to associate with them.
It is this elevated form of fidelity that we would insist
upon as preeminently to be noticed in Thackeray ; and
were it on this ground alone we should not hesitate to
place him in the very first rank of novelists.   In this
essential particular, in truth, he has no rival.   Others
may excel him in various arts of fiction, but with this
passport, even his superiors in minor detail will accord
to him a perfect equality, if not a superiority, in the
manifestation of the cardinal principle of novel-writing.

The subjectiveness of Thackeray is another quality which has greatly enhanced the value of his works. It is generally admitted that subjective writers have a more powerful influence over humanity than those of the class styled objective. It is natural, perhaps, that the external descriptions of circumstances or scenery should not move us nearly so much as the life-record of a breathing, suffering, rejoicing human being. Be his station what it may, we are interested in every individual of the species whose career is faithfully pictured. The author of ' Vanity Fair' is one of the few men who have been able to endue their characters with being and motion. When there were few writers who had either the courage or the gifts to be natural, Thackeray gave a new impetus to the world of fiction. So eminently subjective are his works, that those of his friends who knew him well are able to trace in them the successive stages of his personal career, and to show in what manner the incidents of his own life operated upon his novels. There are but few occurrences in the whole series that were not drawn either from his individual history or the history of some one of his friends or acquaintances. This is, doubtless, one of the most influential causes of the reality of his stories. No stiff, formal record of events, dispassionately told, is to be witnessed. If the

E

reader reads at all, he must perforce become interested in his work. There probably never were novels written in which there was so little exaggeration of colouring. His dear Harry Fielding has been his guide, but the author of 'Tom Jones' has been almost outstripped by his pupil. The latter has been able to throw away more effectually the folds of drapery in which character has generally been presented to us. In his model he was happy, for, previous to Thackeray, Fielding was the most subjective writer in the annàls of fiction. One can understand the charm which those writings exercised over his successor, and the desire which he felt to construct his novels after the fashion of which he had become so greatly enamoured. But the pupil has the greater claim to our regard in the fact that his work is such that not a line of it need be excised in public reading. He is Fielding purified. All the vivacity and the life-giving strokes which belonged to the pencil of the earlier master are reproduced in the younger, and the interest is also preserved intact. But with the later age has come the purer language, and Thackeray may be said to stand in precisely the same relation to the nineteenth century as Fielding stood to the eighteenth. The absence of exaggeration in Thackeray's drawing of character is very remarkable. Notwithstanding the multiplicity of his personages, there are not two which in any sense resemble each other. The faculty is very rare of being able to transfer the lineaments of commonplace people in such a manner as that others will care to study them. Yet this is the result which Thackeray achieves, and without labour. Nothing transcendental, or that which is beyond human nature, is thrown in as a means of bribing the reader into closer acquaintanceship. As men passed Thackeray he observed them; as they interested him he drew them; but in doing so he felt that to add to the original would destroy the identity, and the consequence of his consummate art is that throughout the whole of his varied picture-gallery there is no portrait which bears the impress of falsity or distortion. To say the truth, and to describe what he saw before him, was always the novelist's own boast. There could be no nobler ambition for any writer, but there are few who have attained the perfect height of the standard.

Leading out of his subjectiveness, or rather being a broader and grander development of it, we come to the fourth great characteristic of Thackeray—his humanity. That is the crown and glory of his work. And yet this man, who was sensitive almost beyond parallel, was charged with having no heart! Shallow critics, who gave a surface-reading to 'Vanity Fair,' imagined they had gauged the author, and in an off-hand manner described him as a man of no feeling—the cold, simple cynic. It will be remembered that the same charge of having no heart was made against Macaulay; but its baselessness was discovered on his death, when it became known that 'the heartless' one had for years pursued a career of almost unexampled benevolence. So superficial are the judgments of the world! Against Thackeray the charge was doubly cruel; he was one of those men who are naturally full of sensibility to a degree. Men who understood him best knew that it cost him an effort to subdue that part of his nature which hastened to sympathise with others. Selfishness was as foreign to him as insincerity. The man was true as the light of heaven to the generous instincts of his nature. To veil at times this side of his character was essential in order to give play to that satire which kills. If his mission was to exalt the good and the pure, it was also as decidedly his mission to abase the false. To do this he must necessarily appear severe. But who that reads him well can fail to perceive that the eye accustomed to blaze with scorn could also moisten with sympathy and affection? What man without heart could have written such passages

as that episode in the 'Hoggarty Diamond'? Titmarsh
is describing his journey to the Fleet Prison, accompanied
by his wife :—

' There was a crowd of idlers round the door as I passed
out of it, and had I been alone I should have been ashamed
of seeing them ; but, as it was, I was only thinking of my
dear, dear wife, who was leaning trustfully on my arm, and
smiling like heaven into my face—ay, and took heaven too
into the Fleet Prison with me—or an angel out of heaven.
Ah ! I had loved her before, and happy it is to love when
one is hopeful and young in the midst of smiles and sunshine ; but be *un*happy, and then see what it is to be loved
by a good woman ! I declare before heaven, that of all the
joys and happy moments it has given me, that was the
crowning one—that little ride, with my wife's cheek on my
shoulder, down Holborn to the prison ! Do you think I
cared for the bailiff that sat opposite? No, by the Lord !
I kissed her and hugged her—yes, and cried with her likewise. But before our ride was over her eyes dried up, and
she stepped blushing and happy out of the coach at the
prison-door, as if she were a princess going to the Queen's
drawing-room.'

Or is there to be found in all fiction a scene more
pathetic than the one describing the death of Colonel
Newcome? To have written that alone would have
deservedly made any man great. Though it is doubtless familiar to every reader, it will be impossible to
illustrate fully the human tenderness of the author with-

out quoting some portion of it here. The scene is at
Grey Friars:—

'Ethel came in with a scared face to our pale group. " He
is calling for you again, dear lady," she said, going up to
Madame de Florac, who was still kneeling ; " and just now
he said he wanted Pendennis to take care of his boy. He
will not know you." She hid her tears as she spoke. She
went into the room where Clive was at the bed's foot ; the
old man within it talked on rapidly for a while ; then again
he would sigh and be still ; once more I heard him say
hurriedly : " Take care of him when I am in India ;" and
then with a heart-rending voice he called out, " Léonore,
Léonore !" She was kneeling by his side now. The
patient's voice sank into faint murmurs ; only a moan now
and then announced that he was not asleep. At the usual
evening hour the chapel bell began to toll, and Thomas
Newcombe's hands outside the bed feebly beat time. And
just as the last bell struck, a peculiar sweet smile shone over
his face, and he lifted up his head a little, and quickly said,
" Adsum !" and fell back. It was the word we used at school
when names were called ; and lo ! he, whose heart was as
that of a little child, had answered to his name and stood in
the presence of The Master.'

The principal defect alleged against Thackeray is
that he is a mannerist. But when it is considered that
the same charge could be laid against every writer in the
roll of literature with the exception of the few imperial
intellects of the universe, it must be conceded that the
charge is of little moment. All men, save the Homers,

Shakspeares, and Goethes of the world, are mannerists. There is not a writer of eminence living at the present day who is not a mannerist. Tennyson, Browning, and Carlyle are all mannerists. It is impossible to quarrel with that which sets the stamp of individuality and originality on the productions of the intellect.

To assign Thackeray's ultimate position in literature is a difficult task, for nothing is less certain than the permanence of literary attractiveness and fame; but we think that his works will be read and as keenly enjoyed after the lapse of a century as they are now. Fielding has survived longer than that period, and weightier reasons for immortality than could be advanced in his case might be advanced in favour of Thackeray. If his works ceased to be read as pictures of society and delineations of character, they would still retain no inglorious place in English literature from the singular purity and beauty of their style. It is style even more than matter which embalms a literary reputation. To the faithfulness with which he spake the English tongue we believe future generations will testify. Whatsoever was good, honest, and true found in him a defender; whatsoever was base, unmanly, or false shrank abashed in his presence. A man with less pretence, less assumption, less sham never existed: he revolted from appearing that which he was not. His works were the reflex of the man, and like a shaft of light, which, while it pierces into the deepest recesses of dissimulation and vice, smiles benignantly upon those aspirations and feelings which are the noblest glory of humanity.

ELIZABETH BARRETT BROWNING

[CORNHILL MAGAZINE]

WHAT are the essential attributes of the Poet's art which cause him to be adorned with the noblest crown it is in the power of humanity to confer? From the period when 'the blind old man of Scio's rocky isle' thundered that music which was to reverberate through all time, along the swift revolving centuries, even to our own somewhat prosaic day, we witness an unbroken succession of kings of song, whose thrones have been more permanent than those of the Pharaohs and the Cæsars. What allegiance do we bear, or what sworn fealty have we kept, truer than that which we own towards those who have touched into activity the secret springs of our sensibility? All the grandeurs of birth, and dignities which have blossomed at the touch of monarchs, fail to move our admiration as compared with the simple majesty of genius, which has its rise in higher soi', and whose fruition is not dependent upon the smile of human potentates. One has somewhat bitterly said of good princes, that all their names might be graven within the gem of one ring. The

same cannot be said of the royal race of poets. Theirs
is not the accidental title to reverence which, with the
majority of princes, ceases with the yielding up of life.
There is nothing perishable with the poet but that clay
which has hemmed him in, and restricted the flights of
his burning and ever-aspiring spirit. His soul is immortal in his verse. And he possesses the gift beyond
all others of transferring his mind and his heart into his
effusions. But a momentary consideration will demonstrate the fact that the poet must, of necessity, have the
largest fellowship with humanity. He it is who converses
with our veritable selves, and not with our shadows;
other men affect us at a point somewhere on the surface
—by varied means, but all failing to reach the chord that
has its root in the heart's blood, and which vibrates
whenever the true singer touches his fellow-man. What
matters it whether the poet begs his bread through
opulent cities, as the godlike Homer is affirmed to have
done, or wields a powerful sceptre like that of David,
' the sweet singer of Israel'? The ultimate glory of all
is the same, the difference one of degree only. Posterity
gives the crown which cannot wither. Again, the poet
appears before mankind not only as the most independent teacher, but the most sympathetic—apparently a
contradiction in terms. While the least biassed of all

teachers who instruct us, he has also the extraordinary power of reaching to the profoundest depths of our nature. We should regard the matter with comparative unconcern if we witnessed the world moved from its orbit beneath the lever of an Archimedes, provided our own gravity were preserved; the astounding achievement would excite little or no emotion in us; but when the poet gives birth to a new idea, or when he revivifies old ones by the plastic and life-giving touch of his genius, the world is ready with something better than its applause —it reverences and it loves. It is not our intention here to magnify the Poet's office; the unanimous verdict of men, from the remotest ages, has raised him to the highest pinnacle of fame, and in the great Valhalla of the universe there are no dead so illustrious as those in whom was perfected the divine melody of song. The poet is enthroned of man by virtue of a nobility which comes from God. His mission is to show us that to feel nobly is to be great, and to insist, with a lofty eloquence and in an impassioned strain, upon the importance and sacred character of truth, beauty, and virtue. We are not of those who restrict the scope of poetry, and consider it chiefly as a refinement and a delight; that is to do wrong to its majestic spirit, whose wings touch the earth, but whose glorious eyes look into Heaven.

All true poets themselves have felt that their marvellous gift meant infinitely more than the mere utterance
of melodious numbers.   The outer music is but the
shadow of that deeper soul-music which originated with
the apprehension of a new truth, or a new phase of
beauty.   He is not a poet who does not possess this
strange insight, which distinctly marks off the real singer
from that adventitious writer who, in a happy moment,
may throw off verses which a simply cursory examination
might induce men to accept as the genuine presentment
of poetry.   It was the neglect to take due account of
this matter which led the supporters of Pope to assume a
much higher ground in the famous controversy upon his
merits than his claims warranted.   Soul, and not criticism,
is desiderated in poetry.   The foibles of humanity are
excellent things as marks for the shafts of novelists and
satirists ; but the man who would assure us of his divine
mission in poetry takes a nobler range than that.   He is
for ever in search of, and thirsting for, the beauty of the
universe, that he may interpret it to others.   He brings
it to us from the humblest places and in the humblest
guises ; but his contact, while placing it before our
vision, has glorified it, and shown that within it of whose
existence we had never dreamed.   Has Pope, or any
other man who taught us how to think in measured

cadence, and delighted us with rhyming intellectualism
—ever got beyond didactic assertions, and seized that
fire which the real Prometheus of song invariably gains?
The poet has impulses, gigantic and irresistible ; he has
also love, ever operative and inextinguishable. His
rhyme is an accident ; his poetry is eternal. He finds
his divine manna everywhere ; he is the high-priest of
nature and of God. He sings not so much because it is
pleasant, or to direct attention to his own great and
wondrous ability, but because he must. While he lives,
he cannot avoid it. And the strange faculty of diving
into the mystery of things extends to everything he sees
around him. From no path where intuition can be of
avail is he shut out. In this respect poets might well
appropriate to themselves those lines of delightful old
George Herbert, who himself possessed some share of
the mystic gift :—

> ' For us the winds do blow,
> The earth doth rest, heaven move, and fountains flow ;
> Nothing we see, but means our good,
> As our delight, or as our treasure ;
> The whole is either our cupboard of food,
> Or cabinet of pleasure.'

Now the main charge against the poetry of the Vic-
torian age, if we read it rightly, is this—that however

admirable much of it may be as regards finish, it is in-significant in conception. Emerson, who is unable to find any poetic genius in his own country to satisfy him, thus asks despairingly of England—'Shall I find my heavenly bread in the reigning poets? Where is great design in modern English poetry? The English have lost sight of the fact that poetry exists to speak the spiritual law, and that no wealth of description or of fancy is yet essentially new, and out of the limits of prose, until this conviction is reached. Therefore the grave old poets, like the Greek artists, heeded their designs, and less considered the finish. It was their office to lead to the divine sources, out of which all this, and much more, readily springs ; and if this religion is in the poetry, it raises us to some purpose, and we can well afford some staidness, or hardness, or want of popular tune in the verses.' To say that the standard aimed at by this language is high, is a very inadequate description of it. Emerson's ideal is evidently one that is only reached every five hundred years. He would appear to look for a Homer or an Æschylus with every generation of humanity ; forgetting that we are not gods, but only summed up into one with the fulness of time— as Shakspeare succeeds to the great ancients after the lapse of centuries of mediocrity. But is it true that the

age has exhibited no design in poetry? Did not Wordsworth exhibit any, in spite of his stuttering articulation—
a helplessness probably partly induced by his excess of
spiritual vision? Are Browning's grapplings with magnificent subjects to be accounted altogether as failures?
As for Tennyson, he has, it must be owned, never failed
in anything, for he has been careful not to overweight
himself.[1] He is the perfect singer of the time. Yet
he would fall under the reproach of Emerson—if it be
a reproach—that he gives the age what it asks for,
instead of striving after loftier ideas. Sympathising, however, to a certain extent with the position assumed by
the distinguished American essayist, we must admit that
what we want is not so much the laborious poet as the
emotional. Tennyson is undoubtedly both, but by no
means in the same degree. His melody is stately and
rich, but not overwhelming. He delights by grace, but
never swells by passion. ,The light of consummate art
gleams forth from all he does, but his moments of high
exaltation of soul are very rare.

The contrary is the case with regard to the poet

---

[1] To this statement some critics, judging from their published
opinions, might object, alleging 'Queen Mary' as an instance to
the contrary; but while that drama is not so satisfactory as much
of Mr. Tennyson's previous work in the poetical sense, it is surely
so in the dramatic.

F

whose works we propose to discuss. She, at any rate, has demonstrated what emotional poetry really means, in contradistinction to the poetry of simple art; and it cannot be said, either, that she has altogether come short in the matter of design—the design which stamps the greatest poets. Sensibility and intuition, those endowments of supereminent importance to individuals whose greatness is to grow in proportion to their understanding and interpretation of human life, were in her united in a degree seldom witnessed. Her history, sparse as it is in facts as yet given to the world, is one of intense interest. It is well known how that existence with her was almost one long round of continuous suffering. Her retired life sent her more closely to the companionship of the dead, though she had naturally an eager and insatiable thirst after knowledge. Her own sufferings could never daunt her in the pursuit of learning, and accordingly we find that as a scholar she was distinguished for the ripest erudition. Her account of the Greek Christian poets will serve to show in what direction a large portion of her studies lay; and it is in this work, we imagine, that we discern what was her own ideal of the true nineteenth century poet. 'We want the touch of Christ's hand upon our literature,' she says, 'as it touched other dead things; we want the sense of the saturation of Christ's blood upon the souls of our poets, that it may cry *through* them in answer to the ceaseless wail of the Sphinx of our humanity, expounding agony into renovation. Something of this has been perceived in art when its glory was at the fullest. Something of a yearning after this may be seen among the Greek Christian poets, something which would have been much with a stronger faculty.' This idea recurs again and again in different forms through her works. She yearns for poetry to be sanctified, to be made holy. This is how it was with the grand old Greeks, and how it should be now. It is because poetry is losing its sense of its intimate relations to God that it is in danger of dying out. And how is the sacredness of poetry to be truly apprehended? By the method which Mrs. Browning adopted, of looking boldly into the human heart, and reading it fearlessly and trustfully. 'Foole, saide my muse to mee, looke in thine hearte, and write.' And poetry thus produced is that which preserves an everlasting freshness and fragrance. The human heart first, and Nature afterwards, were the teachers at whose feet our poet learned the deep lessons she subsequently transmitted to her species. By these were fostered in her a tenderness which breathes through all her writings, and whose spirit is mirrored therein as the blue sky mirrors itself upon the bosom of the deep.

To her, also, it may be said that poetry brought ' its

own exceeding great reward.' In the company of the deep-browed poets, the monarchs of all the ages, she found consolation as well as intellectual life. With the fellowship of Æschylus, and Pindar, and Plato, and Sophocles, and Euripides, of the olden world, and Chaucer, Spenser, and Shakspeare, of the modern, the burden of existence, that would otherwise have been insupportable, became comparatively light with her. When but a girl she was able to read in the original some of the greatest masterpieces of antiquity; and indeed almost her first work was an excellent translation of the ' Prometheus' of her great favourite amongst the poets. Her introduction to and intimate acquaintance with Greek literature was in a large measure due to the influence of her well-appreciated and cherished tutor, Boyd, the blind author of a work upon the Greek Fathers, to whom she addresses some of the best of her sonnets. But though the Greek was the language which afforded her the most delight, her acquaintance was not confined to this, her knowledge of the Hebrew being also most intimate, whilst the Bible in that language was amongst her most continuous studies. Little would men suspect in meeting her for the first time that within that slight and spiritual frame burned so much of the celestial fire. It was, perhaps, in consequence of the chance introduction of some literary question, that it was discovered how much learning existed beneath so unpretending an exterior. She was like those branches which hang nearest the ground because of the prodigious crop of luscious fruit which is not always at first apparent to the eye. The love of knowledge, however, deep and lasting though it remained, never subdued or modified in her that great gift of the poet, a burning earnestness or enthusiasm. At the end, as at the beginning of life, the flame shone brightly. It was no flickering, artificial light, kept alive because the poet must simulate an earnestness that is not possessed; but it left an impress and a character upon her work which could not be mistaken. Her song resembled that which fable has associated with the name of Sappho—a living voice, eloquent with passion. Something of her own intensity of feeling breathes in the lines when she speaks of

> ' Electric Pindar, quick as fear,
>   With race-dust on his cheeks, and clear
>   Slant startled eyes that seem to hear
>
>   The chariot rounding the last goal,
>   To hurtle past it in his soul.
>   And Sappho, with that gloriole
>
>   Of ebon hair on calmëd brows—
>   O poet-woman! none foregoes
>   The leap, attaining the repose.'

Had song been less to her than indissolubly bound up
with her life, one thinks she must have wavered in her
devotion to it.   But in truth her appetite grew by what
it fed on, and the weakness of the body only led to a
further development of soul.   We like to think of her as
accepted amongst the gods for her power over the divine
art, and yet dear in her human relations for the exercise
of a tenderness and a sympathy associated with the sex
which make home a second paradise.

Elizabeth Barrett Browning was born in London, in
the year 1809, and was the daughter of Mr. Barrett, an
English country gentleman.   At a very early age she
had written much that was worthy of living, though it
was kept from all eyes save those of her father, whom
she mentions in the first collected edition of her poems
as ‘my public and my critic.’   Miss Mitford has described her as a ‘ slight, delicate figure, with a shower of
dark curls falling on each side of a most expressive face,
large tender eyes, richly fringed by dark eyelashes, and
a smile like a sunbeam.’   She possessed a grace and
delicacy which almost defied representation.   With so
perfect a mental and spiritual organisation it was not
given to her to be equally blessed in the physical.
Always frail, it was her misfortune further to endanger
her existence in 1837 by the bursting of a blood-vessel

on the lungs. The extremest care preserved her life, though the incident was succeeded by a long period of weakness and suffering. Two years afterwards, before she had quite recovered, she was again assailed by misfortune, experiencing the keenest anguish on witnessing the death of her favourite brother, who was drowned at Torquay. A long period of danger followed this catastrophe, and when she was at length able to be removed to her father's house, it was only to become an invalid, with the prospect of a life couch-ridden to its close. For seven long years this period of seclusion lasted; but during that time Miss Barrett devoured all the books she could bring within her reach, and cultivated the art which was afterwards to bring her immortality. In 1846, that is, when she was in her thirty-seventh year, came the principal event of her life—viz., her marriage with Mr. Browning. He bore her away to Italy, where softer skies brought back that health which had so long forsaken her in her native land. The union was most felicitous, and the influence upon Mrs. Browning's genius must have been great. On this influence, however, we cannot now enlarge, for the husband of the author of ' Aurora Leigh ' still lives. Mrs. Browning died in Florence in 1861, after testifying, in some of the noblest strains ever penned, her extraordinary devotion to the land of her adoption.

One beneficial result of the comparative seclusion of Mrs. Browning's life was the habit of introspection which it induced, and which, fortunately for posterity, led to the production of some of the finest subjective poetry extant. We can understand to some extent her admiration for Wordsworth, after noticing the tenor of her own existence, which ran in somewhat similar grooves. Where, but for the seclusion of her life, would have been that wealth of ancient lore which, while not destroying the freshness of her poetry, has added to it a classic grace and a finish most admirable and remarkable? The excellent balancing of her faculties had a happy effect on her work, which is always good in conception, however defective it may occasionally be in expression. Her intellect was keen and comprehensive, not deficient even in masculinity ; and it was only in her theories—witness, for instance, references to social questions in her greatest poem—that she occasionally failed to exhibit that solidity of judgment, or practicality of judgment rather, which is generally associated with the opposite sex. As a poet she undoubtedly looked at men and things from the intensely personal view, in the sense, we mean, of individuality. Instead of taking a broad sweep as Dante— whom we conceive as being merged in the mighty conceptions of his spirit—she had rather that other gift of the poet, of making herself, the individual, apparent in all her writings. It is this quality which adds so greatly to the force of her lyrical effusions—indeed, without this quality no poet had better attempt the writing of lyrics. So far as regards this form of poetry, we understand its force and value to be that it is an appeal from one individual mind to another; and the most successful lyrics have been those which have excited in us a particular, and not a general, interest. A momentary reflection upon the lyrics of Burns and Béranger will attest the truth of this assertion. It was a portion of Mrs. Browning's strength—and by no means an unimportant one—that she was able to achieve this result. Who will not continually feel indebted to her for many of her shorter poems, which have revealed so much of the human heart in them, and awakened impulses and sensations which have delighted and cheered the spirit? That was a happy observation passed upon her by one critic, who described her as Shakspeare's daughter. The same large-heartedness which pertained to the great dramatist is shown by the later poet. The benevolent eye looks out on men and nature with the same imperishable love. If the world has at any time possessed its ideal poets, she is worthy to be counted one of them.

From her earliest years, as will, indeed, have been

discovered already, Mrs. Browning appears to have had
the passion for books—a passion which is referred to
more than once in ' Aurora Leigh '—and her studious
habits, as well as that of writing, were encouraged by her
father.   Her early years are a reproach to any who, with
stronger health and equal opportunities, take no heed to
the storing and assimilation of knowledge.   In all that
we read of her subsequent works, the value of those early
habits of insatiable study is apparent.   Knowledge has
made the full mind, and the richness of the stores is not
without effect upon her original compositions.   How
must her fragile frame have thrilled when, in the course
of her reading, as she says—

> Because the time was ripe,
> I chanced upon the poets.

Doubtless, the slumbering possibilities in her nature were
touched by this, and it must have been with wonder that
the lights of the great bards first flashed across her vision :
something, it would have appeared to her, of the nature
of coming into a priceless inheritance.   And the time
arrived when all that she had acquired became of real
moment to her.   Let those who would despise erudition
in a poet place Mrs. Browning beside other female poets,
and see how they lose by comparison—not only in that

original power in which she was undoubtedly stronger. The poet cannot gain one fact too many; the poorest and commonest coinage which he receives from other mints may be transmuted into the purest gold in his own. The best minds have recognised this, and have laboured diligently after the perfection of knowledge, feeling that none are so gifted, even the gods, but that they may learn somewhat from men.

To attempt to pass in review all that Elizabeth Barrett Browning has left as her legacy for future ages is not our intention. We purpose, however, to examine some of her works individually before offering any criticisms of a general character upon her genius. 'A Drama of Exile,' which was a comparatively early production, is acknowledged to possess great sublimity in its ideas, though the conception as a whole is asserted to be a failure. For ourselves we were struck with the poetic wealth which it displays, and failure as applied to it must be taken in the comparative form. There are those whom the majestic Milton has not satisfied by his *chef-d'œuvre* ; but the most fastidious will admit that if he has not touched the highest heavens he has come very near them. Of course, it is not pretended for a moment that the 'Drama of Exile' stands forth as magnificent a conception as 'Paradise Lost,' which Mrs. Browning's poem

compels us to bring to memory, being upon the same
subject ; neither can it be said to be perfectly original,
coming after that epic : but in the later poem we find
much in point of sustained language which reminds us of
Milton's work. Milton's feet were more firmly set, and
he has the stately march of a conqueror. Mrs. Browning
can only in this work show her possibilities, not her
ultimate perfection. This is an excellent touch, due,
probably, partly to the fact that it was written by a
woman; Gabriel, addressing Lucifer, says :—

> ' If thou hadst gazed upon the face of God
> This morning for a moment, thou hadst known
> That only pity fitly can chastise :
> Hate but avenges.'

These lines, put into the mouth of Adam, are also exquisite :—

> ' The Highest being the Holy and the Glad,
> Whoever rises must approach delight
> And sanctity in the act.'

But for a passage of unfaltering eloquence, and one
instinct with true poetic fire, take the address of Adam
to Eve after the twain have left Paradise. To demonstrate Mrs. Browning's power over blank verse, we cannot
refrain from citing a portion of it :—

'Raise the majesties
Of thy disconsolate brows, O well-beloved,
And front with level eyelids the To come,
And all the dark o' the world !

*   *   *   *   *   *

Thy love
Shall chant itself its own beatitudes
After its own life-working.   A child's kiss,
Set on thy sighing lips, shall make thee glad ;
A poor man served by thee, shall make thee rich ;
A sick man helped by thee, shall make thee strong ;
Thou shalt be served thyself by every sense
Of service which thou renderest.   Such a crown
I set upon thy head,—Christ witnessing
With looks of prompting love—to keep thee clear
Of all reproach against the sin foregone,
From all the generations which succeed.
Thy hand, which plucked the apple, I clasp close,
Thy lips, which spake wrong counsel, I kiss close,
I bless thee in the name of Paradise,
And by the memory of Edenic joys
Forfeit and lost,—by that last cypress tree
Green at the gate, which thrilled as we came out,—
And by the blessed nightingale which threw
Its melancholy music after us,—
And by the flowers, whose spirits full of smells,
Did follow softly, plucking us behind
Back to the gradual banks and vernal bowers
And fourfold river-courses—By all these,
I bless thee to the contraries of these,
I bless thee to the desert and the thorns,
To the elemental change and turbulence,

And to the roar of the estranged beasts,
And to the solemn dignities of grief,—
To each one of these ends,—and to their END
Of Death and the Hereafter.'

It will be apparent that for one who had not yet
attained the full maturity of her powers to write like this
there must have been a great future in store. Whatever
deductions might have to be made as regards the want
of stupendousness in her conceptions, there was still
sufficient breadth in her earlier work to prove that there
were scarcely any heights to which she might not subsequently attain. In the chorus of Eden spirits which
comes into the ' Drama of Exile ' there is an abundance
of lyrical music and power, given in metres which have
since been most successfully adopted by other poets.
In another poem, ' The Seraphim,' we observe the
same noble moral glow which pervaded the drama to
which we have just alluded. The time of the poem is
that of the Crucifixion, and the sublime tragedy is
handled with a delicacy and at the same time a force as
nearly befitting so lofty a subject as we can well imagine.
The deep religious spirit which pervaded Mrs. Browning
led her frequently to the choice of topics in some way
connected with the great verities of the Christian religion,
in which she had a profound and intense belief, as will

have been gathered, not only from repute, but from the attitude assumed in her works, by anyone who has made acquaintance with them. The faults which are principally to be noted in her earliest poems are those related to art, a knowledge of which rarely comes at the outset to the most precocious. Before art can be exhibited, there must not only be capacity, but work accomplished —work compared with previous work, and each stage showing an advance upon that which went before. Although Mrs. Browning was never at any period of her career as distinguished for finish as she was for other and more important qualities, there is yet a considerable difference in this respect between her first effusions and her later lyrics. Her strength and pathos, however, generally overwhelm all other considerations in the reader's mind, whose attention is seized and retained by personal influence. It is the poet who does not throw himself entirely into his creations who is mostly eminent for finish. The value of the diamond to him consists in the way in which it is set, and he would prefer a stone of inferior water if it exhibited excess of polish to one much more massive if some touches of the rough still adhered to it. Yet, we are by no means contending that great poets are not also great in art. We are speaking only of finish, which is but a portion of art, and that not the most important. In art are combined the larger qualities of fitness, proportion, and truth, which are the masters of finish the world over. In all these three points Mrs. Browning was the successful artist; and he who objected to her because he discovered here and there a false rhyme or a defective line, would have lost sight of the towering mountain ahead in stumbling over a mole-hill. Having said thus much, let us at the same time frankly admit that the sense of adequateness is not strongly perceived in the lengthy poems to which we have adverted. We discover it in the highest degree in 'Paradise Lost,' and ought, of course, to find it in all work which is the matured result of a grand imagination —work that has attained solidity by frequent communing with and lifelong study of the bases on which it was grounded. So, had these poems of Mrs. Browning's been written at a later stage the beneficial result would have been apparent, in this one point at any rate upon which we are insisting. The unevenness in her execution would also have been considerably diminished, a matter of no small importance in conceptions of that nature. But take the poem and the drama as they stand, with all their faults, and we repeat there is still room for a feeling of genuine admiration over the result achieved.

Mrs. Browning's chosen field of study was the one

productive of her first work of great importance, viz. her rendering of the ' Prometheus Bound' of Æschylus. She had most probably been incited to this work by the companion, before mentioned, of her studies in Greek. It is a deed of no small magnitude for a young lady to accomplish this at all, and might well daunt even deeper students; but she had a profound appreciation of the old poet, and brought her love for his sublime tragedy to bear upon the task. It was scarcely to be expected that she would obtain a complete success, and she herself admitted that the translation was defective. She accordingly recast it, substantially changing the form of many passages. Though on reading it we gain the impression that it is a considerably Anglicised Greek drama, the vigour exhibited, and the true poetical fervour which is thrown around it, make it very welcome. The vocabulary of passion employed is rich and varied, whilst the rhythm affords scope for considerable poetic effects. In this, as in her other translations, she desired it to be understood that her one great idea was to catch the spirit of the original. The choruses are excellent, and possess, in addition to much music, all the fire that it is essential should burn in poems which have for their aim the depicting of the ecstasies and the writhings of passion. 'A Lament for Adonis,' from Bion, is very happy and

G

full of a warm imagery, and indicates, besides, the instinct and apprehension of the original poet.

The genius of Mrs. Browning had two sides—the lyric and the dramatic : she had little special gift for either the idyllic or the epic. For the idyllic she was not either sufficiently didactic or intransitively calm ; for the epic her emotions were too keen and her sensibilities too quick and lively. Her longest poem has nothing of the epic about it, being in fact neither more nor less than a series of dramatic scenes. It does not profess to give the triumphant progress of a hero or a heroine, but to unfold to us the inner life of its principal character. In a word, it is an Autobiography in verse.

Considering first her lyrical capabilities—for it is really by means of these that her immortality is most secured—we are bound to say that they are of the highest order. Campbell was a great artist, but on reading his lyrics we are struck with the fact that they are in a large measure the product of a skilled mind rather than of a real singer. He has been succeeded by Tennyson in verbal perfection ; but to our mind neither of these true poets is the equal of Mrs. Browning in the matter of the lyric. Yet so high is our estimate of the authors of 'Hohenlinden' and 'Locksley Hall' that no other poets in these later times, save Mrs. Browning and perhaps two others, can be put into comparison with them for real lyrical power. One of the two latter is Shelley, the other Burns, who is the superior of Shelley, and indubitably at the head of his race : and for this reason, that he invariably put his heart into his verse. Soul, not culture, thus gave us the best of our lyric poets. It is on the ground assigned in regard to Burns that we should give Mrs. Browning the next place amongst the moderns for lyrical genius, though these two poets were as wide asunder as the poles in all other respects. Let the reader dispassionately compare the lyrics which have been written by our principal singers during the past two or three generations. He will find, we think, that the position we have assumed is one which can be maintained. Shelley undoubtedly exhibits the true lyrical fire, but his poems are not so varied as those of Mrs. Browning ; while her pathos is deeper than his and that of all his compeers. His imagination was, perhaps, somewhat higher, and he soared into cloud-land more frequently ; but the heart, which gave Burns his power, was the strength of Mrs. Browning. Shelley was almost too ethereal, too spiritual, and the consequence was that the human was somewhat overshadowed. His sensibility was of the keenest description, and many of his lyrics bear testimony to the truth of his averment that

G 2

'Most men
Are cradled into poetry by wrong ;
They learn in suffering what they teach in song.'

One cannot help thinking that Shelley's natural place in the world would be that of a spiritualised Spenser ; and if that calm could have come to him which alone can furnish the poet with the opportunity he ought to have, there is no knowing but he might have given us a work rich enough to justify this fancy of him. As it is, between writhings and groanings, the paroxysms of a much-tried spirit, he wrote those exquisite lyrics and poems, which we should be indeed loth to lose from our literature. Mrs. Browning had not the intense naturalness of Burns, and though both felt acutely, yet in character and temperament they had nothing in common. But, as we have said, the mainspring of the power of both was in the heart. They worked upon different principles and under different circumstances. Burns was moved to joy or sorrow by the impressions he drew from outward nature ; Mrs. Browning, on the contrary, found that nature received a tinge of melancholy or happiness from her own emotions. They are thus perfect contrasts in everything except the one great endowment of genius. And if the word epigrammatic may be used to denote that power which Burns had of describing an object in nature or a human emotion, Mrs. Browning was certainly not so epigrammatic as the northern singer. Leigh Hunt once referred to our poet as the sister of Alfred Tennyson, but the relation does not strike us as of the happiest. It does not set in the proper light either relatively to the other. In the first place, there is a good deal that is feminine (in the best sense) about the genius of Tennyson, whilst occasionally there is that in Mrs. Browning's poetry as masculine as anything to be found in the Poet Laureate. In truth, we do not see much good in these comparisons at all; the happiest expression yet given utterance to is the one previously mentioned, which describes her as Shakspeare's daughter. We are able to see some meaning in this; we can feel that her genius stands in the same relation to that of the transcendent poet of the world as does a daughter to her parent. The lesser is the true miniature representation of the greater.

The precise order in which Mrs. Browning's lyrics were written has never been stated, and it is not possible to arrive at a correct chronology with regard to them by internal evidence. The dates of several, however, are well known : and amongst the earliest of her productions was that entitled 'A Vision of Poets,' written in a very attractive, though unusual metre. This vision of men of 'foreheads royal with the truth,' as beheld in the magnificent temple of poetry, is one of her most successful as well as most graphic conceptions.   No words are wasted in painting the portraits ; to each of the world-famous men are appropriated but a few lines, yet how telling these are !—

> ' Shakspeare, on whose forehead climb
> The crowns o' the world : O eyes sublime
> With tears and laughters for all time !'

The national poet's eminence was never more felicitously indicated than in these simple words—that is, more of him can be grasped than pages of criticism could accomplish, though the poet's description is by no means exhaustive.   Other excellent touches are those devoted to Euripides, Lucretius, ' nobler than his mood,' Goethe, Chaucer, Milton, Schiller,—

> ' And Burns, with pungent passionings
> Set in his eyes : deep lyric springs
> Are of the fire-mount's issuings.

> ' And poor, proud Byron, sad as grave
> And salt as life ; forlornly brave,
> And quiv'ring with the dart he drave.'

And the lesson—it is worthy of the ' Vision.'   Is it well for the poet to be born to suffer, and to die unrecognised and unrewarded?   Verily so ; he has lived for truth and beauty—scarcely two as the author tells us

—and should therefore be content. His experience has been, after all, better than that of the lower man, with lower pains and less transporting pleasures. He will be crowned, but crowned with no ordinary crown. His highest glory is to *know*, however the end is gained. And after death he will have two lives—one in the Beyond, and one in the Past, in the songs he has left behind him. Thus the end of the whole matter is reached, the conclusion being that ' Knowledge by suffering entereth, and Life is perfected by Death.' The lesson in some of its applications is not new ; the martyrs to truth in whatever shape have always taught it, but now the poet-martyrs teach it. For they are martyrs too frequently ; and that is not martyrdom simply which affects or destroys the body. The spirituality of Mrs. Browning's nature shines in this poem ; she affords some clue as to her ideal. It is a strain singularly pure and lofty, and shows a developing imagination which augured powerfully and well for succeeding work. Its burden is more cheerful than that of ' The Two Voices,' a poem cast in the same mould, and to which the thought of the reader inevitably reverts while reading the ' Vision.' Its meaning is not to be restricted alone to the class of beings with whom it deals upon the surface, for the con-clusion is a triumphant one for the whole of the human race, whose ends of life are also made sacred by the same method. Having read this poem, one rises with a more hopeful heart to engage in the world's conflict.

We pass on from such poems as 'The Romaunt of Margret' and 'Isobel's Child' with reluctance, for there is much in them both of concentrated strength and music which we could wish to have pointed out. Some have chosen them as well-nigh the happiest efforts of the poet, and they certainly are amongst the most beautiful notes of her lyre. Even the rhymes seem to possess a melancholy befitting the subjects, whilst the mere repetition of the words 'Margret, Margret,' attains to real pathos in the cunning hands of the writer in the former poem. A singular affection for subjects which have in them the deepest anguish and suffering was early apparent in Mrs. Browning. The spirit very seldom danced, though when it did, the music was as true and fitting as the funeral dirge, which she more frequently gives us. Wandering amongst her poems is like standing in the forest alone, with the wailing wind and the flying rain as the only assurances of an existence sublimer than our own. But the profoundest depth of our heart is reached thereby. We would there had been no need for the lament and the sorrow, and yet we would not have lost those mysterious thrills of the soul which her power has evoked.

We must follow the poet in her quest of truth, follow her wherever she leads us, for by these means shall we emerge out of the thick folds of darkness into the broad light of day. This is one reason why we have such an admiration for, and attachment to her genius. Wherever she leads us, it is to make us better. Does she show us the poor whom we too often oppress? It is that we may know wherein we have erred, and that in the future our hands may be washed clean from oppression and cruelty. Does she sometimes apparently darken the spirit? It is only to make it reflect so that it may endeavour to grope through the mysteries of life and nature up to God. Intellectual doubts are frequently disposed of in a very summary method, and one which has at sundry times in the world's history been most effective ; she sees their lowering forms gradually attenuate and disperse before the calm eye of Faith. Whatever of evil was rampant in the world, this could not be crushed out of her. To her, it was not always necessary to understand all the wrong that she beheld ; she saw it, and hated it. She has helped men by her writings to do something towards making an end of it. She has been a mouthpiece for the poor and miserable ; the light of love beams on her forehead and dwells in her eyes ; the Divine feeling of compassion has swelled in her bosom, and for this reason, as for others, she has her place with those who are beloved of the human race.

In proceeding to indicate what we consider some of Mrs. Browning's most admirable lyrics, we must decidedly name among the chief, 'The Rhyme of the Duchess May.' This ballad has in it not only a quaintness which conveys us back to the days of chivalry, but a strength of expression which is generally absent in the productions of that period. It bears unquestionably the stamp of genius. The poet for the time has completely forgotten herself, projecting her thoughts so far into the subject as to realise a most intense and tragic phase of human existence. There is the ring of melancholy in the lines, which is deepened by the constant recurrence of the allusion to the passing bell. The whole conception is well worked out, and the powers of the writer are not frittered away before the close of the poem, as is too frequently the case with lyrics of similar length. The perfection of what is touching is reached in ' Bertha in the Lane,' where the dying maiden tells with simple pathos the incident which has led to her own heart's breaking. There is nothing forced here ; indeed, the language in some passages does not rise higher than that of actual conversation, the only adventitious poetical aid given to the setting of the story being that of the rhyme, which again is well chosen. The author has wisely avoided the slightest straining after effect, leaving the natural pathos in the story to accomplish the end which she desires. 'Lady Geraldine's Courtship' is a romance which almost necessarily challenges comparison with 'Locksley Hall,' and what is strange about the two, Mrs. Browning has, in our judgment, most truthfully drawn the male characters, while Tennyson has been the happier in all else in his poem. The poet who loved Lady Geraldine has many excellences, but his vocation has not properly imbued him with the kingly spirit, and he fails in the strength and robustness which we should expect. Besides, we quickly grow indignant that he should be so slow in reading that which should have been patent to his eyes. The character of the Earl is well drawn, his natural dignity being admirably caught in the few lines devoted to his limning. The old story of love springing where it listeth, unforced and unexpected, is once more dilated upon, and brought in this instance to a satisfactory consummation. As another specimen of the perfection of lyric art we may cite 'The Romance of the Swan's Nest,' one of the most beautiful and strangely-attractive series of stanzas ever penned.

But let us pass on to 'The Cry of the Children,' that noble and striking remonstrance against the greed and oppression of mankind. Its intense pathos could surely only spring from a woman's heart, wounded in its love for the human by deeds enough to make the heavens blush. We have heard something of the sorrows of the factory children, but these lines have brought them close to us, and compelled us to feel that the poorest and weakest are our brethren and sisters. When was the anguish of a young spirit grasped so clearly as in the following lines, which are supposed to be spoken by the little workers amongst the iron wheels—those wheels which roll on ruthlessly, scarcely giving time for rest?—

' Two words, indeed, of praying we remember,
    And at midnight's hour of harm,
  " Our Father," looking upward in the chamber,
    We say softly, for a charm.
  We know no other words except " Our Father,"
    And we think that, in some pause of angels' song,
  God may pluck them with the silence sweet to gather,
    And hold both within His right hand, which is strong.
  " Our Father !" If He heard us, He would surely
    (For they call Him good and mild)
  Answer, smiling down the steep world very purely,
    " Come and rest with Me, my child." '

England has cleared herself from something of the re-proach contained in the poem from whence these lines are taken, and by God's grace she will be, perhaps, wholly free from stain in the (let us hope not far distant)

future.   There are other poems which exhibit the same
large sympathetic heart as the one founded upon the
miseries of the factory children, such as ' Mother and
Poet,' and ' The Cry of the Human,' which latter reminds
the world how many

> ' Lips say, " God be pitiful,"
> Who ne'er said, " God be praised ! " '

She felt as did that other poet of the poor, of whom we
are proud, for all who are in any way crushed or bruised
by the pressure of society and of social distinctions, or
of social misfortunes.   To be despised or to be sad was
the way to be sure of her deepest interest.   This is a
trait which will serve to keep her memory green, for who
among us will willingly let die the names of our philan-
thropists—those who have been genuine in the active
and written expressions of their sympathy?   One likes
to linger over the point how lofty genius steps down with
more sincerity from its high estate to acknowledge fellowship with the mean and the wretched, than do the
quasi-philanthropists who consider that the claims of
humanity are met by the doling out of a pittance to any
who may appeal to their condescension.   Not always,
yet very often, the great intellect is the index to the
generous and simple spirit.

To mark the range of our author's powers, compare such poems as 'A Child's Thought of God' with those on Napoleon, or 'Casa Guidi Windows.' How sweetly and beautifully the first-named closes !—

> ' God is so good, He wears a fold
>   Of heaven and earth across His face,
> Like secrets kept, for love, untold.

> ' But still I feel that His embrace
>   Slides down by thrills, through all things made,
> Through sight and sound of every place :

> ' As if my tender mother laid
>   On my shut lips her kisses' pressure,
> Half waking me at night, and said,
>   " Who kiss'd you through the dark, dear guesser ? " '

This is better theology than the orthodox damnation with which we were terrified in our youth by narrow-minded bigots, who have probably ruined many a soul by preaching that God is powerful and vindictive, instead of God is love. We want more of the teaching which we get in the pages of this woman-poet. Then note how from these sweet and happy thoughts we can turn to matter more bold and striking, as in 'The Dead Pan,' which has a truly musical ring with it ; ' Cowper's Grave,' an immortal tribute to a suffering singer; ' Crowned and Buried,' an appreciation of the great and deathless Napoleon; but, above all, in this class of effort, to ' Casa

Guidi Windows.' This poem exhibits Mrs. Browning in her greatest intellectual strength. The fabric is solid and enduring; the poem as sustained as anything which she has written, and more perfect than her remaining longer one. Clearly her feeling was in this work as well as her imagination, and the combined powers have given us something which cannot fail to live.

Everyone who knows anything at all of the poet is familiar with her great love for Italy, one of the strongest passions of her life. It is in this poem that she chiefly unfolds to the world her feelings with regard to the emancipation of that country. From the Casa Guidi windows at Florence, her favourite city, she watched the struggle for liberty in which Italy engaged against Austria, and the assistance rendered towards this object by Napoleon III., without whom probably it would never have been accomplished. It was in praise of this champion that she wrote some of her most impassioned strains. She knew the deceased Emperor at his best, when there seemed strongly upon him an enthusiasm for the cause which he had espoused that would be sure to go straight to the heart of the generous and impulsive poet; and in her utterances, therefore, she was lavish and unrestrained. To many in England this over-warmth of feeling will seem strange, but till we have felt all the bitterness which

she felt for a degraded nation, and have seen the conqueror arise to lift her from the dust, we cannot say
how deep our gratitude might be to such conqueror, his
subsequent career notwithstanding. Our concern, however, is with the poems, including those entitled ' Poems
before Congress,' in which Mrs. Browning set forth that
patriotism, to be true, should not be manifested in
behalf of one's own country alone. In ' Casa Guidi
Windows' the imagery is rich and the language flowing,
worthy partners of the idea which engrossed the mind.
In the course of the poem beautiful legends of Savona-
rola and Michael Angelo are laid under contribution to
heighten the charms of the song of their country ; and
the closing pages of the poem contain an attractive
episode in relation to the poet's infant son, whom she
calls her young Florentine, he having been born in that
city. She has thus connected her native land and that
of her adoption more closely together, and claims nearer
relationship to Italy than she ever felt before, through
the link furnished in her child. It is impossible to do
more than refer to the extraordinary wealth and strength
of imagery which the poem contains; but as some justification for the high opinion we have expressed concerning
it, we must not neglect to extract the passage in which,
as before mentioned, the poet addresses her son :—

' The sun strikes through the windows, up the floor ;
Stand out in it, my own young Florentine,
   Not two years old, and let me see thee more !
It grows along thy amber curls, to shine
   Brighter than elsewhere.   Now, look straight before,
And fix thy brave blue English eyes on mine,
   And from thy soul, which fronts the future so,
With unabashed and unabated gaze,
   Teach me to hope for, what the angels know
When they smile clear as thou dost.   Down God's ways,
   With just alighted feet, between the snow
And snowdrops, where a little lamb may graze,
   Thou hast no fear, my lamb, about the road ;
Albeit in our vain-glory we assume
   That, less than we have, thou hast learnt of God.
Stand out, my blue-eyed prophet !—thou, to whom
   The earliest world-day light that ever flowed,
Through Casa Guidi windows chanced to come !
   Now shake the glittering nimbus of thy hair,
And be God's witness that the elemental
   New springs of life are gushing everywhere.'

It is, we imagine, almost universally accepted that to write the sonnet excellently is about the most difficult performance in the domain of poetry.   At any rate, it is the one branch of the art least frequently successfully achieved.   It is questionable whether we have more than three or four English poets who can be credited with the highest execution in this respect.   But to these three or four must be added the name of Mrs. Browning.

After Shakspeare, we should be inclined to maintain that
she is the equal of any.   For proof of this, let the reader
turn to her 'Sonnets from the Portuguese,' which, under a
disguised name, are her own sonnets.   To us they seem
to fulfil all the requisites of the sonnet, including strength,
imagery, sweetness, proportion or art, and massiveness.
They are certainly equal to any of Wordsworth's and
most of Milton's.   The sonnet, with the great poets, has
been generally most successful when personal to themselves.   They appear to have caught their passion and
confined it within bounds, so that the sonnet, in master
hands, becomes, as it were, 'foursquare to all the winds
that blow.'   There is no weak corner—all is solid and
compact.

These sonnets by Mrs. Browning bear upon them her
own very distinct individuality, and, as a means of setting
her truly before her readers, are more explanatory than
any other of her writings.   Let us study them for a
moment.   In the first, the poet presents us with a picture
of her mind at the period when she looked for Death as
the release from a mortal imprisonment, whose shadow
was laid deeply athwart her.   The sonnet is exceedingly
fine, and is as follows :—

'I thought once how Theocritus had sung
    Of the sweet years, the dear and wished-for years,

Who each one in a gracious hand appears
To bear a gift for mortals, old or young ;
And, as I mused it in his antique tongue,
I saw, in gradual vision through my tears,
The sweet, sad years, the melancholy years,
Those of my own life, who by turns had flung
A shadow across me.   Straightway I was 'ware,
So weeping, how a mystic Shape did move
Behind me, and drew me backward by the hair ;
And a voice said in mastery, while I strove :—
"Guess now who holds thee ?" "Death," I said. But there,
The silver answer rang, "Not Death, but Love ! "'

Then comes a description of love, whose powei
nothing can conquer, and which man is helpless to
destroy. Spirits ' but vow the faster for the stars.' Yet,
following on, we come to a declaration of her own un-
worthiness, on the part of the singer, to be thus discovered and made blessed. The gloom is still too heavy
about her, and will not be dispersed. She is fain to
cry—

' What hast *thou* to do,
With looking from thy lattice lights at me,
A poor, tired, wand'ring singer, singing through
The dark, and leaning up a cypress tree ?
The chrism is on thine head,—on mine, the dew,—
And Death must dig the level where these agree.'

How beautiful and how pathetic are these lines! And
the strain is continued, with no diminution of sadness,

through several succeeding sonnets. The soul has found
its counterpart, yet bids it begone; the proffered happiness is too great for it; it must not be. 'Go from me!'
is now the cry; but the spirit is evidently yielding to the
conqueror, for it adds :

> 'The widest land
> Doom takes to part us, leaves thy heart in mine,
> With pulses that beat double.'

The record of life progresses, and the great argument is
discussed, 'Can it be right to give what I can give?'
Witness the seventh and immediately subsequent sonnets,
for their dissection of the love passion, as it thrills
through and permeates the being. Truly autobiogra-
phical, indeed, are these confessions ; the seal of genuine
experience is upon each one with its alternating hopes
and fears, and its unfolding of a woman's heart. Surely
finer subjective poetry than this was never written. The
poet speaks to us without veils, and we listen eagerly to
the revelation. From the sadness and gloom we emerge
at length into daylight ; the cypress has yielded to the
rose. Love is justified ; it asks for and gives all. Troths
are exchanged, and the singer has given up the grave for
the sake of him who is now to be her life. We then see
the plan of the whole work. First, we had the soul
expecting death, then Life revivified by Love ; then the

grave put behind the soul ; and lastly, comes the sequel, the marriage of those whose history has been traced in the series of poems now about to conclude. Thus the poet muses, as she stands midway in her existence—the past behind her, the blissful future immediately in view :—

' " My future will not copy my fair past."
   I wrote that once ; and, thinking at my side
   My ministering life-angel justified
   The word by his appealing look upcast
   To the white throne of God, I turned at last,
   And there, instead, saw thee, not unallied
   To angels in thy soul ! Then I, long tried
   By natural ills, received the comfort fast,
   While budding, at thy sight, my pilgrim's staff
   Gave out green leaves, with morning dews impearled.
   I seek no copy now of life's first half :
   Leave here the pages with long musing curled,
   And write me new my future's epigraph,
   New angel mine, unhoped for in the world ! '

But to show what the wonderful depth of woman's love is, and to reach what seems the absolute fulness of human expression, we have the following triumphant song at the close of this personal history we have been examining :—

' How do I love thee ? Let me count the ways.
   I love thee to the depth and breadth and height

My soul can reach, when feeling out of sight
For the ends of Being and ideal Grace.
I love thee to the level of every day's
Most quiet need, by sun and candlelight.
I love thee freely, as men strive for Right ;
I love thee purely, as they turn from Praise.
I love thee with the passion put to use
In my old griefs, and with my childhood's faith.
I love thee with a love I seemed to lose
With my lost saints—I love thee with the breath,
Smiles, tears, of all my life !—and, if God choose,
I shall but love thee better after Death.'

We have thus glanced briefly through this remarkable
series of psychological poems, one of the most precious
bequests which a poet can leave us, revealing, as they do
so clearly, the inner life of the writer. After their
perusal, just as in the case of a study of Tennyson's ' In
Memoriam,' we feel that we have done more towards
grasping the character of the poet than we are able to do
by an intimate acquaintance with all her other works.
The unity of the 'Sonnets from the Portuguese' is precise and definite ; no link in the chain can be withdrawn without destroying the value of the whole. There
is no hesitancy in the utterance ; we here see Mrs.
Browning at her highest, when she has passed through
the noviciate of her art, and risen to the perfection of
song. The sonnets glow with rapture, are exquisite in

expression, and perfect in form. Taken collectively, and in the light of the one passion which they trace, from its inception to its culmination, we know nothing anywhere to compare with them. Intellect and passion are combined in an equal degree, and together fused into wondrous music.

The love poetry from the hand which wrote thus passionately—and including compositions other than the sonnets—would in itself, and in its entirety, form a complete study, for its variety, sweetness, and pathos. But there yet remain to us some remarks on the work upon which, chiefly, the author's fame is conceded to rest—' Aurora Leigh.' A wide diversity of opinion exists with regard to its merits, and to the position which it ought to occupy in modern literature. The writer herself, in inscribing it to her cousin, described it as the most mature of all her works, and the one into which her ' highest convictions upon Life and Art have entered.' Our own view of it is that, as a whole, it is somewhat inconsequent; it lacks unity, for a poem of such magnitude; but even in these higher respects, though not perfect, it is little beneath anything produced this generation. When we come to regard it in other aspects, however, our praise is almost necessarily unbounded. It is a poem which we could imagine Shakspeare dropping a

tear over for its humanity. Its intense subjectivity will
exempt its influence on men from decay. Were we not
amazed with the beauty and fulness of its poetry, we
should be struck with its philosophy. The following
lines might almost be taken as a digest of the whole
teaching of Carlyle : —

> ' Get leave to work
> In this world—'tis the best you get at all ;
> For God, in cursing, gives us better gifts
> Than men in benediction. God says " Sweat
> For foreheads," men say " crowns," and so we are crowned,
> Ay, gashed by some tormenting circle of steel
> Which snaps with a secret spring. Get work, get work ;
> Be sure 'tis better than what you work to get.'

The author's views on Art are set forth with some
fulness. Art, we presume, notwithstanding all the darkness which has been cast around it by much speaking,
means (if we are bound to describe it as concisely as
possible) the closest and most perfect realisation of the
various forms of Truth which it is in the power of man
to attain. Some such idea as this certainly possessed
the mind of Mrs. Browning ; and it was her opinion that
that was real art which assisted in any degree to lead
back the soul to contemplate God, the supreme Artist of
the universe. Yet Art, even with her, was not the
highest, the ultimate—

'Art is much, but Love is more !
O Art, my Art, thou'rt much, but Love is more !
Art symbolises heaven, but Love is God
And makes heaven.'

As a solution for many of the problems of social life 'Aurora Leigh' must be pronounced a failure. It exhibits a wonderful sensitiveness to the evils resulting from the imperfect conditions of society, but it shows no powers of reconstruction. Its principal attraction, after its poetry, which stands supremely first therein, lies in the series of pictures of human life, in its varied phases, which it presents, and in its power of analysis of the human heart. Sincerity is also a prominent characteristic of the revelations which it makes ; it is an autobiography in which nothing is kept back, and the inner workings of a woman's heart were never more clearly transcribed. Unevenness characterises the narrative, but daring speculation and rich thought are embraced within the lines. There are passages of poetry as lofty and impassioned within the covers of this one book as are contained in any single lengthy modern poem of which we have knowledge. From the level of occasional mediocrity we pass on to sublime imaginative heights. In this poem we have a vantage ground from which we survey the panorama of human life, illumined by the sun of genius. To attempt to extract its beauties would be futile; it is a garden in which every flower of sweetness blooms. Its aroma is amongst the most fragrant in literature. Or again, to change the figure, the poem is like a mine which yields more and more as the human digger presses it. When he first enters into possession he beholds the faint yellow streaks which betoken the golden treasure, but it is the subsequent labour which brings to light the actual El Dorado.

One grand result of Mrs. Browning's literary career has been to disprove the assertion that women cannot write true poetry. Such a taunt may be considered as disposed of for ever. If we are to believe tradition, Sappho wrote the finest lyrics the world has seen; but our own generation has beheld woman's genius take even a wider range. No woman, as yet, has written a great epic, or dramatic poetry of the highest order; but how restricted is the number of men who have done this! What there is in the nature of woman, however, to forbid her rivalling even the highest we do not know; all we can say is, that genius, the dower of the gods, in its most transcendent manifestation, has, up to the present, been bestowed upon man. It may be, nevertheless, that we shall yet see the female complement of our great men— only, it cannot be obtained unless woman have a wider personal sphere. Still, it is most interesting to note that, in this nineteenth century she has demonstrated the possibility of a future equality. What novelist, for instance, has more conclusively made good his claim to rank almost with the highest, than George Eliot? How many of our artists have excelled Rosa Bonheur in her own special gifts? What writer has exhibited a greater breadth of imagination and power than Georges Sand? Lastly, where is the poetry which can be considered superior to Mrs. Browning's? In poetry, fiction, and art, at any rate, man has little supremacy to boast of for the last forty or fifty years. We do not mean that his genius may not have overtopped, in individual cases, that of woman, but the difference has not been so perceptible as in past ages. Woman is now more abreast of man. Her altitude is no longer, when compared with him, that of Mont Blanc beside Chimborazo. It is more than probable that we shall never behold a female Homer, Plato, or Shakspeare; but anything short of these woman may, and most probably will, become. Her passion is as deep, if her ambition be not so great, as man's. As her sympathies widen and she bears more of that burden of the world, experience—which, in its greatest depths and most extended scope, has hitherto largely pertained to man— she will produce work which shall be as potent and

beautiful as his, and possess the same inherent powers
of immortality.

Meanwhile, let us be just to what she has already
accomplished.   A dispassionate examination of the
poems of Elizabeth Barrett Browning can, we maintain,
only lead to this result—that she is the equal of any poet
of our time in genius.   In particular qualities she may
appear inferior to some who could be cited, and whose
names will irresistibly suggest themselves ; but in others
she is as indubitably their superior; and, until we can
decide who is greater, Byron or Wordsworth, Shelley or
Coleridge, Homer or Shakspeare, we care not to assign
her precise position.   One thing is certain, however, her
immortality is assured—she stands already crowned.   As
long as one human heart throbs for another she will be
held in high esteem.   Her poetry is that which refines,
chastens, and elevates.   We could think that with herself,
as with one of her characters, 'some grand blind Love
came down, and groped her out, and clasped her with a
kiss ; she learnt God that way.'   And who were her
teachers?   Can we ask that of one who said, 'Earth's
crammed with heaven, and every common bush afire with
God'?   The emerald beauty of a thousand valleys,
embroidered by the silver threads of meandering rivers ;
the grandeur of the everlasting hills with their lofty and

majestic calm ; the terrible rolling of the restless and unsatisfied sea ; the stars that at midnight shine, looking down upon us like the eyes of those we love ; above all, the whisper of God as it thrills through the human heart —these were her informers and teachers, the sources of her eminent inspiration. She sang of all these that men might be nobler, freer, and purer. Her apotheosis follows of Divine right with that of all the leaders of mankind : God endowed her, and we exalt her.

THOMAS LOVE PEACOCK

[FORTNIGHTLY REVIEW]

ONE trembles to think what the world would have become without its literary scourges. The soft irony of Montaigne, the withering gaze of Voltaire, the lightning flash of Swift, have now and again made it ashamed of its meanness and its vanity, and have discovered the pigmy concealed beneath the folds of the giant. There is no power touching whose exercise the whole of mankind is so sensitive as that of ridicule. Man always has objected, and always will object, to being called a fool: how much greater, then, must his horror be at having the fact demonstrated. Agreeing with the critic in his condemnation of the aphorism attributed to Shaftesbury, that 'ridicule is the test of truth,' we must still hold that it divides power almost equally with all other correctives of the public taste and morals. Wit dissects and destroys, but it has no creative force, is almost devoid of enthusiasm, and is no respecter of dignities and persons. There is much truth, however, which can in nowise come

I

within its scope ; hence it is a fallacy to call it the test of truth. It is rather the discoverer of error. There is something in the mental constitution of the satirist which prevents him from taking an optimist view of things. He is all the more useful on that account. The negative gifts of the satirist, while not lifting him to an equality with the being who originates, still entitle him to a high place in the world's regard. It should be borne in mind, too, that though it will be generally found he lacks enthusiasm, yet he possesses a sensitiveness as real, while differing in quality, as that of the artist and the poet.

Thomas Love Peacock had every opportunity for becoming the calm, contemplative cynic. His life was long but uneventful. His fourscore years did not embrace ten events to be remembered even in an ordinary life. He was born at Weymouth in 1785, and when a little over thirty years of age, obtained a post in a public office, as many others have done who afterwards enriched the national literature by their works. Peacock entered the East India House in 1818, and was Examiner of India correspondence from the death of James Mill in 1836 until March 1856, when he retired on a pension. He died January 23, 1866. He was a friend of Charles Lamb and of Shelley, for the latter of whom he acted as executor, and his wrongs doubtless made him still more sympathetic and friendly. His hatred of oppression in every guise is to be gathered in his novels, which breathe of liberty of thought, speech, and action. There were few, if any, riper scholars in his time. He was distinguished especially for his love of the Greek, Latin, and Italian classics, in editions of which his library was extraordinarily rich. It is not a little singular to find one whose tastes were those of the recluse taking up in his writings the burning questions of the day and mingling in the fray of politics. His observation, however, was most extensive ; like his learning, it seemed to embrace all matters and topics which came to the surface of public life. In his own political views he must have been ardently progressive—Liberal in the highest sense of the word, and to the backbone. He would be as opposed to a Whig job as to a Conservative monopoly. The deep-rooted conviction he had of the rights of man, the individual, caused him to loathe injustice in whatever quarter it was perceived. It is impossible to read his works and not to admire his denunciations of the base, and his scorn of the petty, sins which are sometimes hugged so closely. He had many pagan qualities, and among them a pagan kind of rectitude.

As to his humour, it is exclusively his own; one never

meets with its precise flavour either before or after him. Mingled sometimes with a dash of effrontery, it is very searching, attaining its end by a kind of intellectual travesty. To the quack and the mountebank he is a most dangerous person, wielding a power of castigation that is amazing. To his honour, however, it can be said that throughout his whole works there is no demonstration of personal feeling. Considering his endowment and the great temptation to wield the lash which invariably accompanies it, his self-repression was very great. Principles, not men, were the objects of his satire, and if occasionally individuals recoiled from the smart, it only showed how true had been his perceptions of character. Some humourists gently play with their subjects and tease them as a cat does a mouse; others knock them down with a bludgeon ; whilst others again make them despise themselves by inverting their natures, and showing them their vanity, hollowness, and pretence. Peacock adopted the last method with all the human excrescences he dealt with. To rebuke incapacity in attempting to deal with things too high for it, and to tear the glazed mask from the hollow cheek of pretence, were the objects to which he devoted himself. His success in doing this warrants some reference to the means by which he accomplished it, and justifies us in attempting to recover his name from the comparative indifference in which it has too long lain.

The chronological order in which his works were issued will not be strictly adhered to in the comments it may be necessary to make upon them; in fact there seems to be some doubt as to their order, if not of issue at least of composition. Undoubtedly, however, the public has been right in this instance in its association of his most widely-known novel with the name of the author as being intrinsically equal, if not superior, to any of the rest. Other works may have their own special charm, but that which is richest in the exhibition of the most prominent gift of the author is 'Headlong Hall.' Before the publication of this work there had been no writer who so boldly flung himself into the arena against contemporary humbugs. It is infinitely refreshing to read his straightforward, scathing denunciations, as well as his insinuating facetiousness and inuendo. He seems to revel in a tilt against all that the world praises as proper and respectable. An intellectual and material epicureanism pervades his pages, and when the rollicking wit ceases to flow it is only to give time for the passing of the bottle. We not only get 'the feast of reason and flow of soul,' but an unswerving devotion to those creature comforts in which the clergy—first in good works—have ever been our leaders. Mr. Headlong, the representative of the ancient Welsh family of the Head-longs, claiming superior antiquity to Cadwallader, contracts a strange taste for a Welsh squire—the taste for books. He next desires to pass for a philosopher and a man of taste, and comes up to Oxford to enquire for other men of taste and philosophers; but 'being assured by a learned professor that there were no such things in the University,' he proceeds to London, where he makes as extensive an acquaintance with philosophers and *dilettanti* as his ambition could desire. Several of these he invites to Headlong Hall, and the staple of the volume is composed of their doings and their discussions. The four leading personages who sustain the brunt of the battle are—Mr. Foster, the perfectibilian, who takes the bright view of everything; Mr. Escot, the deteriorationist, who takes the dark view of everything; Mr. Jenkison, the statu-quo-ite, who has arguments to advance on both sides, but is nearly always in favour of allowing things to remain as they are; and the Rev. Dr. Gaster, a worthy divine who can deliver a learned dissertation on the art of stuffing a turkey, and to whom the consumption of a bottle of port is a very slight matter. It is amusing to note how the various class of thinkers are trotted out one after another on their respective hobbies, and how impartial the author is in dividing his favours amongst them. Nor is it a little singular that all the specimens of the clergy whom Peacock has drawn are of one type; they are all jolly men of the world. About fifty or sixty years ago, the time at which he wrote, the conventional parson was very frequently of this stamp. His life was passed between fox-hunting, card-playing, and drinking. Since then the muscular Christian and other excellent men have arisen. But there have also sprung up with them men almost of a more mischievous type than the old fox-hunter. There are too many pitiful shepherds left who, in quiet, out-of-the-way villages make the life of the poor a burden to them. These continually enlarge on the duty of the labourers to keep their proper stations, and to revere the clergy and the squirearchy—the former of whom are to provide for them their opinions and their spiritual food, the latter their temporal comforts. Many of the later clergy are in the eyes of sensible men little less contemptible than the old; the venue of our contempt has been changed, that is all. But there is the same difficulty existing now that there was in Peacock's time, and indeed has been in all ages,—the difficulty of persuading the clergy to take one step towards reform in any direction, till nearly all other classes have taken ten. Progress, to them, has generally meant the destruction of

their cherished rights.   The Rev. Dr. Gaster cared little
about questions which caused the thoughtful intellects of
his day great concern, but in tossing off a bumper of
Burgundy he was equal to the best.   Occasionally he
had a forcible way with him, and said smart things, but
he did not profess to be so proficient in knowledge as
Mr. Panscope, 'the chemical, botanical, geological, astro-
nomical, mathematical, metaphysical, meteorological,
anatomical, physiological, galvanistical, musical, pictorial,
bibliographical, critical philosopher, who had run through
the whole circle of the sciences, and understood them all
equally well.'   The author gives us the portraits of four
critics, Mr. Gall, Mr. Treacle, Mr. Nightshade, and Mr.
Mac Laurel, with accurate descriptions of their various
modes of criticism—the criticism seeming at that period
to be about as deficient in *vis* as it generally is now; but
the happiest passages in the book are those devoted to
the speculations of the various philosophers.   Two
schools of thought are presented to us in the following
few sentences:—

'"I conceive," said Mr. Foster, "that men are virtuous in
proportion as they are enlightened ; and that, as every generation increases in knowledge, it also increases in virtue."
"I wish it were so," said Mr. Escot, "but to me the very reverse appears to be the fact.   The progress of knowledge is
not general : it is confined to a chosen few of every age.

How far these are better than their neighbours, we may examine by-and-by. . . . Give me the wild man of the woods : the original, unthinking, unscientific, unlogical savage : in him there is at least some good ; but, in a civilised, sophisticated, cold-blooded, mechanical, calculating slave of Mammon and the world, there is none—absolutely none. Sir, if I fall into a river, an unsophisticated man will jump in and bring me out ; but a philosopher will look on with the utmost calmness, and consider me in the light of a projectile, and making a calculation of the degree of force with which I have impinged the surface, the resistance of the fluid, the velocity of the current, and the depth of the water in that particular place, he will ascertain with the greatest nicety in what part of the mud at the bottom I may probably be found, at any given distance of time from the moment of my first immersion !"'

All which is rather hard both on the drowning man and the philosopher. The plot of this novel, if novel it can be called, is very subsidiary to the other purposes of the author, and has nothing whatever in it of a striking sort ; but there are scattered here and there through its pages fine descriptions of Welsh scenery, which seems to have possessed a peculiar charm for Peacock. His real strength, nevertheless, lies in another direction—a readiness to grasp instantaneously the views and characters of men, and a singular faculty of reproducing them in dialogue. The entire work, ' Headlong Hall,' is a series of portraits painted by means of opinions, some of them carefully executed and filled in, others drawn in a few rough but unmistakable touches. We have Miss Philomela Poppyseed, the compounder of novels ; Mr. Chromatic ; Sir Patrick Prism ; Mr. Cranium ; Miss Tenorina ; Lord Littlebrain, &c., whose idiosyncrasies are mostly betrayed by their names. The author also exhibits a remarkable power of assimilation from other writers, being able to enforce his points with the most apposite quotations from all sources, in all classes and all ages.

In 'Nightmare Abbey,' another remarkable work, we get the same brilliancy, and again meet with characters whom we have recognised in the world. There is Mr. Scythrop Glowry, heir to the owner of the Abbey, who becomes 'troubled with the passion for reforming the world,' and meditates on the practicability of reviving a confederation of regenerators. He publishes a book on the subject, of which only seven copies are sold ; but that does not deter him. He proposes to his beautiful lady-love, Miss Marionetta O'Carroll, that they should each open a vein in the other's arm, mix their blood in a bowl, and drink it as a sacrament of love—and, in fact, plays transcendental madman to the top of his bent. Then we have Mr. Toobad, who prophesies that 'the devil has come among mankind, having great wrath ; ' the Hon. Mr. Listless, with shattered nerves and a system incapable of exertion ; Mr. Flosky, who considers modern literature is a north-east wind—'a blight of the human soul.' In the mouth of one of the characters two sentences are put which are a deeper, truer comment upon the French character than whole volumes which have been written since. 'A Frenchman,' he says, 'is born in harness, ready saddled, bitted, and bridled, for any tyrant to ride. He will fawn under his rider one moment, and throw him and kick him to death the next ; but another adventurer springs on his back, and by dint of whip and spur, on he goes as before.' An epitome of the history of France since the Revolution of 1789. The following comparison between our own 'enlightened' age and the past, delivered by Mr. Toobad, has in it many points which might well give us pause :—

'Forsooth, this is the enlightened age. Marry, how ! Did our ancestors go peeping about with dark lanterns, and do we walk at our ease in broad sunshine? What do we see by it which our ancestors saw not, and which, at the same time, is worth seeing? We see a hundred men hanged, where they saw one. We see five hundred transported, where they saw one. We see five thousand in the workhouse, where they saw one. We see scores of Bible Societies, where they saw none. We see paper, where they saw gold. We see men in stays, where they saw men in armour. We see painted faces, where they saw healthy ones. We see children perishing in manufactories, where they saw them flourishing in the fields. We see prisons, where they saw castles. We see masters, where they saw representatives. In short, they saw true men, where we see false knaves. They saw Milton, and we see Mr. Sackbut.'

It is impossible even to enumerate here the vast variety of subjects which the writer touches upon. His range is almost unlimited; in every page there is either an old superstition exploded or a new philosophy criticised. The portraits of Shelley and Coleridge will easily be recognised in 'Nightmare Abbey,' for in spite of gross caricature there is also a striking amount of *vraisemblance.*

In 'Crotchet Castle' the author still writes with the pen of wormwood and ink of gall. The motto sufficiently indicates in the outset what a pungency of wit may be expected—'Le monde est plein de fous, et qui n'en veut pas voir, doit se tenir tout seul, et casser son miroir.' The complacency of many people is effectually destroyed by the way the author himself breaks the mirrors in which they have been wont to survey their own perfections. Possibly there may be those who think that in this work he has overstepped the just bounds of ridicule, and endeavoured to bring into contempt persons who are really useful to their generation. This is the conclusion to which a merely surface-reading of his books would lead, and probably many would rise from their perusal with an impression as unjust to the writer as could well be. Because Peacock ruthlessly condemns the pretenders of science, it is not to be supposed, and will not be by the really candid judge, that he has no sympathy with its true and earnest devotees. A Newton would receive his homage equally with an Æschylus or a Homer. He only wishes to prick the windbag ; to show upon what a very little a reputation which the world chooses to honour is sometimes built. It is the bubble which he desires to burst—the unsoundness in our social and political economics he endeavours to expose. Probably there was no one who would have felt it more deeply than he, if he had imagined that what he was writing would be turned from its purpose, either wilfully or ignorantly, and the writer made to appear an enemy of truth. It is hard, at times, to get rid of the idea that he is laughing at all the rest of the world, which, in any, is the surest test of folly, for the mighty wisdom of the cachinnatory great one himself is only a river into which the lesser streams of wisdom in others have flowed. There is no human being who can afford to laugh at and despise the whole race, simply because there is no human being who is not indebted to it. But we absolve our author at once from any such charge as this. Having comprehended in some degree the stand-points from which he has shot his arrows, we are bound to confess, not only that his aim is true, but that he has never chosen his subjects thoughtlessly or unjustifiably. Adam Smith lived long before him, and his principles were well established in the public mind, and acknowledged to be in many respects unassailable. It is not to be imagined for a moment that either he or his true followers were satirised in the person of the Scotch political economist who figures in these pages. Yet, strange to say, there have been critics who have credited him with some such aims, and have employed their acumen in discovering how he has transfixed this and that personage who has hitherto been held as an authority in the branch of literature or science to which he has devoted himself. Nothing could be more fallacious. Peacock was a man who was thoroughly abreast with the intellectual progress of his time ; he was deeply interested in it, and capable of sympathising to the full with all those men whose solid attainments and brilliant talents have been of service to humanity. His satire wants looking at as he wished it to be viewed, and it will be seen clearly of what immense value is the winnowing implement of his ridicule. The principal character in 'Crotchet Castle' is Mr. Mac Quedy, the Scotch political economist aforesaid, or Mac Q. E. D., the son of a demonstration—and certainly the way in which he is dealt with allows of no misunderstanding. Then we have the transcendental schools criticised in the person of Mr. Skionar, with more of the broad farce in his delineation than is conspicuous in the economist, the subject affording better scope for it. Mr. Chainmail is an antiquary, devoted to singing the glories of the twelfth and thirteenth centuries, whilst Mr. Crotchet, the proprietor of the Castle, is one who has made his money in the City with neither more nor less conscientiousness than thousands who are now continually occupied on 'Change in the same operation. Perhaps the best character in the book for life-like vigour and reality is the Rev. Dr. Folliott, the exceedingly vigorous Christian, who batters down the theories of Messrs. Mac Quedy and Skionar with the force of a sledge-hammer, and who is not unlike, in his style of conversation, the great Johnson. When asked if he sets no value upon ' the right principles of rent, profit, wages, and currency,' he answers : ' Sir, my principles in these things are to take as much as I can get, and to pay no more than I can help. These are every man's principles, whether they be the right principles or no. There, sir, is political economy in a nutshell.' The Doctor is wrong ; these are not every man's principles, but they

are very largely every man's practice—which, notwithstanding, amounts to very nearly the same thing. We
should fail in giving an idea of the piquancy of the
various conversations in which the several characters
take part. Peacock has written no work where the
dialogue is more brilliant. From the chapter on theories
we extract only a few sentences, which may serve to
indicate his general style :—

'*Mr. Crotchet, Jun.* There is one point in which philosophers of all classes seem to be agreed ; that they only
want money to regenerate the world.

'*Mr. Mac Quedy.* No doubt of it. Nothing is so easy as
to lay down the rules of perfect society. There wants
nothing but money to set it going. I will explain myself
fully and clearly by reading a paper (*producing a large
scroll*). In the infancy of society—

'*The Rev. Dr. Folliott.* Pray, Mr. Mac Quedy, how is it
that all gentlemen of your nation begin everything they
write with ' the infancy of society'?

'*Mr. Mac Quedy.* Eh, sir, it is the simplest way to begin
at the beginning. In the infancy of society, when Government was invented to save a percentage ; say two and a half
per cent.——

'*The Rev. Dr. Folliott* I will not say any such thing.

'*Mr Mac Quedy.* Well, say any percentage you please.

'*The Rev. Dr. Folliott.* I will not say any percentage at
all.

'*Mr. Mac Quedy.* On the principle of the division of
labour——

'*The Rev. Dr. Folliott.* Government was invented to spend a percentage.

'*Mr. Mac Quedy.* To save a percentage.

'*The Rev. Dr. Folliott.* No, sir, to spend a percentage : and a good deal more than two and a half per cent. Two hundred and fifty per cent. That is intelligible.

'*Mr. Mac Quedy.* " In the infancy of society——"

'*Mr. Toogood.* Never mind the infancy of society. The question is of society in its maturity. Here is what it should be (*producing a paper*). I have laid it down in a diagram.

'*Mr. Skionar.* Before we proceed to the question of Government, we must discriminate the boundaries of sense, understanding, and reason. Sense is a receptivity.

'*Mr. Crotchet, Jun.* We are proceeding too fast. Money being all that is wanted to regenerate society, I will put into the hands of this company a large sum for the purpose. Now let us see how to dispose of it.'

Then follow as many plans for its disposal as there are parties to the discussion. Dr. Folliott denies all Mr. Mac Quedy's positions, and affirms that political economy does no such thing as stand in the same relation to the state as domestic economy does to the family. ' In the family,' says the Doctor, in sentences which are apparently a poser to the economist, ' there is a paterfamilias, who regulates the distribution, and takes care that there shall be no such thing in the household as one dying of hunger, while another dies of surfeit. In the state it is all hunger at one end, and all surfeit at the other.' But

K

we must leave the epicurean Doctor, with his easy jovial manners, his shrewd sense, and also his many fallacies. The end of it all is that Crotchet keeps the money in his pocket, and the scheme for the regeneration of the world falls to the ground.

Amongst other subjects which come under the lash in this volume are the practices of Mr. Puffall, who obtains sketches from Lady Clarinda, and recommends them to the world as the work of a lady of quality, who has made very free with the characters of her acquaintance. The novel appears as ' the most popular production of the day,' but, as the novelist herself slily remarks to a friend, ' the day ' is a very convenient phrase ; it allows of three hundred and sixty·five ' most popular productions' in a year, and in leap year one more. The purse-proud were always the aversion of Peacock, and in this work he is again scathing in his invective upon the greedy appetite for wealth, and the unscrupulousness which so frequently attends its acquirement. The character of Mr. Touch-and-go, the great banker—who, together with the contents of his till, was reported absent one morning—might do duty for many others before and since ; he is one of the ' representative men ' forgotten by Emerson.

' Maid Marian ' is an investiture of the old story of

Robin Hood and Sherwood Forest with new grace and vitality. As with all its author's works, however, it is not destitute of a purpose, though the satire is not so apparent upon the face of the story itself. The narrative is excellently told, and we question whether there was ever a more poetical description penned of the home of the bold outlaw than this. It is put into the mouth of the Friar, who, in answer to the remark of a captured baron that he has fallen into 'fine company,' replies, 'In the very best of company, in the high court of Nature, and in the midst of her own nobility. Is it not so? This goodly grove is our palace : the oak and the beech are its colonnade and its canopy : the sun, and the moon, and the stars are its everlasting lamps : the grass, and the daisy, and the primrose, and the violet are its many-coloured floor of green, white, yellow, and blue : the may-flower, and the woodbine, and the eglantine, and the ivy are its decorations, its curtains, and its tapestry : the lark, and the thrush, and the nightingale are its unhired minstrels and musicians. Robin Hood is king of the forest both by dignity of birth and by virtue of his standing army : to say nothing of the free choice of his people.' The author strikes, through the medium of the old history, at the assumed principle in many quarters in our own day, that Might involves Right,

a matter in which there is no necessity to follow him with
a disquisition at the present moment.

A treatise might be written, with an almost numberless catalogue of instances appended, upon authors who,
from various circumstances and considerations, have
been hurried into too rapid writing. With many minds
the mere fact of publication is a great inducement to
commit the unpardonable offence, for such it must be
regarded in the interests of the general reader. The
time came to Peacock once in his career, and at an early
stage, when the polished steel weapon was seen to be
blunted. The incisiveness which distinguishes most of
his writings is not so apparent in ' Melincourt ; or, Sir
Oran Haut-ton.' Here we have less sarcasm, or rather
what we have is so largely diluted that occasionally we
doubt whether we are drawing from the same spring
which has hitherto given us such delight. The book
bears the traces of hasty composition, and altogether we
should regard it as much inferior to our author at his
best. It partakes more of the form of the ordinary
novel, but, just as much as this is the case, does it lose in
those other qualities which are generally associated with
the name of its writer. Isolated scenes and passages
may be good, but there exists a verbosity to which we
have been unaccustomed, and which we can ill brook.

After the feast of sparkling wines and choice viands which he has again and again placed before us, the palate remains comparatively unexcited and unsatiated with this specimen of intellectual catering. The truth is that Peacock's genius was neither of the novelistic nor the dramatic kind, and his attempt to portray an ordinary heroine in Anthelia Melincourt must be pronounced a failure. Far higher success is achieved in some of the other characters which it is easy to classify amongst the peculiar creations of the author. Sir Telegraph Paxarett, for instance, is a character well conceived and sustained, with a great amount of originality in his development; and so is the Rev. Mr. Portpipe, whose very name is a little idyll upon the course and character of his clerical life. But the best of all the characters is Sir Oran Hautton, and the happiest parts are those referring to political anomalies, which are castigated *con amore*. There are the boroughs of Onevote and Threevotes and Fewvotes, with the peculiarities attendant upon each, and all touched upon with uncommon humour. The book is probably palling and even foolish to those who take no pleasure in intellectual discussions and arguments, but to the thinker who has at heart the purification of society from all that corrupts and degrades, it will not be without a special attraction. But it is writing which needs digesting, not skimming. The assumptions of one of the learned writers in a celebrated Quarterly are very severely handled, the reviewer being credited with the idea that he and those who think with him are the only wise—a fallacy by no means confined to persons holding one set of opinions. We part from the volume, nevertheless, with a decided impression of genius veiled.

Reference has already been made to the attachment which Peacock conceived for Welsh scenery, and another proof of it is afforded by a later work of his, and one of the most pleasant which has proceeded from his pen, ' The Misfortunes of Elphin.' Here we behold a venerable story clothed by genius with all the reality of actual circumstance. The result of the author's labour is perfectly satisfactory. The style is never involved, though the language is now and then pedantic. The history is fixed in the sixth century, when the nominal sovereignty of Britain was held by Uther Pendragon. Amongst the petty kings was Gwythno Garanhir, King of Caredigion. This monarch was not fond of the sea, and built a palace on the rocky banks of the Mawddach, and also erected watchtowers which were subordinate to a central castle commanding the sea-port of Gwythno. In this castle dwelt Prince Seithenyn, who appears to

have been a sort of First Commissioner of Works to the
King. He differs in these considerable respects from
our modern First Commissioner, namely, that he drank
the profits of his office, 'and left the embankment which
was to keep out the sea to his deputies, who left it to
their assistants, who left it to itself.' Elphin, the son of
the King, informs the Commissioner to his momentary
discomfort, one day, that the embankment is rotten, and
should all be made sound, to which the latter replies :—
'So I have heard some people say before, perverse
people, blind to venerable antiquity: that very unamiable
sort of people, who are in the habit of indulging their
reason. . . . There is nothing so dangerous as innova-
tion. See the waves in the equinoctial storms, dashing
and clashing, roaring and pouring, spattering and
battering, rattling and battling against it. I would not
be so presumptuous as to say I would build anything
that would stand against them half an hour; and here
this immortal old work, which God forbid the finger of
modern mason should bring into jeopardy, this immortal
work has stood for centuries, and will stand for centuries
more, if we let it alone. It is well : it works well : let
well alone. Cupbearer, fill. It was half rotten when I
was born, and that is a conclusive reason why it should
be three parts rotten when I die.' Admirable sarcasm !

The policy of masterly inaction was very disastrous, as
of course it always is in matters social and political.
The waves beat high and effected an entrance ; the
tower fell into the surf, and the entire structure was in
danger.   The inhabitants fled, whilst Seithenyn swore
that an enemy had done the deed.   He leaped into the
torrent, from which we afterwards discover he was mira-
culously saved by clinging to a barrel, whose contents had
previously cheered his inner organisation.   Elphin quits
the castle, bearing with him Angharad, the lovely
daughter of Seithenyn.   Then come the lamentations
of King Gwythno over his inundated lands—excellent
stanzas, graphic and concentrated in expression.   Thus
was the kingdom of Caredigion ruined.   Prince Elphin,
who has married Angharad, is very fond of fishing, and
one day he has a miraculous draught (subsequent to a
dream on the subject), which proves to be a little child.
Its surpassing beauty causes Angharad to make the ex-
clamation, ' Taliesin ; ' ' Radiant Brow.'   The found-
ling is adopted by the couple, and in after years becomes
the celebrated bard Taliesin, and marries Melanghel, the
daughter of his foster-parents.   Taliesin grew up in
excellent knowledge, but the science of political economy
being then unknown, he knew nothing of ' the advantage of growing rich by getting into debt and paying

interest.' The author further remarks, ' They had no steam-engines, with fires as eternal as those of the nether world, wherein the squalid many, from infancy to age, might be turned into component portions of machinery for the benefit of the purple-faced few. They could neither poison the air with gas, nor the waters with its dregs : in short, they made their money of metal, and breathed pure air, and drank pure water like unscientific barbarians.' In all which things there is verily much food for reflection. The multiplication of species in a little kingdom like England must be attended with inconvenience and suffering to the majority. The wholesale system of going to the wall is inevitable : but do we not as some compensation for using up the vital force of the labouring class, offer them churches and chapels, regiments of the cloth, 'intellectual' enjoyments, and the brilliant and splendid spectacle for their admiration of an aristocracy which is kind enough to live on the sweat of their brow, and in numberless cases on their absolute degradation? Far be it from us, then, to say that we have made no progress since the time of the Welsh bard.

But, to proceed with the story, leaving all who may be interested in it to pursue their investigations of the constitution of society at that happy period. Elphin succeeds his father as king, but for certain indiscreet boastings, as they are held, he falls into bondage to King Maelgon, who has resolved to seize upon his wife. The rival king attempts to take her during the absence of her husband. But his emissaries are entrapped, and the matter afterwards coming before the great King Arthur, together with other vexed questions, he decides according to his far-famed principles of equity, and an exchange of prisoners is effected. Taliesin, who has been chiefly instrumental in procuring this termination of affairs, is rewarded by Elphin with his daughter's hand. We get glimpses of Enid, Queen Gwenyvar, Sir Gawain, Sir Tristram, and other knights and ladies familiar to the reader of Arthurian romance ; and the volume closes with a Grand Bardic Congress at Caer Lleon. Undoubtedly one of its greatest charms lies in the beauty of the poems which are scattered through the various divisions. They are imbued with more sublimity and tenderness than other poems of the author which may lay claim to be more entirely original in conception. The modern English seems at any rate to have caught the spirit of the old bards, if the form of expression be wanting. We cannot reproduce here the most striking of these poems, but the cultivated mind was rarely more forcibly exhibited than in their composition.

Although travelling over a portion of the ground

already covered in previous novels, ' Gryll Grange,' the
last work by Peacock, is one perhaps intrinsically superior to all except ' Headlong Hall.' Here he bravely
combats many abuses which we regret to say have even
yet not entirely disappeared. It may be commended to
those who would rob us of our national lands and forests,
to the poisoners of our atmosphere and our water, to the
bores in Parliament, and to the useless livers in the
world generally. Hear him on Parliament. ' The
wisdom of Parliament,' says the Rev. Dr. Opimian,
another of those clever epicurean divines of whom we
have had something already, ' is a wisdom *sui generis*.
It is not like any other wisdom. It is not the wisdom
of Socrates, nor the wisdom of Solomon. It is the
Wisdom of Parliament.' The excellent Doctor could
not get much farther than this in our day. But pursue
the analogy between that time and the present. ' The
Wisdom of Parliament has ordered the Science to do
something. The Wisdom does not know what nor the
Science either. But the Wisdom has empowered the
Science to spend some millions of money; and this, no
doubt, the Science will do. When the money has been
spent, it will be found that the Something has been worse
than nothing.' The term ' honourable ' is also objected
to, for ' Palestine soup is not more remote from the true

Jerusalem than many an honourable friend from public honesty and honour.' How much golden advice is compressed into the following words, the spirit lying beneath which would save this most Christian nation from humbling itself in the dust before its Creator for many calamities which might have been prevented !

' Honesty would materially diminish the number of accidents. High-pressure steam boilers would not scatter death and destruction around them, if the dishonesty of avarice did not tempt their employment where the more costly low-pressure would ensure absolute safety. Honestly-built houses would not come suddenly down and crush their occupants. Ships, faithfully built and efficiently manned, would not so readily strike on a lee-shore, nor go instantly to pieces on the first touch of the ground. Honestly-made sweetmeats would not poison children ; honestly-compounded drugs would not poison patients. In short, the larger portion of what we call accidents are crimes.'

Criticism could lend no additional force to such language as this, or more clearly show its appropriateness to our present year of grace. The science of panto-pragmatics, which is described as 'a real art of talking about an imaginary art of teaching every man his own business,' is one that is tantalisingly gridironed, and our system of competitive examinations was never set in a more ridiculous light than in these pages. We have papers which would have excluded Marlborough from

the army and Nelson from the navy : on other matters
hear what our author says :—

' Ask the hon. member for Muckborough on what acqui-
sitions in history and mental and moral philosophy he founds
his claim of competence to make laws for the nation ? He
can only tell you that he has been chosen as the most conspicuous Grub among the Money-grubs of his borough to be
the representative of all that is sordid, selfish, hard-hearted,
unintellectual, and anti-patriotic, which are the distinguishing qualities of the majority among them. Ask a candidate
for a clerkship what are his qualifications ? He may
answer, ' All that are requisite—reading, writing, and arith-
metic.' ' Nonsense,' says the questioner ; ' do you know the
number of miles in direct distance from Timbuctoo to the
top of Chimborazo ? ' ' I do not,' says the candidate. ' Then
you will not do for a clerk,' says the competitive examiner.
Does the Money-grub of Muckborough know? He does
not ; nor anything else. The clerk may be able to answer
some of the questions put to him. Money-grub could not
answer one of them. But he is very fit for a legislator.'

With which compliment to the Lower House we will
close our extracts from this trenchant book. It exhibits
Peacock at his highest, with ripened scholarship, polished
style, and a varied and profound experience.

As might be expected, the poetry of our author was
deeply impregnated with his classical spirit. The vast
weight of his learning, which he seemed to ' bear lightly
as a flower,' was exhibited in numberless erudite allusions,

whilst occasionally the foot-notes to his efforts were even more full of a ripe scholarship than the poems themselves. Naturally, his bent of mind led him, in his quest of subjects, into the realms of romance and mythology, with which he was in a remarkable degree familiar. One of his most successful poems is that entitled ‘ Rhododaphne, or the Thessalian Spell.’ It is a poem which Coleridge might have written. Founded on the ascription of the power of magic to the being from whom it takes its name, the story is worked out with eminent skill and feeling. Anthemion, the flower of all Arcadia’s youth, comes to the festival of Love, which was celebrated in honour of that deity every fifth year in the Temple of Love at Thespia, a town near the foot of Mount Helicon. The flowers he presents at the foot of the altar are suddenly blighted. This fills him with terror. He then hears himself addressed, and, looking up, beholds a maiden before him with more than mortal loveliness. She gives flowers to him, which are accepted at the altar, and so she passes out of sight. In the second canto he is made aware that the flower he has accepted is the fatal laurel-rose, and he is bade to seek the stream that laves the foot of the mountain, and there, calling on his Natal Genius, and with averted face, he is to cast the flower into the stream, looking not upon the running wave again. By this means the magic spell now over him will be dissolved. Immediately he has fulfilled the injunction he hears the cry of his beloved Callirrhoë, and is not proof against looking back ; he does so, but all becomes still. The secret that the bright maiden who has bewitched him is Rhododaphne is revealed in the third canto, where she charges him with having thrown away the flower which she gave him. He pleads its disastrous nature ; at least so he was informed by a reverend seer, and he is thus forcibly rebuked in lines which bear a sting (and doubtless were intended to do so) for nineteenth-century sophistry.

> ' The world, oh youth ! deems many wise,
> Who dream at noon with waking eyes,
> While spectral fancy round them flings
> Phantoms of unexisting things ;
> Whose truth is lies, whose paths are error,
> Whose gods are fiends, whose heaven is terror.'

The spell woven round Anthemion is made stronger by the maiden's kiss, which is to be poison to all lips but hers. He returns to his own Arcadian vale and meets his destined bride. She flies to meet him, her eyes imparting and reflecting pleasure, for, as the author beautifully expresses it,—

'This is love's terrestrial treasure,
    That in participation lives,
    And evermore, the more it gives,
Itself abounds in fuller measure.'

But Anthemion's embrace proves, as predicted, the death
of Callirrhoë, and maddened with despair the lover flies
from the scene. Succeeding cantos are devoted to his
wanderings, and to his meeting again with the magic
maid of Thessaly. At length, for her impious spells,
Rhododaphne is slain by the arrow of Uranian Love,
and the marble palace in which she has been reclining
with Anthemion is riven asunder. By her death the spell
is removed from the latter, and once more he finds himself in his native vale, where he meets the risen Callirrhoë,
and the happy pair raise a marble tomb to the dead
Rhododaphne.

Such is the outline of this poem, which has many
poetic graces : it is not, however, impassioned, as lofty
poetry should be, and therefore very high rank cannot be
conceded to it. It contrasts favourably, nevertheless,
with many modern attempts to render into verse ancient
stories which would seem of themselves to suggest the
loftiest inspiration. The poetry of Peacock is neither
the poetry of sentimental namby-pambyism nor of burning passion. If he does not glow with the fire of Shelley,

he does not pall with the sickly maunderings of later nerveless versifiers, whose genius has had some difficulty in crawling through its long-clothes. While our author's verse is liquid and musical, it is never weak and faltering. He is able to endow his creations with some amount of life-breathing power. It can scarcely be said that he was happier in his poetry than his prose ; rather, indeed, must the reverse be admitted. His intellectual and dissecting strength was greater than his emotional. He knew, probably, that the general reader would take no delight in his verse ; but that mattered little to him ; he could give him none other—consequently all his work in this direction betrays rather the thinking than the feeling man. In only one of his volumes of verse has he dealt after the manner of versifiers generally. The effort was not successful. It was his first attempt in a more popular style and scope, which style he seems afterwards to have abandoned. The truth is that on ordinary topics he had nothing extraordinary to say. It was when he came to re-illume dead torches that his genius shone to advantage. One poem in the work to which we are referring, ' Palmyra '—and which gives its name to the volume—is, however, in spite of what we have said, a splendid ode upon the destruction of the magnificent Oriental city. The last stanza, an adjuration to

L

bow to the will of the Deity, is finely expressed. It reminds one forcibly of Campbell's 'Ode to the Last Man :'—

'Bow thou to Him, for He is good,
 And loves the works His hands have made ;
In earth, in air, in fire, in flood,
 His parent bounty shines displayed.
Bow then to Him, for He is just,
 Though mortals scan His ways in vain ;
Repine not, children of the dust !
 For He in mercy sends ye pain.
Bow then to Him, for He is great,
And was, ere Nature, Time, and Fate
 Began their mystic flight ;
And still shall be when consummating flame
Shall plunge this universal frame
 In everlasting night.
Bow then to Him, the Lord of All,
Whose nod bids empires rise and fall,
 Earth, heaven, and nature's Sire !
To Him, who, matchless and alone,
Has fix'd in boundless space his throne,
Unchang'd, unchanging still, while worlds and suns expire !'

Most of the other poems in this volume are very inferior, and produce the impression that the writer, after having communed with the gods, has descended to the language of the mannikins. A poem of a more ambitious description, entitled 'The Genius of the Thames,' besides exhibiting a considerable infusion of the lyrical spirit, breathes also of the patriotic. The pre-eminence of the noble river is demonstrated in many smooth, flowing lines, and the opportunity is seized to recapitulate all the old traditions in connection with it. The beliefs in tutelary genii are dwelt upon, and the contemplative mind of the author has free scope for exercise. Silvery, however, as the lines are, and beautiful frequently as are the thoughts which give substance to them, it is not a work likely to enhance the author's reputation in any considerable degree. It bears traces of the study of poets of the close of last century, not the best models, one would think, for an author just opening on his career. The eye of the poet for natural scenery is just and true. Perhaps it is not sufficiently fresh. The student has stepped from his books into the open air, and his impressions are scholastic and polished. Legends of the Thames valley are touched with some amount of force, and the comparisons drawn between the state of Britain and the old monarchies, Babylonish and others, are vigorous and interesting. Altogether, it is just such work as to tempt a man to perform who had a high taste for poetic art, but it is not by any means a fair test or gauge of his powers.

The same observations would very nearly apply to 'The Philosophy of Melancholy,' a poem marked by

L 2

graceful fancy and many touches of true poetic feeling, but lacking in the higher imaginative power. It is impossible to peruse it with anything but high pleasure, yet the judgment is tempered when we think what such masters of the art as Milton would have made of the same subject. A pensive attractiveness doubtless attached to these themes in the mind of the poet, but his capability of utterance was by no means commensurate with the fertility of his ideas.

Susceptibility, then, or that extreme sensibility which permeates every avenue of the true poet's being, was deficient in Peacock, and in consequence he came short of the standard. We know the real singer when we meet with him. He is not one who is compelled to ransack the stores of recondite lore before he gives us the treasure we need. He is a man whose heart is turned out towards humanity—and, whether the king on the throne or the beggar in the street be his theme, he is able to invest it with undying interest. He is a mirror upon which are reflected all the complex passions of human nature. He reads the secrets of humanity and of Nature as one would read the pages of a book, without faltering, and with a clear apprehension of their meaning and import. There is no need for him to go back into past ages to discover subjects for his muse : the records of the very lives by which he is surrounded furnish him with material as tragic as the death of Cæsar. The gloom and the glory of his own time strike as deeply into his soul as do those of any past age. The great poet of every period has always been the man who was able to interpret the human life which encompassed him, and to paint it as he beheld it. Realities are what he achieves, and these are always recognised, transcending a thousand failures in attempting to revivify the beings of antiquity. In the sense, then, in which such a man as Burns, for instance, was a poet, Peacock was none at all. Impulsiveness was foreign to him. He had too much of the cynic and the critic in his composition to be possessed of the divine afflatus. His verse is ever correct and musical, not burning and overwhelming: it is like the silvery stream which meanders pleasantly through the meadows, and not the roaring mountain cataract, or the tempestuous waves which beat against the rock-bound shore.

We have left ourselves no space to speak of Peacock's miscellaneous works,—his 'Paper Money Lyrics,' his translation of 'Gl' Ingannati,' a comedy performed at Siena, in 1531, his 'Reminiscences and Correspondence with Shelley,' &c. This is the less to be regretted, however, as these fugitive pieces are to be shortly collected, and republished with his more important works in a uniform and permanent edition.[1]

Sufficient ground has, we trust, been shown for turning back to this too-long neglected author. With a chosen few he has ever been a favourite, but to the admirers of a vapid and invertebrate style he must necessarily remain an abomination. To glance at the mere list of works of fiction at the present day which seem to afford most delight to the general reader is a disheartening operation: it will not have been in vain if these observations on one of the most remarkable writers of several generations should induce, in however small a degree, a reaction. In all those respects in which an author is of permanent benefit to mankind the author of ' Headlong Hall ' is worthy of occupying an eminent position. His vast learning, his precise style, his great research, his boundless sarcasm, his intense abhorrence of cant, are all so many claims upon our regard. With the ordinary novelists he has little in common ; in most respects he cannot be put into competition with them ; for, whilst he has many virtues which they do not possess, he exhibits few of their vices.

[1] Since the above was written, as I have intimated in the Preface, the Edition referred to has been issued.

NATHANIEL HAWTHORNE

[NEW QUARTERLY MAGAZINE]

AMERICAN genius is as yet in its youth. Its slumbering forces have not had time to develop themselves. A nation, like an individual, when first it becomes conscious that it possesses the precious boon called life, endeavours to gratify the selfish propensities of its existence, and from this stage moves on gradually to the manifestation of the higher intellectual and spiritual qualities. So progresses the Transatlantic mind, which has not yet culminated in the exhibition of genius of the first order. The shrewdness of the race has already passed into a proverb, and the world-wide reputation acquired in this respect has latterly been almost equalled by the fame attaching to its new school of humourists, who so singularly reflect in themselves all the angularities of the national character. In poetry, philosophy, and the drama, however, that which has yet been accomplished is mainly of a tentative character. The Transatlantic Milton, Bacon, and Shakspeare have yet to be born. Longfellow, Bryant, Whittier, Lowell, and Walt Whitman are the only planets which burn with a noticeable degree of brilliancy on the poetical horizon ; while of dramatists not one has yet arisen with a clear title to the world's regard. In philosophy, the name of Emerson at once occurs to the mind ; but with all his excellences—and in some respects he is the most remarkable man America has yet produced—he is unable to stand alone. It is questionable whether the world would have heard of Emerson had it not first heard of Carlyle ; and in this country Emerson could not have occupied that conspicuous position to which he can justly lay claim in his own country. In one important pursuit only can we cede to our Transatlantic brethren the possession of a class of thinkers large enough to be distinctive—and that is in theology. With all their shrewdness and great worldliness, there is a bent in the mind indubitably theological, and the result has been the appearance of such strong and earnest theologians as Jonathan Edwards, Channing, and Theodore Parker—names which deserve and obtain the profoundest respect on this side the water.

The imaginative faculty is generally the last to reach its destined width and fulness, and nations have patiently to await its growth for centuries. It is like the oak, which beholds its fellow-trees of the forest grow old and die before it attains to perfection. When it has at length reached its full growth, it even then knows no perceptible decay, but remains with a nation as its most permeating and abiding influence. It is not surprising, therefore, to find that in the literature of the imagination America still occupies but an inferior place. She has yet to cast her giant arms about her, to ascertain of what she is capable, to gauge her resources, and to consolidate her strength, before she arrives at that grand and profound calm which is necessary for the appearance of the great novelist and poet. As an earnest, nevertheless, of what she will yet accomplish in this direction, we have selected for consideration the writer whose genius is, perhaps, universally acknowledged to be the most striking and unique among his own countrymen, and whose works will, without doubt, at no distant date, be cherished as classics, just as we in England preserve men so dissimilar as Fielding and Goldsmith.

The silentness with which genius frequently assimilates the stores of knowledge and experience was never more clearly exemplified than in the life of Nathaniel Hawthorne. The facts of his personal history are very sparse, and those which are known are not of any special import. He adds another example to the many, that those men who have exercised the most permanent influence over the human race have by no means been noisy and turbulent spirits, but just the reverse. Men of action are the waves which break boisterously upon the seashore ; men of thought are the deep quiet undercurrents which are the veritable ocean itself. Activity and enterprise are the fringes of time ; intellect, soul, spirit, *is* Time. The world lives by the throbs of this inner and unseen power. Yet, though it is of little consequence to know what an author has done outwardly, compared with what he has said, suffered, and felt, there is a genuine interest attaching to the life of any who have risen beyond the ordinary altitude, and occupied exalted niches in the temple of Fame. That interest finds its completest satisfaction when an author vouchsafes to explain to us the various mental processes through which he has passed before realising the product which has been of so much benefit to the species. We see, then, that not only is his work far in advance of the average intellect, but his volitions have been deeper and his aspirations proportionately higher. The apparent quietude of his life has been a season of really more rapid growth in thought and feeling than is the lot of the ordinary mortal. The man of genius has lived ceaselessly, not by fits and starts, and his life has been a constant series of intellectual and spiritual surprises, each achievement or revelation being but a landmark on that road to perfection which he travels with unwearied feet. When his individual experience is thus unfolded by himself, and the inner recesses of his spirit laid bare, the life of the man of genius becomes a strong complementary force and element to that of his work.

On Independence Day—the fourth of July, 1804—the day which we suppose of all others would be regarded by citizens of the United States as the most auspicious on which to make entry into this world—Nathaniel Hawthorne was born in the town of Salem, described as one of the most quaint centres of life in the colony of Massachusetts. The ancestors of the novelist were amongst those responsible for the persecution of the Quakers ; and one of them, Justice John Hawthorne, frequently passed sentence upon witches arraigned before him for their supposed familiarity with disembodied spirits. The Hawthorne family declined from a state of affluence and importance in the course of a century to one of comparative insignificance in the social scale; and we learn from Mr. H. A. Page's excellent memorials of Hawthorne that his more immediate ancestors ran on for generations in a long line of mariners and inconsiderable merchants. Prosperity forsook them, and he who was to shed the greatest lustre upon the name has given the fol-

lowing description of his predecessors: 'From father to
son, for above a hundred years, they followed the sea ;
a grey-headed shipmaster in each generation retiring
from the quarter-deck to the homestead, while a boy of
fourteen took the hereditary place before the mast, con-
fronting the salt spray and the gale which had blustered
against his sire and grandsire. The boy also, in due
time, passed from the forecastle to the cabin, spent a
tempestuous manhood, and returned from his world-
wanderings to grow old and die, and mingle his dust
with the natal earth.' The knowledge he gained of the
strange passages in the lives of his ancestors, coupled
with his inheritance of many of their traits, had a strong
influence on the bent of Hawthorne's mind. His own
nature was of a reflective and somewhat melancholy cast,
and its bias was probably deepened by the life he spent
with his mother after his father's death. Captain
Nathaniel Hawthorne, a bold seaman, never returned
from one of his long voyages ; and his widow, the future
novelist's mother, who appears to have been a woman of
considerable endowments, retired from the world with
her two girls and only boy, and spent the remainder of
her years in strict solitude. It is a well-ascertained fact
that a great number of men who have in every age become distinguished in the world, inherited the mental

characteristics and constitution of their maternal parent,
and Hawthorne affords another example of what, by
many, is asserted to be a universal rule.   We can readily
imagine the kind of influence Mrs. Hawthorne would
exercise upon her son's earlier years, with her strong
intellect ; and when it is remembered that the facts and
traditions respecting that town to which she had retired
with her family were of the most thrilling and weird description, we can almost see the mind of the son taking
its tinges of wonder, melancholy, and pathos.   In Salem
was to be beheld the Witch-house, where old women had
been condemned to death by those whose piety was as
vindictive as it was severe ; and there was also to be
seen the Gallows-hill, where the hangings took place, the
restless sea moaning almost at the foot of the hill.
Besides all these reminiscences, which must have had
the strongest possible effect upon an impressionable imagination, Hawthorne, at the early age of eight, was driven
to seek much of his enjoyment in the quietude of home,
in consequence of an accident that befell him in the
cricket-field, which crippled him for some years.   We
are not surprised to find that the first book he purchased
with his own money was Spenser's masterpiece, or that
his greatest favourite in all literature was 'The Pilgrim's
Progress.'   The immortal 'Dreamer' of Bedford had a

miniature successor in the dreamer of Salem ; and there
was not a wide divergence, in some respects, in the
character of the genius of the two men.   Longing for a
yet more secluded existence, Mrs. Hawthorne removed
with her family to her own property near Sebago Lake,
her son at this time being nearly eleven years of age.
Here his opening mind acquired a still more sombre
tone, though one not incompatible with the intensest
enjoyment ; for speaking of this period in later years, he
recalls all its pleasures, and concludes with the reflection
that ' everything is beautiful in youth, for all things are
allowed to it.'   This had reference to the utter freedom
from restraint which marked the life in Maine, when the
glorious pine-woods, magnificent sunsets, and absolute
solitude fed him with the true food of the poets.   Three
years of close communing which he then had with
Nature were a valuable period to him, for he was able
to assimilate, undisturbed by the world, all the riches
which a seclusion in so eminently romantic a spot could
afford.   At the age of sixteen (and after two years spent
in Salem at the conclusion of his residence in Maine),
Hawthorne became a scholar of Bowdoin College, where
he sufficiently distinguished himself, and had for companions Longfellow, Cheever, Horatio Bridge, and
others.   The closest tie of friendship he seems to have

formed, however, was with Franklin Pierce, whom he afterwards defended from his traducers with that straightforward manliness and courage which were peculiar to him. Graduating with honours, Hawthorne left Bowdoin and returned to Salem in 1825, where he once more resumed strict habits of retirement. But what of literary projects meanwhile ? There are indications that he had not been idle for several years prior to this, and an anecdote is related of him to the effect that when he had carefully prepared a small volume of tales for the press he unhesitatingly burnt it, and resumed work again. How much the world might have been saved had but other young authors dealt thus kindly with the crude emanations of their intellect ! The first work published by Hawthorne, and issued anonymously, was never acknowledged by him, though the reader is able to discover in it certain of the like singular powers which impressed his later work. One has remarked of this early romance, that 'it is a dim, dreamy tale, such as a Byron-struck youth of the time might have written, except for that startling self-possession of style and cold analysis of passion, rather than sympathy with it, which showed no imitation, but remarkable original power.' His heart, however, had not widened yet, to allow of its great sympathetic capacity having full sway. The immediate

M

successors of this repudiated story were ' The Twice-told Tales,' of which we shall speak with more fulness presently.   At this juncture, it will be sufficient to observe that two influences are distinctly traceable in them— that of the objects and the moods of nature upon a sensitive mind, and that of a strong introspective faculty. The criticism that would compare these stories to Brummell's failures we cannot understand.   They are, in fact, no failures at all ; that is, when regarded in their proper light, and alone.   An injustice is done to them when they are compared with the riper romances from the same hand, with which, of course, they will not bear comparison ; but, considered by themselves, they not only possess interest but cleverness, and a certain amount of intuition.   They have interest as indicating the groove in which the young writer was hereafter to acquire his fame, and they are to his ultimate productions what sketches are to completely elaborated pictures.

Hawthorne once described himself as ' the most obscure man of letters in America,' and the definition— thanks to the slight amount of discernment possessed by the reading public—had the merit of being strictly accurate.   His first essays before the world were not successful.   Probably the total newness of his style repelled many, who did not care to dive for what was valuable in it, or who judged from a hasty perusal of one or two of his sketches that a hypochondriac had arisen in litera- ture. Some men—noble writers—go all through their lives with the recognition only of a very limited circle of admirers ; while others (of which class Hawthorne was one) spend many years in obscurity, though they even- tually obtain a wide celebrity. Unknown by society, Hawthorne wrote much in a serial form, and he had a short experience of editorship, which was as unsatis- factory as it was brief. It appears that in 1836 he com- menced editing the 'American Magazine of Useful Knowledge,' published at Boston, and for which he was to receive the not very munificent salary of six hundred dollars per year. Conscientious and something more, he kept on at his work, even after the proprietors became insolvent. The magazine was supposed to be 'illustrated in the best style,' but, as is too often the case with lavish promises, the reality was nearer the exact opposite. Combined with this disadvantage, Hawthorne had no contributors to the magazine except himself, and he wrote nearly the whole of it, filling up the interstices with extracts, the drudgery of selecting which was also personally performed. The issue of this could be only one thing, resignation, and the editor took farewell of his readers. Very few events, however, are without some useful or pleasant side, and Hawthorne's position as editor had the good effect of bringing his name before those who were likely to be of service to him. Accordingly, we find that partly through his magazine connection he was able at length to get the appointment of collector at the Custom-house at Boston. The duties of this post he continued to discharge till 1841, when the revolving wheel of political circumstances sent him down, and he was again stranded without an occupation.

The next passage in his life is, perhaps, of all the most important and the most interesting. We refer to the part which he took in an enterprise regarded as quixotic by New York society, and which excited much comment and animadversion. Various are the stories which have been circulated respecting Brook Farm, the scene destined for the exhibition, in a concrete form, of theories which had been pretty extensively ridiculed in the abstract. This was neither more nor less than the establishment of a Socialist Community on the principles of Owen and Fourier. The originators of the idea in America were Dana, Ripley, and Pratt, though, as Mr. Moncure Conway points out in his lucid sketch of the movement, Emerson was largely responsible for exciting the feeling which afterwards found expression in the establishment of Brook Farm. With regard to the views of the individuals who introduced this new mode of life, they were to the following effect:—'They firmly held to the belief that the only thing needed for the grand transformation of society was, that human beings should be placed under new circumstances; that they should live together on principles of commercial harmony instead of those of competition; and that, by a combination of material resources and labour, they should be liberated from drudgery, and gain more leisure for the cultivation of the intellectual and spiritual powers.' With every sympathy for the noble aspiration which breathes through all this, it was obvious that the time had not arrived for the realisation of such a transcendental project. The scheme, notwithstanding, drew together some of the finest spirits of America, including Dwight, W. H. Channing, Dana, and the brothers Curtis; whilst the occasional visitors included Theodore Parker, Emerson, and Margaret Fuller. Hawthorne joined the movement soon after it began; but his residence at Brook Farm gave rise to contradictory statements. Whether there was ever the same intense moral inspiration at the root of his desire to join the society which animated the distinguished people who were its real founders, is open to grave doubt. But, certainly, if he commenced with such a feeling, he was afterwards partially disillusionised, for we find him writing as follows in September, 1841 :—

' Really, I should judge it to be twenty years since I left Brook Farm, and I take this to be one proof that my life there was an unnatural and unsuitable, and therefore an unreal one. It already looks like a dream behind me. The real Me was never an associate with the Community ; there has been a spectral Appearance there, sounding the horn at daybreak, and milking the cows, and hoeing potatoes, and raking hay, toiling in the sun, and doing the honour to assume my name. But the spectre was not myself. Nevertheless, it is somewhat remarkable that my hands have, during the past summer, grown very brown and rough, insomuch that many people persist in believing that I, after all, was the aforesaid spectral horn-sounder, cow-milker, potato-hoer, and hay-raker. But such people do not know a reality from a shadow.'

This is obviously language that would not be held by the writer towards any project for which he cherished a deep feeling. The fact seems to be, that Hawthorne was not permeated by such an enthusiasm, and he doubtless joined the Community mostly with a view to pursue the psychological studies which had so strange a fascination for him. Here was something entirely out of the common modes of life, brought close under his own observation, and which he felt afforded an opportunity for analysis that could not be passed over. As he remarked, ' I must observe, and think, and feel, and

content myself with catching glimpses of things which
may be wrought out hereafter.' His residence accordingly, as a member of the Community, was entirely a
tentative one, he being on the outlook to see whether he
really had any call for that new and singular existence
as far as in him lay, while penetrated by the spirit of the
student of human nature rather than by that of the trans-
cendentalist. Hawthorne did his share loyally towards
making Brook Farm a success. Its founders were not
more true and staunch than he, though working from
different motives. Miss E. Peabody wrote an interesting
sketch of the movement, from which it appears that
commercial interests were by no means lost sight of. All
who took in property received stock, together with a
fixed interest thereon; house or board was kept in
common, as the members severally desired, at the cost
of provisions purchased at wholesale or raised on the
farm. All in the Community were to labour and to be
paid at a certain rate, choosing their number of hours as
well as their kind of work. They were to pay their
board with the results of their labour, or the interest of
their stock, and to purchase whatever they might require
at cost price from the warehouses of the Community.
All labour, whether bodily or mental, was to be paid for
at the same rate of wages, and no one was to do bodily

work wholly. Intellectual improvement and social inter-course were not to be neglected, and the Community was also to traffic with the world at large. The members even went so far as to offer to sell education to as many young persons as could be domesticated in the families, and who would enter into the common life with their own children. If parents were too poor to pay, their children could be educated gratuitously, on the condition that they should work for the Community afterwards. This programme seemed sound and liberal, and it was, in fact, neither more or less than the ordinary conditions of society considerably improved upon, and an air of poetry and romance given to the whole from the fact of the isolation of the Community from the rest of the world. But it was not carrying out thoroughly the principles of Robert Owen and Fourier. The Com-munity was for a time very successful; it owned upwards of two hundred acres of land, and at the close of two years had accumulated thirty thousand dollars. Various reasons are assigned for its failure, and one invidious critic affirms that had it not been brought to an end by other causes, 'the picnic of poets and lovely women' was in a fair way of being broken up through female rivalries. This statement is emphatically denied by another writer, whose facilities for coming to a right judgment are unquestioned, so far as the outward circumstances of the Community were concerned. But even he has not gone deeply enough into the matter. He affirms that the causes of its failure were purely economical : alleging the unsuitability of the spot for an experiment whose basis must be necessarily agricultural. His reason is insufficient, when we remember that for two years this same spot had proved very fruitful and well adapted to the end in view. Besides, it was competent for the Community to introduce into their sphere of labour all the mechanical improvements and appliances which were possessed by the outer world. The apologist for Brook Farm goes on to say that so far from its failure being a proof of the inherent weakness of the associative principle, he regarded the existence of the Community for so long a time, under very unfavourable circumstances, as a demonstration of the great vitality there is in the principle. The real state of the case, however, appears to be that the nearer the Community approached that ideal condition desired by its most earnest promoters, the more clearly its impending failure became apparent. The attempted application of Fourier's principles closely, is believed to have been the cause of the decline of the movement. Hawthorne left it at this time, probably foreseeing the beginning of the

end. Society has not yet attained to that perfection
when it can be content with a common purse ; though
we are far from alleging that the attempt to disregard
the pecuniary relations of society was the real cause
of the failure of Brook Farm.   Our present concern
with the Community, however, is of a far different
nature from that of the mere anxiety to understand
fully its fortunes and its vicissitudes.   We know that
the residence of a powerful novelist there led to the
production of one of his finest works, and at the same
time one of the most remarkable and beautiful fictions
with which America has yet enriched literature. Not only
was Hawthorne repaid for his associations with Brook
Farm, but the world has been at least an equal gainer.

Hawthorne's marriage to a lady of great personal
attractions, mental and physical, to wit, Miss Sophia
Peabody, took place in 1843.   If the fervour of youth
ever leaves some men, it may be expected to have
left him at this period, for he had now arrived at the
somewhat mature age of thirty-nine.   He would seem to
have been singularly free from all that care which
generally besets the youthful Benedict, regarding his
future prospects without any fear whatsoever, and not
caring to draw gloomy drafts upon the Bank of Fate.
He describes his mode of life as one of easy trust in

Providence, affected only by the varieties of the weather; and his chief anxiety consisted in watching the progress of his vegetables. In the retirement of his own room, however, his brain must have been busy, for it was in the Old Manse of Concord, where he settled after his marriage, that there grew and gathered together those ' Mosses ' which have made the Old Manse and its immediate vicinity one of the greenest spots on earth. One can imagine him rambling through the orchards or wandering by the river side in search of wild flowers, of which he was passionately fond, and which seemed to speak with far more natural voices to his heart than the human voices of the busy city. But this delicious poet-reverie could not last for ever ; however noble his dreamings, they must come to an end. The responsibilities of the condition upon which he had entered at length made themselves felt, and he roused himself for mental work, writing in the Old Manse many books which satisfied the public taste. Nor was he deprived of congenial society when he chose to enjoy it, for within easy distance lived Emerson, Longfellow, Thoreau, and others, who thoroughly comprehended his nature, and with whom he could feel himself *en rapport*. Indeed, when this condition could not be attained with those into whose society he happened to be cast, Haw-

thorne was of all men the most miserable; never exhibiting his chagrin, however, because of the great gentleness
of his nature.   An anecdote is related of Hawthorne by
his friend Curtis which is too admirable to be passed
over, as it affords not only a glimpse of the former's
personal appearance, but of that strange demeanour for
which he was known, and which was always respected
and understood.   The occasion was an æsthetic tea
at Emerson's, during the cold winter months, with a
cheerful fire blazing upon the hearth.   The narrator
proceeds :—

' There were various men and women of note assembled ;
and I, who listened attentively to all the fine things that were
said, was for some time scarcely aware of a man who sat
upon the edge of the circle, a little withdrawn, his head
slightly thrown forward upon his breast, and his black eyes
clearly burning under his black brow   As I drifted down
the stream of talk, this person, who sat silent as a shadow,
looked to me as Webster might have looked had he been a
poet—a kind of poetic Webster.   He rose and walked to the
window, and stood there quietly for a long time, watching
the dead white landscape.   No appeal was made to him ;
nobody looked after him ; the conversation flowed steadily
on, as if everyone understood that his silence was to be respected.   It was the same thing at table.   In vain the silent
man imbibed æsthetic tea.   Whatever fancies it inspired did
not flower at his lips.   But there was a light in his eye
which assured me nothing was lost.   So supreme was his
silence, that it presently engrossed me to the exclusion of

everything else.   There was very brilliant discourse ; but
this silence was much more poetic and fascinating.   Fine
things were said by the philosophers : but much finer things
were implied by the dumbness of this gentleman with heavy
brows and black hair.   When he presently rose and went,
Emerson, with the slow, wise smile that breaks over his
face, like day over the sky, said, " Hawthorne rides well his
horse of the night." '

Verily ! this man was after Carlyle's own heart !   For
does not the Chelsea philosopher regard himself as the
Apostle of Silence, and declare that the dumbness of a
great portion of humanity would be for the infinite good of
the rest ?

From the garden of the Old Manse could be seen
the monument of a battle fought during the War of
Independence, and the occupant of the Manse has left
upon record how this fact, and the traditions associated
with the neighbourhood generally, strongly affected him.
One story was to the following effect:—During the noise
of battle which agitated the district, a servant of the
clergyman who formerly occupied the Manse, ran from
his work across the intervening field to see what was
going forward.   The British had retreated, and the boy,
who had a battle-axe in his hand, found two soldiers
lying upon the ground.   One was a corpse, but as the
New Englander came near, the other Briton raised him-

self painfully upon his hands and knees and gave a ghastly stare into his face. 'The boy—it must have been a nervous impulse, without purpose, without thought, and betokening a sensitive, impressible nature rather than a hardened one—the boy uplifted his axe, and dealt the wounded soldier a fierce and fatal blow upon the head.' Hawthorne turned over this melancholy incident repeatedly, following the miserable youth by a mental process through his subsequent career, and wondering to what depth his soul was tortured by the blood-stain so irresistibly, but perhaps not very criminally, incurred. Many years elapsed before the story was elaborated in the pages of the novelist, but it was not to be expected that so graphic a detail could remain finally neglected.

From the Old Manse, Hawthorne went to Salem, having been appointed surveyor of the port there by Mr. Bancroft. In less than a year after he had entered upon his new duties, was completed the first sketch of the most famous work by which his name is remembered; yet, strange to say, the author of 'The Scarlet Letter' was almost indifferent to his own handiwork, and showed no desire for its production. Fortunately, the insight of inferior men was too keen to allow of this extraordinary romance being lost. We behold in it the greatest embodiment of remorse ever achieved. Terrible in its gloom, the spirit of the reader asks again and again for some relief. Even the writer of it had experienced the same feeling, but 'found it impossible to relieve the shadow of the story with so much light as he would gladly have thrown in.' This unmatched story having been written, Hawthorne found himself yet once more subjected to change. Losing his place as Custom-house officer after three years' service, he retired to Lenox, where his life seems to have been of a rather more genial character than hitherto. His compositions did not stand still either; for in addition to the 'Wonder Book,' and 'The House of the Seven Gables,' he planned the novel based on his experiences amongst the Community of Brook Farm. Matters went on calmly till 1851, when he had an attack of illness which incapacitated him from intellectual exertion, and as the result of which he again went to Concord to reside. Here he lived for two years, till in 1853 he was appointed United States Consul at Liverpool. His five years in England were very pleasant, and many dear friends were made during that period; while he also found much to satisfy his tastes in the quaint and venerable nooks and buildings with which the old country abounds. In 1858 he quitted England and went to reside in Italy, and one of his

later works well exhibits the marvellous faculty he possessed of extracting all that was best from the different
human spheres in which it was his lot to be cast.   He
returned to America in 1860, and although he occasionally devoted himself to literary work, the illness of
certain members of his household, coupled with various
other causes, greatly impeded his operations.   Four
years more, and the end of his career was touched in the
town of Plymouth, New Hampshire.   Not a little singular is it that his oft-expressed wish to die suddenly was
granted, and the exact time of his passing away was
unknown, for no spasm of pain attracted the attention of
those who were with him in his last hours.

The growth of the modern novel has been marked by
many changes and developments, but it may be said
that its psychological interest was first exhibited in a very
high degree by Hawthorne.   His deep study of the soul
had scarcely been equalled before by writers of fiction.
His stories do not of course display all the gifts which
we witness in profusion in such men as Fielding and
Scott; but in their deep concentration of thought upon
the motives and the spirit of man, they stand almost
alone.   Examining now these works a little more closely,
there comes first that early and disjointed collection,
entitled 'Twice-told Tales.'   They possess several points

of attractiveness, first among which is that they are the blossoms of that tree which afterwards yielded such rich fruit. We find here in the germ those special qualities which finally asserted themselves with great prominence. As they severally appeared they excited little or no interest amongst their author's countrymen; but he has since been amply justified for their republication. They undoubtedly demonstrate, even in embryo, a strange capacity for the perception and illustration of lofty spiritual truths. Through the framework of the sketch is to be seen the moving of a restless soul. Hawthorne was always anxious to have it understood that he was never drawing character as it had existed in real life, but the fact seems to be unquestionable that he did discover and use types by which he was surrounded. Whether consciously or unconsciously it matters not, but the result is there—the characters have been reproduced, though that was not the chief end the author had in view. A fair description is given of these Tales by the writer himself, when he says:—'They have the pale tint of flowers that blossomed in too retired a shade, the coolness of a meditative habit, which diffuses itself through the feeling and observation of every sketch. Instead of passion, there is sentiment; and even in what purport to be pictures of actual life, we have allegory,

N

not always so warmly dressed in its habiliments of flesh
and blood as to be taken into the reader's mind without
a shiver.' Those who have read the sketches will attest
the truth of these observations; but they will scarcely be
able to agree with the succeeding remarks, that ' Whether
from lack of power, or from an unconquerable reserve,
the author's touches have often an effect of tameness :
the merriest man can hardly contrive to laugh at his
broadest humour ; the tenderest woman, one would
suppose, will hardly shed warm tears at his deepest
pathos. The book, if you would see anything in it,
requires to be read in the clear, brown twilight atmosphere in which it was written ; if opened in the sunshine
it is apt to look exceedingly like a volume of blank
pages.' Hawthorne's self-depreciation and exclusive
habits of thought led him to be a little unjust here to his
readers, who are able to discover something of the moral
he would enforce in whatever mood his stories are read.
What a striking and powerful sketch is that of ' The
Minister's Black Veil,' where the subject of it is made to
go about the world shrouded, as a symbol that man is
always in a veiled condition before his God and his
fellow-man. It is founded on the original fact in connection with a clergyman of New York, who had the
misfortune in youth to kill accidentally a beloved friend,

and who from that time forth kept religiously to the resolve of hiding his face from men. One can see at a glance how so singular a subject would commend itself to Hawthorne, and he has absolutely made us realise the wretched being in flesh and blood. Another sketch, permeated, this time, with a love for humanity, and showing how it can overcome all the prejudices of tribes and people, is that where the Puritans take in the gentle outcast boy, and are made to suffer for it in consequence. Hawthorne well rebukes religious bigotry, and makes it appear the loathsome thing it is. 'A Rill from the Town Pump' is a well-known paper of entirely another stamp and infused with a rich humour which is not general amongst the sketches. We cannot but smile at the conceit which describes the pump as the chief person of the municipality, and also as a most admirable pattern to its brother officers for the steady and impartial discharge of its business, and the constancy with which it stands to its post in all weathers. The search for the 'Great Carbuncle' has much amusement, notwithstanding that it is open to the charge of wild extravagance. This mystery of the White Mountains is an excellent illustration of the way in which Hawthorne delighted to mingle facts and impossible incidents together.

In the search for that which will never be discovered
he starts persons whom he has himself met, and all the
differing specimens of humanity which are found in the
tale were seen in actual life by the writer. His alle-
gorical genius is well displayed, for the reader is irresistibly forced to arrive at the conclusion that he is
endeavouring to depict as a second and hidden purpose
the search of mankind after the perfect good—which is
still in existence somewhere, but whose secret has not
yet been attained by man. In a slight sketch, headed
'The Prophetic Pictures,' the author asks, 'Could the
result of one or of all our deeds be shadowed forth or
set before us, some would call it Fate, and hurry onward,
others be swept along by their passionate desires, and
none be turned aside by the prophetic pictures.' So
intent is man upon attaining the object of his pursuit.
We cannot linger long over this repertory of interesting,
and in numbers of cases, thrilling stories—all bearing
upon them a warranty of good. Some of them are weird,
like 'The Snow Image,' some beautiful, and some tragic.
So far from being without a purpose, all seem to bristle
with lessons. We can say of each page that 'thoughts
and fancies gleam forth upon it, like stars at twilight, or
like violets in May;' but unlike those fading objects in
nature, the light and the bloom remain.

Contrary, perhaps, to the general verdict, we are almost impelled to the conclusion that the most perfect work left by Hawthorne is the ' Blithedale Romance.' This is the novel already alluded to as being founded upon his experiences at Brook Farm, and while it does not exhibit such a centralisation of passion in the individual as is the case with the ' Scarlet Letter,' it manifests qualities which are absent in the latter. Its thought and language are superior, and as regards composition alone, it may be pronounced a perfect work. The masterpiece of Oliver Goldsmith is brought to mind whilst reading it, though the two novels differ in most aspects as widely as possible. In each, however, there is a charming style, whose easy flow has never been excelled, while in Hawthorne's story there is a poetic beauty which is not to be found in the ' Vicar of Wakefield.' The drawing of characters is also very satisfactory. The *dramatis personæ* are few in number, but all are realised with extraordinary vividness. In Miles Coverdale is beheld the novelist himself, and Hawthorne's peculiarities are touched off with a free and unbiassed hand. There is the same half shy, retiring demeanour which characterised the original, and which prevented Coverdale from being that hearty member of the Community which his friends desired. Hollingsworth is an individual of great power, and yet we are divided in mind as to whether he most attracts or repels us. Full justice is, however, done to his remarkable force of character, which stirred in Zenobia so profound an admiration and love for him. The gentle Priscilla, fragile and beautiful as a daisy, adds to the charms of the society at Blithedale ; a perfect contrast, in her quietude and simplicity, to Zenobia herself, who brings to mind the famous queen of old whose name she bore. The novelist has thrown a tinge of the deepest poetry, sad, and yet enthralling, round his whole narrative. Where would have been its power had he only given us but a dry record of the daily life at Brook Farm ? He keeps himself judicially aloof from expressing an opinion upon those principles for whose practical working the Community was instituted, and simply goes thence because something is to be gained, he imagines, by travelling out of the beaten track of the novelist. He asserts, moreover, that his characters are entirely fictitious, but the world generally will only regard them so in the same light that it regards a very faithful portrait—the fictitious representation of the real man. Identification is clear and palpable with several of the leading individuals in the story, and his sister-in-law has admitted the fact that his creations have not entirely sprung from the imagination. But this fact is

one of little moment in connection with the story. It is
given to us—in what form we care not—to be a delight
to every succeeding generation. After the poetic halo
which envelops it, we notice the philosophy of the
romance, which gleams out in detached sentences preg-
nant with deep allusion or ripe wisdom. How truly
the author is led on to speak of the better life in man,
in connection with the project which forms the basis of
his narrative! 'The greatest obstacle to being heroic,'
he says, 'is the doubt whether one may not be going to
prove one's self a fool; the truest heroism is to resist the
doubt; and the profoundest wisdom, to know when it
ought to be resisted, and when to be obeyed.' Never
can it be said that Hawthorne casts a shadow over enthusiasm. Often, doubtless, in his own mind he had
asked the question which has puzzled most thinking men
at some period of their lives, *cui bono?* but on no occasion does he pour contempt either upon the ardour of
youth, or upon those deep feelings and aspirations which
survive youth, as in Hollingsworth's case, but which
have not the remotest chance of attaining their ends.
His own eye is too clear in gauging the impossible
barriers which intervene between human desire and perfect fruition; and to this, we could almost believe, is to
be attributed the sadness which pervades all that he has

done. Come whatever else may, he must at any rate
be true to his genius; and here lies partially the secret
why he laboured for so many years before he obtained
the popular ear. He had only the truth to tell, and it is
so difficult for *that*, at any time, to make way, unless
assisted by many brilliant and striking flashes of falsehood. To Zenobia, that magnificent creature, from
whom came an influence ' such as we might suppose to
come from Eve when she was just made,' he awards the
most miserable lot of all. With so great a capacity for
reverencing all that is grand and noble in man, she sees
the love of Hollingsworth—who meets every requirement
of her great and ardent nature—poured upon the little
maiden who trembles in her glance, and who appears
no more than a drop of rain sparkling in the sun. What
can she do when she fails of attainment? Even the
great purposes for which she joined the Community pale
into insignificance compared with the intensity of her
unrequited passion. She misses that union for which
Nature evidently destined her, and without which she
cannot live and breathe. All the paraphernalia of philanthropy fade away into nothingness; she discovers that
life, after all, cannot be transformed into a commonwealth; it is made up of the union of two, and not of a
hundred; her soul yearns for that portion of itself with-

out which she cannot be happy. Despair seizes upon
her spirit, and the tragedy of existence is completed by
that plunge into the dark waters which alone can bring
oblivion to her woes. The whole story is mournful and
thrilling to the last degree, and we know not whom
to pity most, the beautiful woman who so miserably
perishes, or the man Hollingsworth who so miserably
survives. In the latter, Hawthorne says he sees 'an
exemplification of the most awful truth in Bunyan's book
of such—from the very gate of heaven there is a byeway
to the pit!' Rarely does the novelist moralise in his
stories, but he is perforce compelled to do this when
brought face to face with the final wrack and ruin which
overtakes Blithedale and its little company. 'The moral
which presents itself to my reflections' (the author is
speaking) 'as drawn from Hollingsworth's character and
errors, is simply this—that, admitting what is called
philanthropy, when adopted as a profession, to be often
useful by its energetic impulse to society at large, it is
perilous to the individual whose ruling passion, in one
exclusive channel, it thus becomes. It ruins, or is fear-
fully apt to ruin, the heart, the rich juices of which God
never meant should be pressed violently out, and dis-
pelled into alcoholic liquor, by an unnatural process, but
should render life sweet, bland, and gently beneficent,

and insensibly influence other hearts and other lives to the same blessedness.' And upon the lines indicated in this deliverance, the ' Blithedale Romance ' is constructed. Formulated, mapped-out benevolence was clearly a thing for which Hawthorne had little sympathy; and there are certainly many nobler modes of rendering the philanthropic sentiment concrete than by self-imposed exclusion from the bulk of the human species.

The two forms of genius, the subjective and the objective, were blended in Hawthorne, the former, nevertheless, greatly predominating. A fine example of the two styles combined is to be found in the ' House of the Seven Gables.' This romance possesses an interest from its general excellence rather than from any definite distinctive trait of character or directness of purpose. Yet the novelist had a particular end in view in the construction of the story, namely, to show the evil consequences which are entailed through the commission of error or crime. He himself admits that he would feel it a great gratification if the narrative should impress upon others the folly of accumulating golden gains in order that they should descend to posterity as an incubus and a snare. But in a story like this, although the moral cannot be forgotten or utterly lost sight of, it is relegated to a secondary position. Moral truths are to be picked out of novels as the reader passes along, but they should never be so prominent as to obstruct the view, and shut out those artistic merits without which any novel must be worthless. Picturesqueness is eminently the characteristic of the history of the old Pyncheon family, and additional interest is created through its semi-legendary character. The writer has traversed backwards for some generations, and given a present-day interest to a bygone age and romance. We can well understand that it cost Hawthorne more labour than most of his other stories. He was deeply conscious of the fact that he had undertaken to bear a sad burden, and strenuously endeavoured to lighten the shadows here and there. Not very successful, however, was he in this, and the narrative stands as another tomb of dead hopes, like so many builded by the hand of this melancholy genius. His fondness for the out-of-the-way, the grotesque, and the abnormal, is appeased a little by the introduction of the mesmerist element into the composition, which further serves to show that he was always abreast with what was going on in science and the world. The critic is almost deprived of his work in regard to Hawthorne, from the fact, unusual with authors, that he has left behind him his own opinions upon almost every work that he has written.

The judgment, for instance, that we will venture to say any careful reader would have passed upon this work of the ' House of the Seven Gables,' viz., that in parts it is finished with all the minuteness of a Dutch picture, has been anticipated by the brain which conceived it ; so that there is little left to do, except to admire his manipulation.   The great difficulty which he experienced, of avoiding too close and careful an analysis of the human soul in its more sombre aspects, has been partially, but not altogether surmounted.   Phœbe Pyncheon, however, gleams like a ray of the summer sun across the dark pages of the story.   She is a bright, loveable, and beautiful creation, elaborated with softness and tenderness.   As a sweet poem lingers in the brain, and its undying music is ever present with us, so do such characters as this leave an impression on the memory and the heart.   As the author says, her ' natural tunefulness made Phœbe seem like a bird in a shadowy tree ; or conveyed the idea that the stream of life warbled through her heart as a brook sometimes warbled through a pleasant little dell.   It betokened the cheeriness of an active temperament, finding joy in its activity, and therefore rendering it beautiful ; it was a New England trait— the stern old stuff of Puritanism, with a gold thread in the web.'   And yet this girl, of whom her uncle said he

' never knew a human creature do her work so much like one of God's angels as this child Phœbe does,' found the one great happiness of her life in being a sacrifice for others. She is a noble moral type, as near the perfection of human nature, in her utter absence of selfishness, as it is possible to conceive. Before we part from her, we ought not to omit giving the author's description of her, both on account of its being a fair specimen of his painting of individuals, and for the portrait's own sake :—

' Out of New England it would be impossible to meet with a person combining so many ladylike attributes with so many others that form no necessary (if compatible) part of the character. She shocked no canon of taste ; she was admirably in keeping with herself, and never jarred against surrounding circumstances. Her figure, to be sure, so small as to be almost childlike, and so elastic that motion seemed as easy, or easier, to it than rest, would hardly have suited one's idea of a countess. Neither did her face, with the brown ringlets on either side, and the slightly piquant nose, and the wholesome bloom, the clear shade of tan, and the half-a-dozen freckles—friendly remembrancers of the April sun and breeze—precisely give us a right to call her beautiful. But there was both lustre and depth in her eyes. She was very pretty, as graceful as a bird, and much in the same way ; as pleasant about the house as a gleam of sunshine falling on the floor through a shadow of twinkling leaves, or as a ray of firelight that dances on the wall, while evening is drawing nigh. Instead of discussing her claim to rank amongst ladies, it would be preferable to regard Phœbe as the example of feminine grace and availability combined, in a state of society, if there were any such, where ladies did not exist. There it should be woman's office to move in the midst of practical affairs, and to gild them all, the very homeliest, with an atmosphere of loveliness and joy.'

But this is not the only portrait drawn with realistic power. Those of Hephzibah and Judge Pyncheon are superior to it in force if inferior in delicacy. That passage in which the stirrings of conscience are revealed in the Judge, is instinct with energy; whilst the author's own delineation of the miserable soul tinged with blood— and like a pool of stagnant water, foul with many impurities, beneath the show of a marble palace—is amongst the most graphic passages in this branch of literature. The story itself, as we have seen, is concerned with retribution—retribution after long years. A Colonel Pyncheon had sought and accomplished the destruction of one Matthew Maule, who was executed for the crime of witchcraft. While he had the halter about his neck, and just before the moment of execution, Maule addressed the Colonel, who stood calmly gazing upon the scene, in words which were preserved through history, as well as fireside tradition: 'God,' he said, 'will give him blood to drink!' The deed apparently dies, but in Judge Pyncheon the full results are borne. That gross, sensual, villainous life, is the answer to the original sin—the re-verberation which comes from Heaven's gate to assure man that acts which seem to bear no consequences in their dark folds, yield, in the far-off time, their black and bitter fruit. In Pyncheon's fearful death is that percep-tible reckoning for former deeds which the eye of man is not always able to trace.

We pass from this really wonderful work to pause before that with which Hawthorne's name has been im-mortally associated. 'The Scarlet Letter' has been not inaptly described as 'the great New England epic.' In the absence of any work of stupendous genius in America, this definition may well be accepted ; it has no equal, either in Transatlantic poetry or prose, for its dramatic strength. For the accident of its form, which is very striking, we are indebted to Hawthorne's stay at Boston. Not without significance to mankind was his discharge of the ordinary duties of the Custom-house officer. It is related that one day, while searching among the old re-cords of the Custom-house, he lighted upon a sentence decreeing that a woman convicted of adultery should stand on the Meeting-house steps with the letter A marked upon her breast. The problem how to deal with sin, in the shape of a romance, is supposed to have then flashed upon him in full artistic form ; and the friend who was beside him at the moment very shrewdly remarked, 'We shall hear of the letter A again.' Never, perhaps, was so powerful a story constructed out of materials so slight. The one prominent object of the writer seems to burn through every line, even when he has apparently no thought of its doing so. That great trait of Hawthorne's, his diving into the recesses of the human heart, and laying it bare to the gaze of the world, finds here its full expression. And one lesson, which seems to have been missed hitherto in connection with the novel, is this, that the author intended by it to illustrate and enforce his belief in Providence. For whatever may have been the case as regards man, his faith in the Deity was strong enough. Not in vain is the burden laid upon poor Hester Prynne and Arthur Dimmesdale. They are to suffer here and to expiate their offence, but mercy is to be granted to them hereafter—that mercy which the severe, so-called Christian code refused them on earth. Such, we think, is the great moral Hawthorne had in view. Is it possible ever to erase from the memory the scene upon the scaffold, where, the minister who has suffered years of torture for his sin, has at length courage given him to make known his guilt and to bear the punishment? 'God is merciful!' he cried. 'Let me now do the will which He hath made plain before my sight. For, Hester, I am a dying man, so let me make haste to take my shame upon me.' Then, addressing the people of New England in solemn and majestic tones, he made known the burden of his woe. He identified himself as the one sinner of the world. The scarlet letter of cloth which Hester wore was more terribly represented in him, for years of remorse had printed it in blood upon his own breast, and it was also reproduced on his very heart. But let the author give the final words which passed between the clergyman and his deeply-wronged Hester—words which set forth Hawthorne's own view of the expiation of the long past crime :—

' " Shall we not meet again ? " whispered she, bending her face down close to his. " Shall we not spend our immortal life together ! Surely, surely, we have ransomed one another with all this woe ! Thou lookest far into eternity with those bright, dying eyes. Then tell me what thou seest ! "

' " Hush ! Hester, hush ! " said he, with tremulous solemnity. " The law we broke—the sin here so awfully revealed ! Let these alone be in thy thoughts. I fear ! I fear ! It may be, that, when we forgot our God—when we violated our reverence for each other's soul—it was thenceforth vain to hope that we could meet hereafter in an everlasting and pure reunion. God knows; and He is merciful ! He hath proved his mercy most of all in my afflictions. By giving me this burning torture to bear upon my breast ! By send-

ing yonder dark and terrible old man to keep the torture
always at red heat ! By bringing me hither to die this death
of triumphant ignominy before the people ! Had either of
these agonies been wanting, I had been lost for ever !
Praised be His name ! His will be done. Farewell !"'

Thus is taught the moral that to be true is worth
more than life ; and collaterally with this is exemplified
in Roger Chillingworth the folly of the passion of re-
venge. Little did he imagine that by the exhibition of a
sublime courage and virtue Arthur Dimmesdale would
escape him at the last, and leave him to gnash his teeth,
a disappointed man, with such a glance as he had never
before taken into the contemptible depths of his own
nature. Like the foul and noxious weed, he was up-
rooted from his very base, and cast forth to encounter
the opprobrium of the world.

In other respects the romance is noteworthy. Besides its passion we have its beauty. The description of
the Custom-house is written with a minute and delicate
pencil, no strokes, however small, being omitted, which
could add to the perfection of the picture. Occasionally,
there is a humourous touch in the introduction, as when
he slyly informs us that ' neither the front nor the back
entrance of the Custom-house opens on the road to
Paradise.' How delightful is that touch of poetry in

which he refers to the wild rose-bush at the door of the prison, which seemed to assure the prisoner that the deep heart of Nature could pity and be kind to him ! The author's fondness for allegory comes out even here, when he goes on to observe—'This rose-bush, by a strange chance, has been kept alive in history ; but whether it had merely survived out of the stern old wilderness, so long after the fall of the gigantic pines and oaks which originally overshadowed it, or whether, as there is fair authority for believing, it had sprung up under the foot-steps of the sainted Ann Hutchinson, as she entered the prison door,—we shall not take upon ourselves to determine. Finding it so directly on the threshold of our narrative, which is now about to issue from that in-auspicious portal, we could hardly do otherwise than pluck one of its flowers, and present it to the reader. It may serve, let us hope, to symbolize some sweet moral blossom, that may be found along the track, or relieve the darkening close of a tale of human frailty and sorrow.' But the fragrance of the rose is scarcely distinguishable as the narrative of sad import proceeds. Surely never was the human spirit so put upon the rack as in these pages ; it suffers torture till the final moment which we have rehearsed. The romance is a monograph of anguish. In its deep, utter, and absorbing psychological interest it stands without a peer. The beauty of Hester, and the angelic sweetness and purity of little Pearl, are only streaks of light which, flashing across the darkness, serve to show the abysses of that darkness. The hell of human suffering was never more accurately gauged, and the thunders of conscience never reverberated with more terrific fury and power.

Our purpose is not to consider Hawthorne's works in strict chronological order, nor indeed is it our intention to review them all specifically. Many of his slighter sketches, though all tinged with the same spirit as his larger stories, afford little scope for saying more than this in reference to them. The 'Mosses from an Old Manse' are valuable as indicating the class of subjects for which he had an affection. In the introduction the writer seems to be filled with a more cheerful spirit than usually animates him, though it is a great mistake to jump at the conclusion, as some have done, that Hawthorne was a gloomy man. Behind all that power of dissection which he possessed, and past the shadow which falls across his works, was a trustful spirit—one which never let loose the anchor of faith. 'Oh, perfect day!' he exclaims on one occasion, 'Oh, beautiful world! Oh, beneficent God! It is the promise of a blessed eternity! for our Creator would never have made such lovely days, and have given us the deep hearts to enjoy them, above and beyond all thoughts, unless we were meant to be immortal. This sunshine is the golden pledge thereof. It beams through the gates of Paradise, and shows us glimpses far inward.' Strong, therefore, it will be seen, was the religious instinct in Hawthorne. Looking at his Note-book, we get some insight into his method, which is here beheld in its rough and early stage. His first process is to seize upon the local colouring, or upon the naked passion. This is slightly elaborated in the short sketches, as, for instance, the ' Mosses,' where, nevertheless, he gets little further than just clothing the simple leading ideas, and it is perfected in his longest stories, where art has been called in to give all possible aid to nature. The germs of a hundred stories could be found in a few sentences culled from his Note-books. ' Our Old Home ' and the brief romances which have been collected since his death, call for little special mention, for the reasons, first, that the former work has so long been known to Englishmen, and, secondly, that the new stories are not distinguished for their strength, though they are very characteristic of the writer's manner.

' Transformation,' however, is a novel which cannot be thus passed over. The idea of Donatello, the Faun-like man, which gives so singular an interest to this work, was most probably derived by Hawthorne from the details of the examination of Byron's dead body given by Trelawney, in his 'Recollections of Byron and Shelley.' ' I asked Fletcher,' says the author, ' to bring me a glass of water ; and on his leaving the room, to confirm or remove my doubts as to the cause of his lameness, I uncovered the Pilgrim's feet, and was answered—both his feet were clubbed, and the legs withered to the knee ; the form and face of an Apollo, with the feet and legs of a sylvan Satyr.' This is a tolerably fair description of the being whose destiny was linked with Miriam, that remarkable character in Hawthorne's novel. We ought also at the same time to note that a friend of Hawthorne's asserts it was Henry Thoreau's wonderful intimacies with animals which first suggested this being. But however interesting its origin may be as an incident personal to the author, it is immaterial when we come to regard the story itself ; and those who assume that the chief attraction of the romance consists in its singular blending of the natural and the unnatural, commit, we think, a profound mistake. Its real gist lies in the revelation of the reflex action of one human heart upon another, and in the *facilis descensus Averni* of the spirit, when it has once commenced a certain career. Is it Fate—or if not, then what is it ?—which seems from the very commencement of the narrative to be welding adamantine chains with which to interlock Donatello and Miriam? No more pathetic story could well be conceived, and no plainer moral indicated, than we find here. Even the bystander Kenyon saw clearly how these links had been forged, for addressing the darkly beautiful Miriam, he said, 'On his behalf, you have incurred a responsibility which you cannot fling aside;' and then, turning to Donatello, he added, 'The mysterious process by which our earthly life instructs us for another state of being, was begun for you by her. She has rich gifts of heart and mind, a suggestive power, a magnetic influence, a sympathetic knowledge, which, wisely and religiously exercised, are what your condition needs. The bond betwixt you, therefore, is a true one, and never—except by Heaven's own act—should be rent asunder!' These words were prophetic, for the speaker recked not of the dark secret which had knit together indissolubly those whom he was addressing. This inter-dependence of humanity, then, brought about by destiny, is what is clearly taught in the novel; and its general leaning to fatalism is very marked. In one passage the author affirms that as the future likeness exists in the block of marble which the sculptor takes for his work, so does the fate of the individual man exist in the limestone of time. Man may fancy that he carves his own future out of the marble, but its ultimate shape was already known before any action on his part. This is a gloomy view to inculcate of man, that being who is generally accredited with the possession of godlike capabilities and will. And as though to correct the impression which may be formed, Hawthorne hastens to put himself individually right with the reader on the matter by drawing another character, whose life is to be moulded by other influences, and to develop under the sway of other principles. In Hilda we have at once the contrast and the counterpart of Miriam. Not a shade of the evil which affected the latter comes near the graceful child of Nature, who goes singing through the world happy in herself, trustful in God, and free as the bird to whose music her own soul makes answer and tender response. Besides indicating, therefore, the fondness of the author for meddling with questions which have a great charm for the Darwin school, we perceive that this work deals with spiritual truths of the highest significance. Whether or no Donatello be really the outcome, after many generations, of the progress of the Faun, the fact is well demonstrated of the close relation each unit of humanity bears to the other, and of the inferior fellowship which he possesses with the lower creation. The story itself has its triumph in the artistic sense ; while disclaiming the intention of giving a portraiture of Italian manners and character, the author has nevertheless been most successful in imbuing his romance with the atmosphere of Southern skies. Italy, with all its beauty, its traditions, and its tragic history, was exactly the land for Hawthorne to select in which to fix the *locale* of his novel. In that country it seems almost impossible for the most prosaic not to be moved to poetic paroxysms.

That extraordinary book, the ' Dolliver Romance,' did not find Hawthorne a whit nearer writing the ordinary novel of society. To the general romance-monger it would have possessed no charm, had the plot been originally suggested to him to work upon. Severely simple to a degree, it had one leading thought only, and that weird and strange as usual, viz., the idea of a deathless man ! True, there is a beautiful woman in it, Panzie, who affords a gleam of sunshine to a page surcharged with gloom, but the bulk of the story is impregnated with sadness, which nevertheless in the hands of the writer possesses a resistless enchantment. The fragment bears upon it sufficient indication of what it would have ripened to had fortune been propitious. Old Doctor Dolliver was to live on and on through far generations, loving and guarding Panzie, till the world in time forgot to measure his days and years, and began to count him

immortal. For her youth, hope, and vitality, he was to
make the exchange of wisdom and love ; and thus,
moving hand in hand, life was to be made divine for
both, and desolation thrust back into oblivion. Then,
again, in 'Septimius,' the last work from this gifted hand,
we behold the same great craving after immortality embodied in the person of the hero, mingled with other
strange elements which make him not the least striking
of Hawthorne's creations. The picture of the pale
student, with his unquenchable thirst after the deep
knowledge of the mysteries of life which he has set himself to attain, is one that no other conceptions can
obliterate. We watch him from those early days in
which he first made love to Rose Garefield, and see how
circumstances or fate gradually make him their own, till
he, who was the most inoffensive of God's creatures by
nature, feels that irresistible impulse to shed blood which
develops in him so rapidly. Next he obtains possession
of the document which changes the whole current and
purpose of his life. His love for Rose, his love for
himself and the world, and all created things, evaporate
in the presence of a more terrible longing and burning
for knowledge. Finally, at the hand of his enemy he
learns the lesson that 'the wish of a man's inmost heart
is oftenest that by which he is ruined and made mise-

rable.' One can see what a wonderful story Hawthorne would have made of this had he lived to complete it. The passages which are finished are distinguished for a full, rich style, elegant language, and well-poised sentences. Altogether, it suffers little by comparison in literary merit with the 'Blithedale Romance,' which, from the artistic point of view, as we have already intimated, may be pronounced his masterpiece. Art and passion are in both works blended in a very rare degree.

Compared with the writers of his own country, there is no difficulty in assigning his proper position as a novelist to this illustrious writer. He has no equal. It is rare to meet with his artistic qualities anywhere ; it is rarer still to find them united to the earnestness which so distinguished him. Whether as the result of an inheritance of the old Puritan blood or no, matters little, but in him there was apparently a sincerity truly refreshing amongst so many writers whose gifts have been vitiated by the lack thereof. Admirably did Russell Lowell depict him when he wrote the following lines in his 'Fable for Critics !'

'There is Hawthorne, with genius so shrinking and rare,
   That you hardly at first see the strength that is there ;
   A frame so robust, with a nature so sweet,
   So earnest, so graceful, so solid, so fleet,
   Is worth a descent from Olympus to meet ;

'Tis as if a rough oak that for ages had stood,
With his gnarled bony branches like ribs of the wood,
Should bloom, after cycles of struggle and scathe,
With a single anemone trembling and rathe ;
His strength is so tender, his wildness so meek,
That a suitable parallel sets one to seek,—
He's a John Bunyan Fouquè, a Puritan Tieck ;
When Nature was shaping him, clay was not granted
For making so full-sized a man as she wanted,
So, to fill out her model, a little she spared,
From some finer-grained stuff for a woman prepared.
And she could not have hit a more excellent plan
For making him fully and perfectly man.'

That Hawthorne will ever be what we call a very popular novelist is open to much doubt. The habits of abstraction to which he was accustomed from his boyhood had their influence upon his thought, which is not always expressed in a manner adapted to the average reader. At times he appears to be living away from the world altogether ; and society likes now what is concrete, something which it can handle and appraise, whether in literature, science, or art. It has little reverence for the conscientious worker, unless he can contrive to make a noise about his work. This, of course, was precisely what the writer whose claims are under discussion could not do. He knew what conscience was, and he revered knowledge ; but he never understood the rage for popularity. The real admiration for his books, which had its root in sympathy with the intellectual and spiritual throes of the author, was the highest reward he felt he could receive ; for that was intelligible. He had a shrinking from the lionising which is done on trust, that unpleasant phase which has crept over society during the last few years. The principle of giving the highest praise to the man who can play the loudest on the big drum was a hateful one to him. A silent rebuke to the fussiness of the nineteenth century, and to its fulsome adulation of what is unworthy, may be traced in his pages. This man had a strong and fearless spirit, and though he discussed questions occasionally which have been found too high for settlement in all ages, he did so with humility and on reverent knee.

Hawthorne had unquestionably, moreover, as will have been gathered, a strong poetic element in his nature, sublimated by constant contact with the various forms of sorrow. Through worldly loss he came to an insight into spiritual truths to which he might otherwise have been a stranger. At times he appears almost to distrust men, but it is never really so ; he laments man's indecision for the right, the evil growths which enwrap his soul, and that dark veil of sin which hides from him the smiling face of his Creator. 'Poet let us call him,' with Longfellow; but, greater still, an interpreter, through whose allegories and awe-inspiring creations breathe the soul that longs after the accomplishment of the dream of unnumbered centuries, the brotherhood of man. The world has been enriched by his genius, which is as a flower whose fragrance is shed upon man, but whose roots rest with God.

THE BRONTËS

[CORNHILL MAGAZINE]

No soil has the monopoly of Genius. Alike in the barbaric empires of the East and the Christian nations of the West, we behold numberless proofs and monuments of that force which has been irresistible in bursting the narrow bounds by which it was sought to be confined, and which men call Genius. This power, or adaptability, or whatever name is chosen to be given to it, is seen to be independent of the conditions which affect men generally, or at least it rises superior to them ; it is a law to itself; in the world's darkest ages it has endeavoured to pierce the secrets of the universe, and has uttered language which has been the seed of wisdom for succeeding generations. Humanity has been more indissolubly knit together, and the gulf of time bridged over, by a Confucius and a Bacon. Truly independent, indeed, of the accidents of time or place, ' the light that never was on land or sea '—to give a broad application to Wordsworth's graphic expression—beams forth upon all ages and peoples, but in gleams as fitful as the light-

P

ning which cleaves the dense thunder-cloud. Yet the greatest unbroken succession of the earth is this same genius, yielding those potentialities which have operated for the evil or the good of mankind. Wars and enthusiasms have been kindled by it, and dying hopes have been revivified by its life-giving influence. It cannot die. Its light may be obscured, but never extinguished. Where the Divine spark exists it must become manifest, for it is imperishable.

But our present purpose is to look at genius from a point which possesses even more of interest than its imperishability. It is to note its appearance in scenes which it has ever favoured, and where it has always disappointed the world. How frequently in history has it taken up its abode in the most unpromising soil, where there seemed no root for its rare and extraordinary growth ! Where nature has most darkly frowned, and the sterile aspect of her moors and hills has had a corresponding influence upon the population, thence have sprung some of the choicest spirits, whose lives were fragrant, and whose memories still

Smell sweet and blossom in the dust.

Perhaps no example could be cited in illustration which more clearly demonstrates the irrepressibility of genius than that of the remarkable trio of sisters who were known originally as Currer, Ellis, and Acton Bell. The truly surprising vigour of their mental constitutions can only be accurately gauged by a consideration of the natural and other disadvantages which they successfully overcame. To many persons, we suppose, they will ever remain but a name, though one almost synonymous with sturdy independence of character; but to those who more deeply study their separate individualities an untold wealth of interest and profit will be discovered. Their life's history proves that in the most barren regions the power of genius can flourish. The bleak, wild moorlands, with their poverty of natural beauties, were the nursery of rich lives, whose influence —with that of all other lives to whom the Divinity has intimately spoken—still lives, and must live, for long generations. The personal narrative, as related by Mrs. Gaskell, is one of mingled pathos and rarity. Some of the points in the Life of Charlotte Brontë it will be advisable to recall to the reader's attention before the works of the three sisters themselves are passed in review. Haworth village, whose parsonage was so long the residence of the Brontës, is in the West Riding of Yorkshire, and situate only a few miles from three towns of considerable importance — Halifax, Bradford, and

Keighley. The friend of Charlotte Brontë has endeavoured to give some idea of the appearance of the
district, but even she fails to depict it as it existed in
the early part of the present century.   In addition to the
dull, monotonous stretch of moorland, with here and
there a 'beck' or a crag, as the sole variation for the
weary eye, there was a population to be met with which
in some respects exhibited no advance whatever over
that of the Middle Ages. Nor is this scarcely to be
wondered at, for within the knowledge of the present
writer, to whom the whole locality is perfectly familiar,
there were living a few years ago individuals who had
never beheld one of the foremost powers of civilisation—
the railway. Great natural shrewdness undoubtedly was
a characteristic of the inhabitants of the Riding, and in
many cases a rough kind of *bonhomie* was added, which,
however, was frequently made more offensive than positive rudeness. Add to this that there was very little
opportunity afforded to the poor for culture—twelve,
fourteen, and sixteen hours per day being their constant
labour at the factories—and the imagination will have
little left to do in forming an estimate of the exoteric
existence of the Yorkshire character. The people were,
and indeed now are, hard-fisted, but scarcely so much so
as the reader of Mrs. Gaskell would gather ; for many

have a passion for personal adornment, whilst others will spend considerable time and money in attaining proficiency in music, for which they have a natural talent beyond that possessed by the inhabitants of any other county in England. They are good friends and good haters. The misers, mostly, are to be found in the type of small manufacturers or cotton-spinners, who, bereft of many of those graces which should adorn the human character, set themselves with dogged persistency to the making of 'brass,' as they term wealth. With some the passion is carried to a lamentable, and at the same time amusing excess. A characteristic story is told of a person of this class, who was tolerably rich, and had been seized with illness soon after taking out his policy. When the doctor made him aware of his hopeless state, he jumped up delighted, shouting, 'By Jingo! I shall *do* the insurance company! I always was a lucky fellow!' Another trait in people much poorer in station than those just referred to was the fixedness of their religious principles. The doctrine of Election had firmer root in their minds—and indeed has now in those of their successors—than is found to be the case elsewhere. The factory hands would stand at the loom till nature yielded to consumption or to the hardness of the burdens it was called upon to bear, but in the hour of dissolution,

as in every hour of sentient existence in the past, would
be apparent the conviction that as surely as the sun rose
in the morning, so surely were they themselves predesti-
nated to a triumphant salvation, of which it was an
impossibility they could be rifled by the combined
powers of the universe. Amidst this stern and unyield-
ing race, then, was the lot of the sisters cast, and it
would have been strange had not their genius been
directed in its moulding by such distinctive surroundings.
To understand at all the spirit of their works, it is necessary to have some preliminary knowledge of the kind
just indicated. Precocity distinguished the whole trio,
though that is not an unfailing sign of future celebrity.
When children, their answers to questions were clever
and characteristic. Emily, whose intellect was always
singularly clear, firm, and logical, when asked what
should be done with her brother Branwell, if he should
be naughty, instantly replied, ' Reason with him, and
when he won't listen to reason, whip him.' And as
another indication of the quick ripening of faculties in
this remarkable family, it may be mentioned that Mr.
Brontë said he could converse with his daughter Maria
on all the leading questions of the day when she was
only eleven years of age. Charlotte Brontë was at an
early age familiar with all the forms of suffering and death,

and her life, from its commencement to its close, may be said to have been one prolonged endurance of agony. Yet the grandeur of her courage must always strike us as one of the sublimest spectacles. When a child she lost those who were dear to her, and there were none who could understand the vast yearnings of her nature. Then came the stirrings of her genius, and she longed to take flight, but her wings were weighted, and she was kept enchained to the dull earth. A few more years, and another trouble, almost worse than death, cast its horrible shadow over her path. The melancholy story of her brother Branwell, whom she loved deeply, in spite of his numberless errors and terrible slavery to one master-passion, is matter of general knowledge. To his death succeeded that of Emily Brontë, the sister whom Charlotte especially loved. To see her drift out into the great Unknown Sea was trouble inexpressible to that loving soul—which had watched her with fostering care, and hoped to have witnessed the universal acknowledgment of her splendid genius. Seldom was the heavy cloud lifted from the head of our author on those dull Yorkshire hills: can it be matter of surprise, then, that her works should bear the impress of the character of her life? The wonder is, that the sun should break through at all, as it does in 'Shirley,' with beams of real geniality and cheerfulness. But the life was destructive of that gentler kind of humour of which we are sure Charlotte Brontë must have had originally a considerable endowment. She was necessarily propelled towards the painting of what was frequently harsh, and always peculiar and extraordinary. Her perceptions were keen—as will be admitted by the close student of her works—not only of human life, but of nature, and what she wrote must therefore exhibit the qualities of truth and strength. Severe discipline waited upon her through all her history, and its results are graphically depicted in her works, each of which deals with the experience of some stage of her brief existence. One almost wonders, as we follow her career, where her happiness came from. There was no society, no wealth, none of the common delights of life for her, whilst death was always approaching with measured, but inevitable steps, when not, indeed, already in the house. Doubtless her literary occupations yielded her at times intense enjoyment, but she possessed, in addition, a faith in Providence which must have been like that of a child for simplicity and strength—a faith to which many, who boasted of their Christian excellence, were perfect strangers, and to whom its existence in her was utterly unsuspected.

The iron will of this truly great woman was never

broken till the period came when she must yield up her own life. Then the weakness—if such it can be called—which she exhibited, arose not from any fear respecting herself, but for the tender and faithful husband whom she was leaving behind. Desolation, blank and utter, overtook the father and husband when her heart ceased to beat, such as the old parsonage had never experienced before. Charlotte's spirit had nerved others so long as it was with them, and the tenement of hope was not completely shattered till she died. The picture Mrs. Gaskell gives of the closing moments and of the funeral is very touching. With regard to the latter it painfully reminded her of the scene after the death of Oliver Goldsmith. Mr. Forster thus describes it: 'The staircase of Brick Court is said to have been filled with mourners, the reverse of domestic; women without a home, without domesticity of any kind, with no friend but him they had come to weep for; outcasts of that great solitary, wicked city, to whom he had never forgotten to be kind and charitable.' Such would have followed Charlotte Brontë's remains to the grave, but the survivors wanted not the sympathy of strangers, their grief being too keen to be assuaged. The detractors of the writer of 'Jane Eyre' could have had little real understanding of her. Those who knew her best were

the fallen and distressed, to whose wants she had minis-
tered, and, better still, into whose bruised and dejected
souls she had poured the sweet balm of sympathy. Such
shall judge the woman ; as for her genius, that will take
care of itself; its fruits are too genuine to be in danger
of perishing.

The novels of Charlotte Brontë were totally dissimilar
in style to all which had been previously given to the
world, and their quality was not such as to be at the first
moment attractive. Masculine in their strength, and
very largely so in the cast of thought, there could be no
wonder that the public should assume Currer Bell to be
of the sterner sex, and even persist in its delusion after
the most express assurance to the contrary. Certainly
one can sympathise with the feeling of astonishment that
'Jane Eyre' should have been written by a woman.
What vigour there is in it compared with the novels of
another great artist, Miss Austen ! For sheer force, she
has even eclipsed her own chief of novel-writers, Sir
Walter Scott, whilst Balzac, who, as Currer Bell said,
'always left a nasty taste in her mouth,' is also outstripped in the delineation of passion. Many readers
were doubtless repulsed from a fair and candid perusal
of the works of Charlotte Brontë by certain adverse criticisms which had pronounced them extremely coarse.

The unfairness of this charge we think it will not be difficult to show presently. Faithful transcripts of the life she had witnessed they certainly were; distorted they were not. Speaking of fiction, the author of ' The Curiosities of Literature ' has said—' Novels, as they were long *manufactured*, form a library of illiterate authors for illiterate readers; but as they are *created* by genius, are precious to the philosopher. They paint the character of an individual or the manners of the age more perfectly than any other species of composition : it is in novels we observe, as it were passing under our own eyes, the refined frivolity of the French, the gloomy and disordered sensibility of the German; and the petty intrigues of the modern Italian in some Venetian novels.' We accept this as a tolerably substantial appraisement of the *rôle* of the novelist ; but in order to be strengthened in our opinion, let us look at what the eminent philosopher Adam Smith said of the true novelist, and surely no higher praise could be desired by our storywriters. ' The poets and romance-writers who,' he says, ' best paint the refinements and delicacies of love and friendship, and of all other private and domestic affections, Racine and Voltaire, Richardson, Marivaux, and Riccoboni, are in this case much better instructors than Zeno, Chrysippus, or Epictetus.' But surely we

need not stay to argue here that the novel, when in the
hands of a true genius, can be made one of the best
instructors of the human race. It is so because there is
nothing of the abstract about it—which the mind of
mankind generally abhors ; it is a record of the concrete
existence of individuals like ourselves, and must therefore be profitable both for amusement, interest, and
guidance. A good novelist can scarcely be appreciated
too highly. In this class we place Charlotte Brontë ;
she fulfils the requirements glanced at already in the
words of Mr. D'Israeli, and is in every respect a faithful
delineator of the scenes and persons she professes to
describe. How faithful, indeed, few can scarcely tell,
but the mass can darkly feel it on close acquaintance
with her. The charge of coarseness brought against her
works she herself indignantly repelled, but the base
notion of such a charge must have cruelly wounded her
spirit, which, though strong and brave as a lion, was yet
pure and tender as that of a child. She said, ' I trust
God will take from me whatever power of invention or
expression I may have, before He lets me become blind
to the sense of what is fitting or unfitting to be said.'
And it is on record that she was deeply grieved and
long distressed by the remark made to her on one
occasion, 'You know, you and I, Miss Brontë, have both

written naughty books !' Mrs. Gaskell goes so far as to admit that there are passages in the writings of Currer Bell which are coarse ; for ourselves, we can scarcely understand what is meant. Roughness there is, but indecency none, and coarseness seems to us to imply a little more than mere roughness. Several of the characters she has drawn are reproductions in type of the wildest natures, and the over-refined sensibilities of some readers are possibly shocked by their extreme naturalness. Charlotte Brontë simply thought of painting them as they appeared, never thinking for a moment there could be harm in laying in deep shadows where deep shadows were required. Fielding was coarse, Wycherley and some of the other dramatists more so, but their examples show that coarseness is an unfortunate epithet to apply to the writings of Currer Bell. If applicable to them, it is totally inapplicable to her. Her coarseness—if such quality exists at all—was undetachable from her subjects. She would have ceased to be the true delineator and the real artist she aspired to be, had she swerved from the outlines of character she undertook to fill in. In truth, we need only turn to 'Shirley' and 'Jane Eyre' to prove the position that Charlotte Brontë was far beyond the common novelist. In the former story we have characters which for sweetness have been rarely excelled, whilst in the latter we have a Jupiter of rugged strength and passion. The novelist has power to go out of herself—that attribute of the great artist. It is genius which impels, and she must obey. If the characters are occasionally coarse, she is unconscious of it ; she is only aware of their truth. No need for her to lop off the distorted branches in the human forest of her delineations in order to secure a level growth of mediocrity. She could not if she would, and is too intent on the manifestations of nature to do so if she could. Such creations as please the ordinary romance-monger would be an abhorrence to her ; it is because she exalted Art that she could not depart from the True, with which the former, when real, is ever in unison.

'The Professor,' which was the first work written by Charlotte Brontë ostensibly for publication, though not by any means her first effort in fiction (what author does not carry the recollection of many juvenile crudities ?), exhibits a great amount of conscious power, but also an inability on the part of the writer to give herself free scope. A comparison between this and succeeding works will show how she was cramped in its composition. The story is good, nevertheless, though numerous publishers to whom it was submitted decided otherwise. Its author has possibly hit upon the reason for its rejection, when in the preface she says she determined to give her hero no adventitious aid or success whatever. He was to succeed, if he did so, by the sheer force of his own brain and labour. 'As Adam's son he should share Adam's doom, and drain throughout life a mixed and moderate cup of enjoyment.' These principles were of course unpopular ; the novel-readers of the day demanded something which should exhibit more of the romantic and the heroic. Battling well, however, with materials which were in the outset obstructive, Currer Bell achieved a substantial success There can be no doubt that her husband, in consenting to the publication of the volume subsequently, did a wise act. There is much in the work which is characteristic of its author as she appears in her later novels, and the drawing of at least one of the characters, Mr. Hunsden, is masterly. Some of the materials, we are told, were afterwards used in 'Villette ;' but if so they are carefully disguised, and the world could very well afford to welcome the two. Passages occur in 'The Professor' which are almost startling in their strength of passion and eloquence, and which alone would have given to Currer Bell the stamp of originality. All the toilsome way by which the person who gives the title to the volume is led, is marked by the intensest sympathy on the part of the author, and although the reader may not be able to feel much personal enthusiasm for the various characters, he must at once yield the point that he is perusing the thoughts of no common mind. The valuable knowledge which the author acquired abroad is utilised with considerable skill, whilst she is equally at home when she comes to delineate the York-shire family of the Crimsworths. Her ideas of love and marriage, afterwards so fully developed in her other novels, are here touched upon. 'I am no Oriental,' says the Professor : 'white necks, carmine lips and cheeks, clusters of bright curls, do not suffice for me, without that Promethean spark, which will live after the roses and lilies are faded, the burnished hair grown grey. In sunshine, in prosperity, the flowers are very well ; but how many wet days are there in life—November seasons of disaster—when a man's hearth and home would be cold, indeed, without the clear, cheering gleam of intel-lect ? ' Love without the union of souls, the author again and again insists, is a delusion, the sheen of a sum-mer's day, and quite as fleeting. Altogether the idea of ' The Professor' was new, and as an indication of the grooves in which its author's genius was afterwards to run, we would not willingly have lost it. As a psycho-logical study alone it was well worthy of preservation.

But better and more remarkable works followed. The reading world has very seldom been startled by such a genuine and powerful piece of originality as ' Jane Eyre.' One can almost gauge the feeling, after reading it, which caused Charlotte Brontë to be such an enthusiastic admirer of Thackeray. He, at any rate, she knew, would appreciate her efforts, for was he not also engaged (with even more splendid talents) in the crusade against conventionality? He, at least, understood her burning words, when she affirmed that ' conventionality is not morality, self-righteousness is not religion. To attack the first is not to assail the last. To pluck the mask from the face of the Pharisee, is not to lift an impious hand to the Crown of Thorns.' These words will sufficiently show how she endeavoured to tread in the steps of ' the first social regenerator of the day,' and to whom she inscribed the second edition of her most widely known book. ' Jane Eyre ' is an autobiography, and its intention is to present a plain, unbiassed narrative of a woman's life from its commencement to a period when it is supposed to have ceased to possess interest to mankind generally. It is told fearlessly, and with a burning pen. But there is no *suppressio veri;* that, its author would have scorned : perhaps it would have been better for its reception in some quarters—

Q

limited in range we are happy to think—if the narrator
of the story had glossed over some portions of her
heroine's history. She has chosen, however, to adhere
to stern reality, and there it is finally for us, unpleasant
and rough though it be in some of its recorded experiences. The book shows the most opposite qualities
—light, darkness ; beauty, deformity; strength, tenderness. Its pathos is of the finest quality, stirring most
deeply because it is simple and unforced. The situations
are very vivid : several scenes being depicted which it
would be impossible to eradicate from the memory after
the most extensive reading of serial literature. Even
those who regard it as coarse must admit its strange
fascination. It was a book that could afford to be
independent of criticism, and accordingly we find that,
before the reviews appeared, anxious and continuous
enquiries respecting it began to be made at the libraries.
There was not much fiction being written which fixed
the public eye, and the issue of this novel almost created
an era. Forgotten now is the savage criticism of the
reviewer who said of the author of 'Jane Eyre,' 'She
must be one who for some sufficient reason has long
forfeited the society of her sex,' whilst the work which
baffled his judgment, but earned his vituperation, still
remains, a memento of real genius which could not be

suppressed. Although chiefly remarkable for its prominent delineation of the passion of love in strong and impulsive natures, there are many other points which are noticeable about it, and should therefore be mentioned. The keen observation of the writer is manifest on almost every page. Intense realism is its chief characteristic. The pictures are as vivid and bold as though etched by a Rembrandt, or drawn by a Salvator Rosa. Dickens has been almost equalled by the description of the school at Lowood, to which Miss Eyre was sent, and which might well be described as Dothegirls' Hall. Here, however—melancholy lot!— in addition to indifferent food, supplied in very limited quantities, there was a good deal of threatening about 'damnation.' The hypocritical minister, Mr. Brockle-hurst (as drawn by the author), had sometimes the worst of it in his dealings with Jane Eyre, as, for instance, in this : 'What is hell ? ' 'A pit full of fire.' 'What must you do to avoid it ?' The answer was a little ob-jectionable, as the autobiographer says—' I must keep in good health and not die.' As a corrective, she had given to her to read ' The Child's Guide,' containing 'an account of the awfully sudden death of Martha G——, a naughty child addicted to falsehood and deceit.' Cer-tainly if this mental pabulum, combined with the

material one of nauseous burnt porridge, was not potent
in keeping down the old Adam, it would be impossible
to mention an effectual remedy, one would think. As
the story progresses it becomes most thrilling, and we
are introduced to a character which is frequently
regarded, and not without reason, as Currer Bell's
masterpiece of powerful drawing—viz., Mr. Rochester.
Strong and yet weak, a very thunderbolt for strength
and explosiveness, and yet a bundle of ordinary human
weaknesses, this individual stands forth as real and living
a portrait as is to be found existing in word-painting.
He is attractive in spite of his numerous faults, and
where is the character who more stood in need of pity?
Picture him at Thornfield, united in wedlock to a raving
maniac, who in her paroxysms attempted his life, whilst
he, in return, saved hers—that very life which was a
curse, and brought unutterable gloom to him. Then,
too, he saw the form that he loved, but could not retain,
and yet felt the movement of a wicked but ineffable
love towards her—wicked, because of the tie which
bound him to the wild being who bore his name. Add
to all this that his nature was as sensitive as it was
intense, and where is the person who could not pity ·
Fairfax Rochester? Behold him again after he has been
maimed in the fruitless endeavour to save the maniac

from death. He describes himself as 'no better than the old lightning-struck chestnut-tree in Thornfield orchard;' but is the process of purification to be counted as nothing which has brought about this result?—

'Jane! you think me an irreligious dog, I dare say; but my heart swells with gratitude to the beneficent God of this earth just now. He sees not as man sees, but far clearer; judges not as man judges, but far more wisely. I did wrong: I would have sullied my innocent flower—breathed guilt on its purity; the Omnipotent snatched it from me. I, in my stiff-necked rebellion, almost cursed the dispensation: instead of bending to the decree, I defied it. Divine justice pursued its course; disasters came thick on me: I was forced to pass through the valley of the shadow of death. His chastisements are mighty, and one smote me which has humbled me for ever. You know I was proud of my strength, but what is it now when I must give it over to foreign guidance as a child does its weakness? Of late, Jane—only—only of late—I began to see and acknowledge the hand of God in my doom. I began to experience remorse, repentance; the wish for reconcilement to my Maker. I began sometimes to pray; very brief prayers they were, but very sincere.'

Verily, this is the epitome of an experience worthy of being sympathised with, and valuable to be written.

There can be no doubt that the first and greatest cause of the extreme vividness of the writings of Charlotte

Brontë and her sisters is the fact that most of the characters depicted are as faithful copies from real life as
though an artist had sat down and limned their features.
More so : for the artist has nothing to do with psychological characteristics, which, in the case of the authors,
are as accurately described as the features. Having
fixed upon their subjects for analysis, they clung to them
like a shadow or a second self, and the very isolation by
which they were surrounded lent strength to their conceptions. The characters are true to their respective
natures, and their final ends are fearlessly worked out.
Having spoken of the book which made the fame of
Charlotte Brontë, let us glance at her next most important work, and the one which we like best of all—
'Shirley.' It opens with a chapter in which a vein of
humour unsuspected in Charlotte Brontë is manifested,
and we know of no other author whose sketches so much
remind us of George Eliot as does this delineation of
the three curates. The writer has completely unbent, relaxed from the severity which so greatly predominates
in her other works, and given play to a quiet and yet
quaint drollery which is positively irresistible. A little
further on, however, we come to more serious business ;
and the terrible machinery riots which so disastrously
retarded commercial progress at the period at which this

history is fixed, afford excellent scope for those graphic descriptions in which Currer Bell stands almost un-rivalled. The West Riding of Yorkshire, and some parts of Lancashire, were especially subjected to hardships and *émeutes* on account of these improvements and inven-- tions in manufacture, and the sketch of Robert Mocre's campaign against the bigoted factory operatives in his employ and that of his neighbours is only a fancy one as regards the disposition of the events. Such things were common at the time of the Luddite riots, but in adopt-ing these riots as the foundation of her story, the author also took characters living in her own day and at her own door, so to speak, hoping that they would thus pass unrecognised. But the fact that the riots occurred thirty years previously did not blind the people portrayed to the knowledge that they were gazing upon their own portraits. The Yorkes, the three curates, and Mrs. Prior are all portraits, whilst Shirley herself is Emily Brontë idealised, or rather what Emily would have been had she been placed in different circumstances. Though the book is singularly strong in individualities, there is, further, more general merit in its writing. Its scenic effects are beautiful ; the deep love of nature which possessed the soul of Currer Bell is more observable here than elsewhere. It is what we should describe as a novel good 'all round.' It has no weak side ; it is the most perfect piece of writing the author has left behind her. There is not the terrible sweep of passion we see in 'Jane Eyre ;' the roughnesses of life are smoothed down a little, and it seems altogether more humanised and humanising. The most opposite events are touched upon skilfully. Who can forget, for instance, the description of the revival in the new Wesleyan Chapel at Briarfield, when 'Doad o' Bill's ' announced positively that he had 'fun (found) liberty,' and the excitement amongst the brethren was intense. Why can't these worthy people take their religion a little more quietly ? As our author says on this occasion, 'the roof of the chapel did *not* fly off ; which speaks volumes in praise of its solid slating.' A little further on we get another sample of power, occurring in the description of a female character. 'Nature made her in the mood in which she makes her briars and thorns ; whereas for the creation of some women she reserves the May morning hours, when with light and dew she wooes the primrose from the turf, and the lily from the woodmoss.' Again, we find in this novel that although Currer Bell was not a great poetess through the usual medium of measured cadence, she could write fine, genuine poetry in a prose setting. Witness the following description of nature put into the mouth of Shirley :—

' I saw—I now see—a woman-Titan : her robe of blue air spreads to the outskirts of the heath where yonder flock is grazing ; a veil, white as an avalanche, sweeps from her head to her feet, and arabesques of lightning flame on its borders. Under her breast I see her zone, purple like that horizon ; through its blush shines the star of evening. Her steady eyes I cannot picture; they are clear—they are deep as lakes—they are lifted and full of worship—they tremble with the softness of love and the lustre of prayer. Her forehead has the expanse of a cloud, and is paler than the early moon, risen long before dark gathers ; she reclines her bosom on the ridge of Stillbro' Moor ; her mighty hands are joined beneath it. So kneeling, face to face she speaks with God. That Eve is Jehovah's daughter, as Adam was his son.'

Our young poets might well covet a power of poetic description like this. As with all true poetry, there is not only the form but the halo. The expression, coming as it did from the feeling, begets in us the feeling again. Other passages of equal beauty could be culled from ' Shirley,' gems glittering here and there in a great broad field. Nature, love, happiness, misery, loss, gain, are the themes dilated upon, on each of which much is given to delight, to improve, and to engender sympathy. Charlotte Brontë exhibits a marked contrast in one respect to the greatest female novelist at present living, and perhaps 'Shirley' is the clearest example of what we mean. Her faith is unwavering—faith in the Unseen. But because He is Unseen she would teach us that that is no reason why He should be Unknown. Neither does she form impossible ideals. Shirley is as grand a character in her way as Dorothea Brooke, but we can comprehend her better. And though Shirley's soul was deep, and she had yearnings after greatness, her hopes were not placed beyond fruition, as in the case of Dorothea. The former says : 'Indisputably, a great, good, handsome man is the first of created things. I would scorn to contend for empire with him. Shall my left hand dispute for precedence with my right?—shall my heart quarrel with my pulse ?—shall my veins be jealous of the blood which fills them ? ' Some feeling of this kind, of course, Dorothea indulged towards Mr. Casaubon ; but in her case the idol is shattered, whilst Shirley obtains in the love of Louis Moore all that she craves for. It was Dorothea's fate to be always finding humanity fail, and created things insufficient to fill the void in her nature. In this sense Shirley is the superior character. Besides her love, she had a truer insight into the means of procuring happiness. She discovered that it must sometimes be worked for with her own hands. Thus, then, was her nature completely rounded. With reverence to the Supreme were added his richest gift of love and the link of benevolence to bind her to the rest of mankind. Not so serenely beautiful as Dorothea, and not perhaps so lofty in intellect, she is yet a more suc- cessful character. On her forehead there is not written— failure.

If the sisters Brontë had early in life been accustomed to mingle in society, and had not been imprisoned within the walls of Haworth parsonage, there can be little question that we should have had more masterly and more general works from their hands. The skill they exhibit in delineating life should not have been confined to the inhabitants of those northern moors, but should have been employed in other haunts and other scenes likewise. Their field has been necessarily restricted, though their genius had full play on the subjects within their reach. But to demonstrate the capacity to turn experience to account wherever it might be obtained, we only need to direct the reader's attention to Charlotte Brontë's latest work, 'Villette.' It is redolent of the society of Brussels, where the author and her sister spent some years of their lives. To the ordinary English reader it is probably the most uninteresting of all the works of Miss Brontë, as page after page is composed mostly of French, and that sometimes difficult and idiomatic.

This doubtless operated to some extent against its popularity with the mass of novel-readers, though the book seems to have earned the most lavish encomiums from the critics.   It exhibits, however, the genius neither of 'Jane Eyre' nor of 'Shirley:' it is, in truth, superior to the fiction of ninety per cent. of novelists, but it scarcely warranted the extravagant terms of praise which were showered upon it by the reviewers.   These valuable individuals, however, were, as is too often the case unfortunately, wise after the event—that is, they found it tolerably safe to eulogise a new work from the hand of one who had already established her position as amongst the most original writers of the age.   One or two of the *dramatis personæ* evoke sentiments of approval an account of their originality, conspicuous amongst them being Mr. Paul Emanuel and Miss de Bassompierre ; but on the whole the book is disappointing, for there is no one character whose fortunes we are anxious to follow ; and a novel which fails to beget a personal interest must be said to have lost its chief charm.

Emily Brontë—for it is now time that we should say something of the two other persons in this remarkable trio—was, in certain respects, the most extraordinary of the three sisters.   She has this distinction at any rate, that she has written a book which stands as completely

alone in the language as does the ' Paradise Lost' or the
' Pilgrim's Progress.' This of itself, setting aside subject
and construction, is no mean eminence. Emily Jane
Brontë, as is well known, was the youngest but one of
the Rev. Mr. Brontë's children, and died before she was
thirty years of age. Early in life she displayed a singularly
masculine bent of intellect, and astonished those with
whom she came in contact by her penetration, and that
settlement of character which generally only comes with
age. She went from home twice, once to school and once
to Brussels, but it was like the caging of a lioness, and her
soul yearned for the liberty of home. When in Brussels
she attracted and impressed deeply all those who came
across her, and M. Heger declared she should have been
a man, for ' her powerful reason would have deduced new
spheres of discovery from the knowledge of the old, and
her strong, imperious will would never have been
daunted by opposition or difficulty : never have given
way but with life.' On her return to Haworth she began
to lose in beauty but to gain in impressiveness of feature,
and she divided her time between homely domestic
duties, studies, and rambles. Shrinking entirely from
contact with the life which surrounded her, she gave
herself up to nature, the result being apparent in her
works, which reveal a most intimate acquaintance with

the great Mother in all her moods. Her mind was
absolutely free to all the lessons which she should teach,
and she embraced them with the most passionate longing.
' Her native hills were far more to her than a spectacle ;
they were what she lived in, and by, as much as the wild
birds, their tenants, or as the heather, their produce.'
Her descriptions, then, of natural scenery, are what they
should be, and all they should be. Any reader of her works
must perforce acknowledge the accuracy of these observations. Her life, however, seemed to be an unprized one,
except by that sister who loved her profoundly, and who
keenly appreciated her genius as it essayed to unfold its
wings in the sun. But whilst she lived the world made no
sign of recognition of her strangely weird powers. When
illness came her indomitable will still enabled her to
present an unflinching front to sympathising friends.
She refused to see the doctor, and would not have it
that she was ill. To the last she retained an independent
spirit, and on the day of her death she arose and dressed
herself as usual. Her end reminds us of that of her
brother Branwell whose will was so strong that he
insisted on standing up to die and did actually so die.
Emily did everything for herself on that last day, but as
the hours drew on got manifestly worse, and could only
whisper in gasps. The end came when it was too late to

profit by human skill. 'Wuthering Heights,' the principal
work she has left behind her, shows a massive strength
which is of the rarest description. Its power is absolutely
Titanic : from the first page to the last it reads like the
intellectual throes of a giant. It is fearful, it is true, and
perhaps one of the most unpleasant books ever written :
but we stand in amaze at the almost incredible fact that
it was written by a slim country girl who would have
passed in a crowd as an insignificant person, and who
had had little or no experience of the ways of the world.
In Heathcliff, Emily Brontë has drawn the greatest
villain extant, after Iago. He has no match out of
Shakspeare. The Mephistopheles of Goethe's 'Faust'
is a person of gentlemanly proclivities compared with
Heathcliff. There is not a redeeming quality in him ;
his coarseness is very repellent ; he is a unique specimen
of the human tiger. Charlotte Brontë in her digest of
this character finds one ameliorating circumstance in his
favour, one link which connects him with humanity—viz.,
his regard for one of his victims, Hareton Earnshaw.
But we cannot agree with her : his feeling towards
Earnshaw is excessively like that feline affection which
sometimes destroys its own offspring. As to his alleged
esteem for Nelly Dean, perhaps also the less said about
that the better. But 'Wuthering Heights' is a marvellous

curiosity in letters. We challenge the world to produce
another work in which the whole atmosphere seems so
surcharged with suppressed electricity, and bound in
with the blackness of tempest and desolation.   From the
time when young Heathcliff is introduced to us, 'as dark
almost as if he came from the devil,' to the last page of
the story, there is nothing but savagery and ferocity,
except when we are taken away from the persons to the
scenes of the narratives, and treated to those pictures
in which the author excels.   The Heights itself, the old
north-country manor-house, is made intensely real to us,
but not more so than the central figure of the story, who,
believing himself alone one night, throws open the
lattice, and cries with terrible anguish—'Cathy! oh, my
heart's darling.   Hear me this once.   Catherine, at
last!' Then his history is recapitulated, by one who
witnessed his life in all its stages ; and in the passage
where Catherine informs her nurse that she has promised
to marry Edgar Linton, but ought not to have done so,
we get the following example of concentrated force :—

'I have no more business to marry Edgar Linton than I
have to be in Heaven.   But it would degrade me to marry
Heathcliff now ; so he shall never know how I love him, and
that not because he's handsome, Nelly, but because he's
more myself than I am.   Whatever our souls are made of,
his and mine are the same ; and Linton's is as different as

moonbeams from lightning, or frost from fire. . . . Who is
to separate us? they'll meet the fate of Milo. I cannot express it; but surely you and everybody have a notion that
there is, or should be, an existence of yours beyond you.
What were the use of my creation if I were entirely contained here? My great miseries in this world have been
Heathcliff's miseries, and I watched and felt each from the
beginning; my great thought in living is himself. If all else
perished and he remained, *I* should continue to be; and if
all else remained and he were annihilated, the universe
would turn to a mighty stranger; I should not seem a part
of it. My love for Linton is like the foliage in the woods:
time will change it, I'm well aware, as winter changes the
trees. My love for Heathcliff resembles the eternal rocks
beneath: a source of little visible delight, but necessary.
Nelly, I *am* Heathcliff! He's always, always in my mind; not
as a pleasure any more than I am always a pleasure to myself, but as my own being.'

Then comes Catherine's death—when she asks for-
giveness for having wronged him, and Heathcliff answers,
'Kiss me again; and don't let me see your eyes! I
forgive what you have done to me. I love *my* murderer
—but *yours!* How can I?' The tale of woe proceeds;
the despairing man longing for the dead, until at last he
faces death, and being asked if he will have the minister,
replies—'I tell you I have nearly attained *my* Heaven;
and that of others is altogether unvalued and uncoveted
by me.' He then sleeps beside her: the tragedy of
eighteen years is complete. A great deal has been said

R

on the question whether such a book as 'Wuthering Heights' ought to be written, and Charlotte Brontë herself felt impelled to utter some words of defence for it. Where the mind is healthy it can do no harm; but there are, possibly, organisations upon whom it might exercise a baleful influence. With regard to the drawing of Heathcliff, Currer Bell scarcely thought the creation of such beings justifiable, but she goes on to say that 'the writer who possesses the creative gift owns something of which he is not always master—something that, at times, strangely wills and works for itself.' We are afraid that if this opinion were pushed to its logical issues it would be found incapable of being supported. A multiplication of such books as 'Wuthering Heights' without corresponding genius would be a lamentable thing, no doubt; yet, while we cannot defend it altogether possibly as it stands, we should regret never having seen it, as one of the most extraordinary and powerful productions in the whole range of English literature.

Anne Brontë, the youngest of the three sisters, was unlike Charlotte and Emily in disposition and mental constitution. She was not so vigorous, and seemed more dependent upon the sympathy of others. These characteristics are apparent in her works, though in her principal novel there are touches which almost remind one of Emily. She was, nevertheless, deficient in the energy which distinguished her sisters, and was altogether frailer in body, and more tender and serene in spirit. The devotional element in her nature was very strong, as will be seen from a perusal of her poems. Her sensitiveness was great, and apt to be wounded by the bitter experiences she was called upon to endure as one of the class of ill-treated individuals called governesses. Some of these experiences she has commemorated in her story 'Agnes Grey,' which, however, shows no notable powers of penetration and insight such as the world had been accustomed to look for in the authors bearing the cognomen of Bell. It is the most inferior of all the works written by the sisters, though interesting in many aspects. Possessed of a less determined will than Emily, Anne Brontë bore her sufferings patiently, and as the hour of dissolution approached, the terrors which had bound her spirit were dissipated, and she passed away, we are assured, in a calm and triumphant manner. Her last verses are most beautiful in sentiment, and worked out with considerable skill. It is a curious question how this gentle woman, nevertheless, came to write such a narrative as 'The Tenant of Wildfell Hall,' which in some of its details is more offensive and

repulsive than the great *pièce de resistance* of her next
elder sister. The drunken orgies of Mr. Huntingdon
and his companions cannot fail to be disgusting to the
reader, vivid though the relation may be in colour.
Most probably that portion of the story was suggested by
the sad practical acquaintance the author had been
compelled to make of the effects of the vice of drunken-
ness in her brother Branwell. The sorrow entailed by
his conduct weighed upon her deeply, and she gave
relief to her feelings by picturing the sin, with all its
hideous consequences and deformity, through the medium
of fiction. It might be that she had hope such a
revelation would be effective for good, and certainly all
who read the story cannot but be affected by that
wretched portion of it devoted to the delineation of a
drunkard. It is the strongest, the most striking part of
the volume, and the mystery of its production by such a
pure soul as Anne Brontë's can only be explained on the
hypothesis we have assumed. The love of Gilbert
Markham for the attractive and clever widow is a
delightful episode, and excellently told, and the closing
chapters go very far to redeem the unpleasantness we
were compelled to encounter in the body of the work.
As with Emily, Anne Brontë's strong point as a novelist
was in the delineation of one grand master passion from

the moment when it entered into the soul to the time
when it assumed complete and undisputed possession of
it. We see this tyranny of passion in Heathcliff; we
behold the tyranny again in another direction in Mr.
Huntingdon. In both cases, however, it is finally left
with as repulsive an appearance as the graphic pencils of
the artists were able to command. No one can affirm
that vice is ever winked at : it is, on the contrary, drawn
without cloak or veil, in order that its devotees may be
ashamed, or that those who are in danger of becoming
its victims may be arrested and appalled. Such, we take
it, is the great lesson of ' The Tenant of Wildfell Hall,'
and readers, even without sympathy for the author,
would be unjust to affirm that the lesson is not taught
with sufficient distinctiveness and force. There are
some things which only need to be described to be
abhorred ; and this feeling probably led to the production of the work just alluded to.

Of the little volume of poetry written conjointly by
Currer, Ellis, and Acton Bell, and published before their
prose works, there is not much to be said, except that it
might teach a lesson to some of the poets of the present
day, that the best inspiration after all is to be derived
from contact with Nature herself. Many of these verses
are not only Wordsworthian in their simplicity of ex-

pression, but also in their reverent feeling for the Great
Teacher of all true poets. They are rills which spring
from the best source of inspiration, and, whilst they do
not lose the idiosyncrasies of their respective authors, are
all imbued with intense love of outward beauty, and
breathe of the native heath upon which they were in
most part written. The poems which bear traces of the
highest flight of imagination are undoubtedly those of
Ellis Bell. Her genius here attains a more refined
expression, without losing anything of its power. In
several instances she has surrounded an old subject with
new and delightful interest, and even where her choice
has fallen upon more sombre subjects, the originality is
so great that we are lost in admiration, and enter fully
into the theme, glad of the new thoughts even when the
old theme, *per se*, has no charms for us. Amongst the
many fine things which have been said of Memory,
where are there four lines which concentrate so much
regret as are found embedded in this utterance?—

> ' I dare not let it languish,
> Dare not indulge in memory's rapturous pain;
> Once drinking deep of that divinest anguish,
> How could I taste the empty world again?'

This was no maundering of a simply sentimental spirit,
but the outcome of a soul that had suffered, and had not

lost its strength, though a deep sorrow encompassed it, and obscured its vision. There was not the light that shone in the old days, and the regret that has overtaken many a heart found a fine and truthful utterance in one who was gifted with a power of expression beyond her fellows. But the last lines which this wonderfully-gifted woman ever wrote strike us as being specially note-worthy. They are an address to the Deity : space fails us to quote them all, but as a specimen of their strength we may give the folluwing :—

> ' Vain are the thousand creeds
> That move men's hearts ; unutterably vain ;
>   Worthless as withered weeds,
> Or idlest froths amid the boundless main,
>
>   To waken doubt in one
> Holding so fast by Thine infinity.
>
> *　　*　　*　　*　　*
>
>   Though earth and man were gone,
> And suns and universes ceased to be,
>   And Thou wert left alone,
> Every existence would exist in Thee.
>
>   There is not room for death,
> Nor atom that His might could render void ;
>   Thou, Thou art Being and Breath,
> And what Thou art may never be destroyed.'

We will not stay to investigate the theology of this passage, but as a specimen of poetic vigour it is well worthy of reprinting. The poems of Charlotte Brontë strike us as being the least excellent in the collection. Correct as they are in sentiment and expression, they lack the emphasis to be perceived in those of her sisters. The probability is that while Emily and Anne Brontë would have attained considerable eminence as poets, Charlotte would have wasted her powers on a branch of literature to which she was not quite adapted. In the case of Emily, the brief, decisive, epigrammatic form of expression suited her genius, just as the devotional cadence suited that of Anne, but Charlotte had better scope in a more didactic and extended style. One spirit breathes through the poems of Acton Bell—that which animates the trembling suppliant appealing to Heaven. They are all a single cry couched in different, but exquisite language, the cry of a dependent for guidance by a Sovereign hand. The moods may differ, but the substance of the soul's aspiration is the same, and there are few sweeter religious poems than that which contains the last thoughts and wishes of Acton Bell. The verses are so well known that we refrain from reproducing them ; but they may be taken as a good illustration of the spirit which animated the author, and form a touching farewell to a world in which she could never be said to have been at home.

With regard to the position which the Brontës occupy amongst authors, we express ourselves with some diffidence. In summing up their general merits, and pronouncing upon their works, it must be done as a whole, and with no singling out of particular excellences. So, whilst Charlotte Brontë infinitely eclipses novelists of the highest reputation in isolated qualities—such as those we have already endeavoured to point out—it must be confessed that when we speak of her as the artist it cannot be as pertaining to the very highest rank. Her genius is intense, but not broad, and it is breadth alone which distinguishes the loftiest minds. But if she fails to attain the standard of the few writers who have been uplifted by common consent to the highest pinnacle of fame, she is the equal of any authors of the second rank. It is not too much to predict, in fact, that many meretricious works which have been commended for public admiration will lose in popularity, while those of which we have been speaking will increase. It is impossible for two of the works of Charlotte Brontë to fall out of our literature. They have been stamped as genuine gold and will keep continually in circulation. Works which fail to pass this ordeal are those which are either weak or false ; these are both strong and true. We obtain from the author of ' Jane Eyre ' no multitude of characters, but those we do get we become closely familiar with—and one being of veritable flesh and blood is worth a thousand insubstantial imitations. The novels deal with no particular forms of religious belief, or social questions, which the author would doubtless but have regarded as accidents of which she cared to take no account ; and hence we may affirm that after the lapse of fifty years her works would read as freshly as when they first made their appearance. It was humanity she strove to produce ; not its creeds, crotchets, or peculiarities ; and it is for this reason that her labour will triumphantly stand the test of time. The inner life of a soul is very much the same in all ages. Its hopes, its fears, and its joys do not change with the changing seasons and the revolving years. Ages pass away, and those writers and writings which have only appealed to transient phases of thought or particular changes of society are swept away as by a resistless current, whilst those who defy the potency of the waves are the gifted few who have shown the genuine power of interpreting nature, or of dealing with the passions of the human heart.

HENRY FIELDING

[MACMILLAN'S MAGAZINE]

HENRY FIELDING, upon whom we place the distinction
of being England's first great novelist, has for a century past been the constant subject of criticism. His
surpassing merits have compelled even his most pronounced foes to assign him a lofty place in the art which
he adorned. Attempts to depreciate his genius, because
the moral backbone was lacking in some of his characters,
have been repeatedly made, but with no permanent
effect upon his renown. For ourselves, we affirm at the
outset that we consider him the Shakspeare of novelists.
By this, of course, it will be understood, we do not imply
that the sum of his genius was in any way comparable
to that of the illustrious dramatist ; but that he achieved
his results in the same way. He was the great artist in
fiction because he was the great observer and interpreter
of human nature. The novel will never be able to
assume a position of equal importance with the drama,
because of its comparative defectiveness of construction.
But to such perfection as it is capable of being brought,

Fielding almost attained.   It is, then, for the reason
of the similarity of his method to that of Shakspeare
that we have ventured to award him the highest title
of eminence.   It will be our endeavour, while not
hiding his defects, to set forth the grounds of justification for the position we have assumed.

With that perversity which only men of the same
class or profession can exhibit towards each other, it was
the fashion with literary men of Fielding's time—and
indeed for many years subsequently—to compare him
unfavourably with his rival, Richardson.   It is singular
how frequently individuals of professed literary acumen
are willing to accept the *dicta* of others in matters of
criticism.   We are only just now losing the effects of this
empiricism.   Some unfortunate epigram, or some warped
and fantastic judgment, has frequently been passed
upon an author by those who were supposed to be
competent judges, and the depreciatory observations
have had the same effect upon the public mind as that
of the pebble cast into the pool.   The waters have been
agitated and disturbed by ever-widening circles of dis-
content, even to their utmost limits.   Much laborious
effort has been required to exorcise the prejudice thus
established ; and it is just this power which a wrong
judgment possesses over the minds of men in an equivalent

degree with a right one, which makes criticism dangerous. In the hands of an incapable person it is an engine of incalculable mischief. And the fact that now and then this engine destroys its foolish owner is no satisfaction for the wrong done to men of undoubted genius. The self-righting power of criticism certainly moves slowly. We are somewhat diffident, for example, when we find it necessary to differ strongly from such authorities as Dr. Johnson; or at any rate should unquestionably have been so had we been amongst his contemporaries. Now that we are out of reach of his terrible voice and his overbearing demeanour, and regarding him thus from a safe distance, we do not find it so difficult to designate his capacity for judging in literary matters as often shallow and pretentious. Most people admit that his view of Milton is far from a just and worthy one of that sublime poet. He lacked the balance of mind, the intellectual equipoise, which is the foundation of the critical faculty. Consequently, with the lapse of time, his reputation in this respect will crumble away. Even the obsequious Boswell has ventured to insinuate that at times Johnson was so swayed by his feelings that, when making comparisons between writers, he very often contradicted his intellect by his affection; and, while saying the utmost he could of the inferior qualities of his personal favourite, ignored those which were superior in the person with whom he was ranged in comparison. Some such treatment as this was meted out to Fielding when he placed him in juxtaposition with Richardson. Let us reproduce his criticism. 'Sir,' said he, in that pompous manner in which we can fancy the burly old Doctor was wont to settle the affairs of men and mundane concerns generally, ' there is all the difference in the world between characters of nature and characters of manners ; and *there* is the difference between the characters of Fielding and those of Richardson. Characters of manners are very entertaining ; but they are to be understood by a more superficial observer than characters of nature, when a man must dive into the recesses of the human heart.' There is very little in this beyond saying that there is a great deal of difference between things which differ. Yet it is the kind of criticism which bears a deceptive sound with it, and acquires a reputation far in excess of its value, as being an expression of great apparent profundity. We shall hope to show that in his attribution of the one method to Fielding and the other to Richardson, Dr. Johnson came to an erroneous conclusion. For the present his observations lend some force to what has gone before, and it is an undoubted fact that the weakness of Fielding's moral character had much to do with Johnson's estimate of him. The formidable lexicographer was of that class of men who are almost prepared to find fault with the sun because of the spots upon his surface.

Horace Walpole was another of the critics who appear to have been either blinded by envy or unable to detect the effects of true genius, for we find that he was amongst the earliest detractors of Fielding—a prominent member of the school of depreciators which endeavoured to humble him in the eyes of his contemporaries. It is pleasant, however, to think that some who bear great names have expressed the most unqualified admiration for the novels of our author, and the opinion of one master mind outweighs that of a hundred Walpoles. Byron gave it as his belief that 'Fielding was the prose Homer of human nature;' the far-seeing Goethe was delighted with his art; and Gibbon demonstrated his literary sagacity by the following eloquent eulogium :—
'Our immortal Fielding was of the younger branch of the Earls of Denbigh, who drew their origin from the Counts of Hapsburgh, the lineal descendants of Eltrico, in the seventh century Dukes of Alsace. Far different have been the fortunes of the English and German divisions of the family of Hapsburgh ; the former, the knights and sheriffs of Leicestershire, have slowly risen to the dignity of a peerage ; the latter, the Emperors of

Germany and Kings of Spain, have threatened the liberties of the Old, and invaded the treasures of the New World. The successors of Charles V. may disdain their brethren of England; but the romance of "Tom Jones," that exquisite picture of human manners, will outlive the palace of the Escurial, and the Imperial Eagle of Austria.' Ornate as is Gibbon's language, it yet contains a judgment upon Fielding which has been in gradual process of verification since the words were written. Most of those who have dispassionately considered Fielding's works, and compared them with the works of his contemporaries and successors, will arrive at a conclusion much nearer to that expressed by Gibbon than that of the detractor, Horace Walpole. Of course, an argument which we have previously used for another purpose, may possibly be inverted and turned against ourselves. It may be replied that after all criticism is only the opinion of one man, though it is often acted upon by the multitude: and that judgments upon literary works attain an inordinate influence when delivered by individuals of acknowledged reputation. Supposing this were to some extent true, every single reader has the opportunity of righting the matter so far as he is personally concerned. But what we do find valuable about the art of criticism, notwithstanding its numerous and manifest imperfections, is this, that it not unfrequently results in the deposition of much that is unworthy, and in the exaltation of some works which have been threatened with an undeserved obscurity. The critic is really nothing more than a leader of men ; he is supposed to have the capacity of leading in the right way, and when it is found that there is no light in him, and he is incapable of perceiving eternal Truth, we should withdraw ourselves from his guidance. We say, then, that while it is necessary for a man's self-culture and intellectual independence that he should not accept off-hand the opinions of any critic, however eminent, in the bulk and without scrutiny, yet when judgments come to us stamped with the names of those who have devoted themselves to the art of criticism, they should at any rate receive candid, if searching, investigation. The destruction of the empiricism of the critic need not involve the destruction of the eclecticism of the art. It must come to us as a friendly guide, and not as a tyrant. Our own opinion of Fielding stands very little short of the most eulogistic which has been expressed concerning him ; but we trust we have arrived at it out of no slavish regard for other minds.

A glance at the novelist's life is almost a necessity, for it elucidates many points in connection with his works which would otherwise be obscure. There has probably been no instance where the impress of the author's character has been more perceptible upon his writings than that of Fielding. Some of his novels confessedly contain passages from his own life, with very little variation of detail. It will have been perceived by the quotation from Gibbon that Fielding was of illustrious descent, but the wealth of the family must have flowed into another channel, for he got none or little of it. He was born on April 22, 1707, at Sharpham Park, near Glastonbury. His father was a distinguished soldier, having served with Marlborough at Blenheim, and at length obtained the rank of Lieutenant-General. Besides being grandson of an Earl of Denbigh, this warrior was related to other noble families. The mother of Fielding was a daughter of Judge Gold, one of whose immediate descendants was also a baron of the Exchequer. Posterity may thus rest satisfied with the novelist's birth. Fielding, however, was not the only one of his family who appears to have been talented in literature. One of his sisters wrote a romance entitled 'David Simple,' and was also the author of numerous letters, which, with the story, earned the encomiums of her brother. We cannot, of course, now say to what extent she may have been indebted to him in regard to these compositions. There is every reason to believe that he was most accessible to advice and sympathy, while his affection for his relatives was deep and sincere. This—in addition to a warm affection for children—is one of the redeeming traits in a character that was subsequently marred by many imperfections. Having received the earlier part of his education at home, from the Rev. Mr. Oliver, his private tutor—who is supposed to have been laid under contribution as the original of Parson Trulliber—Fielding was sent to Eton, where he became intimate with Fox, Lord Lyttelton, Pitt, and others, who afterwards acquired celebrity with himself, and at various crises in his history sustained towards him the part of real friendship. Unlike many literary men, whose scholastic career has been rather a *fiasco* than otherwise, Fielding was most successful in his acquisition of knowledge, and when only sixteen years of age was acknowledged by his masters to possess a very sound acquaintance with all the leading Greek and Latin writers. Traces of this linguistic proficiency are again and again beheld in his novels. From Eton he went to the University of Leyden, where he immediately entered upon still wider and more liberal studies; but at the threshold of his life the demon of misfortune which seems to have dogged his footsteps all through his

career found him out.   His university career closed
prematurely, for his father, General Fielding, had married
again, and having now two large families to keep out of
a small income,· discovered that his original intention
with regard to his son must be abandoned.   This could
not have been a pleasant intimation to a youth of twenty,
who had just begun to feel the expansion of his faculties,
and doubtless to be conscious that his future 'might
copy his fair past' as regards the accumulation of the
stores of knowledge.   Whatever laxity of mind overtook
him in after life, the earlier years of Fielding show him
to have been enamoured of learning, and in nowise
averse to its routine.   His spirit was keen and eager,
and though at twenty years of age he was somewhat
given to pleasure, he at the same time was always
desirous to excel, and never allowed his recreations and
amusements to bar his intellectual progress.

Undismayed, however, by this rebuff of fortune,
Fielding returned to London with comparatively little
depression of spirits, and even this entirely cleared off
as soon as he began to mingle in the society of the
metropolis.   It was here, as we shall presently see, that
greater dangers afterwards attended him, which he was
less able to withstand than the assaults of adversity.
Fielding was especially distinguished for all those gifts

which make a man the darling of the circle in which he moves : and accordingly we learn that in a very few months after his settlement in London he was an established favourite of its great literary and dramatic lions, Lyttelton and Garrick amongst the number. Under the auspices of the latter he speedily commenced writing for the stage, and at the age of twenty, as Mr. Roscoe tells us in his excellent life of the novelist, produced his first comedy of 'Love in several Masques.' We shall postpone what comments we have to make upon this and Fielding's other works till the close of our remarks on his personal history. Necessity compelled him to turn to the writing of comedies, for though he was supposed to be enjoying an allowance of some 200*l.* per annum, he made a joke about this income to the effect that it was a sum which really anybody might pay who would. At this juncture some of our most brilliant wits were writing for the stage, so that the young author might be pardoned for the degree of nervousness he felt on entering upon the same career. Indeed, although his genius was not naturally that of the dramatist, the probability is that what aptitude he really possessed for it was somewhat cramped by the circumstances in which he was placed, and the diffidence with which he undertook a profession that at the time enjoyed two of its keenest and wittiest ornaments. It appears, nevertheless, that the comedy already mentioned, and his second one of 'The Temple Beau,' were well received, though his success was by no means proportioned to his increasing embarrassments. That his efforts at comedy were well appreciated is testified to by Lord Lyttelton's assertion, when some one was alluding to the wits of the age, that 'Harry Fielding had more wit and humour than all the persons they had been speaking of put together.' This language seems to have been concurred in by others who were continually looking out for some new thing in that age of wit and humour. Fielding must have worked with great rapidity, for during the nine seasons in which he wrote for the stage, and before he attained his thirtieth year, he had written no fewer than eighteen pieces, reckoning both plays and farces.

It was in the midst of his unsatisfactory career in connection with the stage—unsatisfactory because of its restlessness and its recklessness—that an event occurred which promised to change the whole tenor of his life for ever ; and had Fielding been as strong in his will as he was in the perception of what is right, we should now probably have been able to write him in different characters. In his twenty-seventh year he fell in love with a young lady named Cradock, residing at Salisbury.

She was possessed of both beauty and accomplishments, but her fortune was small. Fielding, however, never hesitated in the pursuit of an object wherein his heart was deeply enlisted, and accordingly he married Miss Cradock with her small fortune of fifteen hundred pounds. The old, old passion had thus again its good old way. Shortly after his marriage his mother died, and Fielding became possessed of a little estate in Dorsetshire, worth some two hundred a year. Hither he bore his bride, and made many resolves to lead the life of a model country gentleman. But with all his affection for his wife—and it was genuine and sincere—he was led by the example of others into great extravagance. Setting up his coach, and living as though he could make one pound do duty for a hundred, it can evoke no surprise that at the end of three years he discovered all his patrimony to be gone, and found himself faced by the terrible spectre of absolute poverty which he himself had raised. It is held by many that genius should never be tried by the ordinary standpoints of thrift and virtue. This is a position to which we can give no kind of countenance ; but what we may look at with regard to Fielding, as some mitigation for his conduct at this period, are those social qualities for which he was so famous. Though they ultimately proved his pecuniary ruin, they were marked by a generosity which cannot but beget in us a pity for the man himself. The delights of society were more than he could bear ; he entered into them with a zest which completely overmastered his *aplomb*, and for the time being made him their slave. So far this was unquestionably bad ; but his case must not be confounded with that of the essentially vicious, with the man who never had Fielding's lofty appreciation for the good, and never even felt the most spasmodic striving after an ideal. To the one we can extend our unfeigned sympathy, to the other only our unmitigated abhorrence. As the sequel to the difficulties which overtook Fielding, he was compelled to resume the study of the law, which he had at one time hoped to abandon for ever. Entering himself at the age of thirty as a student of the Inner Temple, he at once began to work with a will, in order to recover himself from his embarrassments. His devotion to his studies was most praiseworthy, and, as he had great natural shrewdness, there is every reason to believe that in the legal profession he would have been most successful. But one cause or another continually interrupted him, and whatever he undertook through life seems to have met with a premature ending. For his failure, however, ultimately to earn distinction at the bar, he was himself in the first instance responsible. He was not only called, but assiduously went the Western circuit for two or three years, though briefs appear to have been very scanty with him. Suddenly, and in consequence of an intimation that he proposed issuing a work upon law, his practice increased immensely, but only, we are told, to decline again as rapidly. Meanwhile physical retribution began to overtake him for the convivial years he had spent in London society; he was seized with gout, in addition to which, his constitution was much weakened and enfeebled; though in justice it must be said that late hours of study, with literary work executed under great pressure, acted as additional causes in the general break-up of his system. The upshot of it all was that after ceasing the active exercise of his profession, and writing two large volumes (a 'Digest of the Statutes at Large'), which remained for many years unpublished, he finally quitted the bar, and returned to literary pursuits. As might be expected from the nature of his talents, he contributed for a time most successfully to periodical literature. But a period of great distress quickly came upon him. With failing health, which interfered somewhat with the operations of his brilliant intellect, his mind was still racked with the consciousness that his wife and family were entirely dependent upon his exertions.

Heroic he undoubtedly was under difficulties, but there
are some odds against which men cannot possibly
contend. Note, nevertheless, how the true spirit of the
man shone through all the darkness which surrounded
him at this trying moment. His biographers, one and
all, bear testimony to the native strength of his mind.
We are assured that 'when under the most discouraging
circumstances—the loss of comparative fortune, of health,
of the fruits of years of successful toil ; his body lacerated
by the acutest pains, and with a family looking up to
him for immediate support—he was still capable, with a
degree of fortitude almost unexampled, to produce, as it
were, *extempore*, a play, a farce, a pamphlet, or a newspaper. Nay, like Cervantes, whom he most resembled
both in wit and genius, he could jest upon his misfortunes, and make his own sufferings a source of
entertainment to the rest of the world.' He did, in fact,
at this precise period, and in the darkest hour of his
misery, indite a rhyming letter to Sir Robert Walpole,
with himself and his position for its subject ; which is
full of the most humourous allusions. One cannot help
thinking, while reading this incident, of the much later
humourist of our own time, Hood, whose experience was
almost its counterpart, with the exception of the
difference in the cause of Hood's suffering, a naturally

frail constitution being the sole reason for his bodily decay. Fielding was now writing because, as he expressed it, 'he had no choice but to be a hackney writer or a hackney coachman.' This was the man who had been the pride of London fashionables, who had doubtless kept a hundred tables in a roar, and whose very enjoyment of life for its own sake was so keen as to cause Lady Mary Wortley Montagu (his second cousin) to say in comparing him with Steele, that 'he ought to go on living for ever.' When writing for the stage, Fielding was frequently obliged to pass off work which did not satisfy his critical judgment. For this he was now and then remonstrated with by Garrick, and he once replied that the public were too stupid to find out where he failed. The consensus of the pit, however, is tolerably keen, and when the audience began on this occasion to hiss the weak part of the comedy Fielding was astonished, exclaiming, 'They have found it out, have they?' An anecdote characteristic both of the man and his times is told of the novelist which affords a clue to some of his pecuniary difficulties, though it is a credit to his generosity. It appears that some parochial taxes had long remained unpaid by Fielding, a fact which need not greatly surprise us. At length the collector—as tax-collectors always will—became rather threatening in his

aspect, and Fielding went off to Dr. Johnson, that friend-
in-need of the impecunious, to obtain the necessary sum
of money by a literary mortgage.   He was returning
when he met with an old college friend who was in even
greater difficulties than himself.   He took him to dinner
at a neighbouring tavern, and emptied the contents of
his pockets into his hands.   Being informed on returning
home that the collector had twice called on him for the
amount, Fielding replied, 'Friendship has called for the
money, and had it; let the collector call again.'   Other
anecdotes could be cited illustrating the *bonhomie* and
natural benevolence of the novelist's character.

It was during the period in which Fielding was most
busily employed upon his literary ventures that he
married a second time (having lost a few years before
the lady to whom it has been seen he was devotedly
attached) ; and we now find him bending to his work
with redoubled energy.   But all his assiduity was in
vain, and he was compelled to announce with regret that
he could no longer continue the publication of 'The
Covent Garden Journal'—a paper he was then editing.
The mental and physical strain had been too severe, and
there were now added to his other ailments the alarming
symptoms of dropsy.   The only hope held out by his
physician for the prolongation of his life was that he

should go abroad ; and this, upon the earnest solici-
tations of his friends, Fielding consented to do. Por-
tugal having been recommended, he tore himself from his
wife and children, and set sail for Lisbon on June 26,
1754.

At this juncture, noting that Fielding makes references to the matter in the introduction to his 'Voyage,'
we may allude to him in another capacity, and one
in which the literary man has seldom an opportunity of
exhibiting himself. In 1748 he had been appointed
Justice of the Peace for Westminster and Middlesex, an
office which, as we learn, was then paid by fees, and was
very laborious, without being particularly reputable. As
affording some idea of the nature of the work which fell
to the accomplished Justice, we may recapitulate certain
facts narrated by himself. While preparing for a journey
to Bath, which it was hoped would result in his restoration to health, there was placed upon his shoulders no
enviable piece of work. When nigh fatigued to death by
reason of several long examinations relating to five
different murders committed by gangs of street robbers,
he received a message from the Duke of Newcastle to
wait upon him the next morning upon business of great
importance. Though in the utmost distress he attended,
and found that what was desired of him was a statement

of the best plan he could devise for the suppression of
robberies and murders in the streets, offences which had
become alarmingly common.   Fielding submitted a plan
that was highly approved of by the Duke, who promised
to lay it before the Privy Council.   All the terms of the
proposal were complied with, one of the principal being
the depositing of 600*l*. in its author's hands.   At this
small pecuniary charge he undertook to demolish the
gangs complained of, and also to put civil order in ·such
a state of security that it should be thenceforth impossible
for these gangs to enrol themselves in bodies and pursue
their nefarious occupations.   It is interesting to note, as
demonstrating Fielding's executive ability in his new
post, that in a few weeks the whole gang of cut-throats
was entirely dispersed.   But the occupation of Justice
was anything save a pleasant one, while its remuneration
was paltry in the extreme.   Fielding himself says that by
refusing to make the most of his position, by composing
instead of inflaming the quarrels of porters and beggars,
by not plundering the public or the poor, and by refusing to take a shilling from a man who would most
undoubtedly not have had another left, he had reduced
' an income of about 500*l*. a year of the dirtiest money
upon earth to little more than 300*l*.,' a considerable
portion of which remained with his clerk.   It was

acknowledged on all hands that Fielding made an excellent justice, and it is moreover affirmed that his charge to the grand jury, delivered at Westminster on June 29, 1749, is to be regarded, for that time, as a very able and valuable state paper. It was most lucid and searching, as were certain legal investigations which he subsequently made. Furthermore, it may be noted that in a 'Proposal for the Maintenance of the Poor,' of which he was the author, Fielding was the first to make the recommendation of a county workhouse, in which the different objects of industry and reformation might be united. The paper also contained numerous suggestions creditable to Fielding's magisterial sagacity, some of which have since been carried into effect. Altogether he appears to have justified the high eulogium passed upon him in the capacity of Justice of the Peace.

The journey to Lisbon was of no avail for the novelist; his poor, shattered constitution had already failed beyond hope of recovery; in fact, it is stated that he was a dying man when he reached the port. He lingered, however, for two months after his arrival, in great suffering, and at length died in the Portuguese capital on October 8, 1754, being then only in his forty-eighth year. It is not too much to say that in that brief span of life Fielding had exhausted both the mental

T

and physical energy of the seventy years' limit allotted to humanity ; and when we consider the wearing and excited existence he led in the metropolis, it is almost marvellous that he should have been able to accomplish so much intellectual labour.   There is something touching in the fate which compels a man whose genius was so native to the soil of England, to die in a foreign land, away not only from those he loved, but from the scene of his literary triumphs.   The last tribute of respect paid to the novelist emanated from the Chevalier de Meyrionnet, French Consul at Lisbon, who not only undertook his interment, but followed his remains to the grave, and celebrated the talents of the deceased in an epitaph.   The people of the English Factory in the city also erected a monument to him.   In Fielding's absence from England, he was not forgotten by his friend Mr. Allen, who, after his death, educated his children, and bestowed pensions both upon them and their widowed mother.   This Mr. Allen was the original of one of Fielding's best and most satisfactory characters.

The title of honour which we have accorded to our author at the outset may seem to need some justification when it is remembered that De Foe and Richardson were writers at and before the same period, and had produced novels anterior to those of Fielding.   De Foe, however, can scarcely be treated as the ordinary novelist, or put into competition with the race of writers of fiction : he was rather the fierce polemic and satiric author. In the fictitious element he was, of course, remarkably strong ; his art was undoubtedly good, but it was the art of the inventor, and not the narrator. Crusoe was a real creation, but not in the same sense as Tom Jones. He was a greater effort of the imagination, and excites the faculty of wonder in us accordingly to a greater degree ; but while Tom Jones was not a being of such strange singularity as Crusoe, he became so realisable to the rest of humanity that his conception must be deemed more admirable from the novelist's point of view. Then, again, De Foe seems to let it be understood, from the general drift of his writings, that he meant them to have a personal interest, that they were to be saturated by his own individuality, that his scorn, his anger, his sorrow, were to shine through them. His energy, his irrepressibility, his misery, all combined to make him one of the strongest writers of his age ; but he must yield the palm to Fielding in the art of novel writing. The latter had individuality too, but it was individuality of a higher stamp than De Foe's. It selected human beings not from the imagination, but from the species itself, and the types are as unmistakably real, and more true, though

not so astounding in conception to the general consciousness.

With regard to Richardson, while, as we have said,
it was the fashion at one time to extol him as the
superior of Fielding, this is a position which has now
been abandoned by the best critics. The man in
possession has necessarily always the advantage of the
man who is desirous to succeed him, and Fielding having
written one novel in imitation of his predecessor, had to
struggle for some time against that fact, which was
continually hurled against him. Richardson was evidently a man of high moral principle ; indeed, he always
strikes us as a perfect compendium of innocence and the
virtues. We are willing not to see in him what others
have seen, merely the priggish moralist, but he comes
terribly near earning that character. Yet let us not be
unjust to him. His 'Pamela' is a very original work,
and its author deserves no small meed of praise for
daring to make it a pure one in an age so strikingly
celebrated for vice. But the fact that Richardson commenced to write at fifty years of age, precludes the idea
of his having possessed lofty creative genius : talent may
slumber, as in his case, but genius never. In some
respects, 'Clarissa' is a stronger novel than the one
which preceded it, but here again it is difficult to avoid

the idea that we are in church, listening to the homilies of the clergyman. The spiritual psychologist is at work again ; he is flinging his code of morals at us on every page. We could admire the strength of his virtuous characters without the endless panegyrics upon morals to which we are treated, but we implore in vain. The strings of conscience were what Richardson desired to lay hold upon, and to do this he thought it necessary to follow both virtue and vice from their very inception, and to write, as it were, their autobiography. How powerfully he has done this let his characters of Clarissa and Lovelace testify. But the permanent impression remaining is that, in spite of his acknowledged power and Puritanical tendencies, he is not one who loves his fellow-men so much as one who would wish to see them made better by the rigid exercise of those virtues to the exposition of which he has devoted his talents. Courage, talent, purity, all these Richardson exhibits, but little genius.

How greatly dissimilar to him was Fielding ! Inheriting the frailties of humanity, and feeling himself bound up with its joys and sorrows, he was gifted with a mind incredibly rich in resource. Richardson had some of the weaker elements of woman's nature mingled with his own, but Fielding had its real tenderness, its compassion. Tripped up repeatedly by his follies, his

nature never hardened ; he was the same genial spirit as
ever.   Betwixt the chariot of excess and the stool of
repentance a great portion of his time seems to have
been passed.   He had the voice of mirth for those who
wished to rejoice, and the tears of sympathy for those
who were called upon to suffer.   He flung no sermons
at the head of men and women overtaken in their sins,
though he never wrote one book wherein he failed to let
it be gathered that he honoured virtue and scourged
vice.   He was not the kind of man to be the favourite of
Richardson.   More magnanimous than the latter, though
not so severe in his morality, his knowledge of humanity
was at once wider and deeper, and he could gauge it to
its greatest depths.   His invention and his naturalness
were far superior to those of Richardson.   His mind was
more plastic, his wit keener, his intellect altogether of
a superior order.   He had, in one word, what Richardson lacked, genius.   In his boyhood the marvellous gift
began to develop itself, and in after years it achieved its
greatest results with the apparent ease by which the
operations of genius are often attended.   In Richardson
there burned the lambent flame which neither surprises
nor destroys; in Fielding there was the veritable lightning of soul.   These, then, are some of the reasons why
we have assigned to Fielding the right to be considered

our first great novelist : but others will be apparent as we proceed.

It is fair to assume that, to a very large extent, those works which attain the widest repute must be national in their character—that is, must bear an unmistakable impress of the national genius upon them. See how that is borne out : Shakspeare, Bunyan, and Fielding in England, Goethe in Germany, Voltaire in France, have each produced individual works in their various languages which have acquired world-wide celebrity. And are not all those works imbued with national characteristics? Do we not find the strength, and at the same time the singular nobility and elasticity of the English mind, developed in the writings of the three authors whom we have named? Are not the speculative thought and transcendentalism of Germany adequately embodied in Goethe? Does not Voltaire sum up in himself the force, the point, the fickleness, and the scepticism, which lie at the core of the French character? An English Voltaire, or a French Goethe, is a sheer impossibility. We feel it to be so in the very nature of things. And with respect to Fielding, he has taken root in foreign soil because of his distinctly national character, and yet, at the same time, cosmopolitan genius, as genius in its highest form must always be. We have no writer to whom we can point who excels Fielding in the art of setting forth his characters by means of strong, broad lights and shadows. The drawing is masterly and accurate. And nothing deters him from telling the whole truth. He is full of a sublime candour. His narrative is no mere record of events, but personal history of the most effective description. Whoever comes in the way of his pencil must submit to the most rigorous and unflinching representation. However great, rich, or powerful, he will be drawn exactly as he is—himself, the veritable man, or, as Cromwell wished to be limned, with the warts on his face. We are getting, through these observations, to the secret of the success of 'Tom Jones.' It is marked by the characteristics to which we have been referring, and all the world has acknowledged the truthfulness of the work. Where is the novel in existence which has reached so many corners of society?

As it is considered, and with reason, its author's masterpiece, we may well devote some space to its examination. Notwithstanding its vast popularity, it is regarded in two lights by opposing classes of readers. The first, those who are overcome by its wonderful power, have no eye for blemishes; the second, those who are afraid of seeing plain truths stated in a plain way, and men and women represented with their masks off, have nothing for it but terms of reproach, on the ground of what they call its indecency. With the excep tion of certain phrases which are redolent of the period at which Fielding wrote, it is one of the purest books in our literature. Pure, we affirm, in its general tendency ; and surely that is the way in which any work should be regarded. If we adopt the objectionable principle of selecting words and phrases which are obnoxious to the sensitive ear, and from them forming an adverse opinion, what will become of some of the finest effusions of Chaucer and Shakspeare, whom these same purists doubtless cherish most closely? We are inclined to agree with the distinguished critic who asserted that the man who read 'Tom Jones' and declared it an essentially evil book, must be already corrupt. Of course, to the evil there is a ministry of evil, which can find sustenance everywhere, degrading even good so that it may become food for their debased natures. But to a really healthy nature we can conceive no ill accruing from an acquaintance with this novel. It is but fair, however, in a matter upon which there is some difference of opinion, to hear the author himself speak, before delivering judgment. In dedicating 'Tom Jones' to Lord Lyttelton, Fielding trusts that he will find in it nothing whatever that is prejudicial to religion and virtue ; nothing inconsistent with the strictest rules of decency, or which could offend the chastest eye. It was obvious that the author had little fear that he would be charged with indecency, and he goes on to declare that goodness and innocence had been his sincere endeavour in writing the history. Further, besides painting virtue in the best colours at his command, he was anxious to convince men that their true interests lay in the pursuit of her. What more exalted end could an author have in his work than this ? and we are bound to affirm that, read in the right spirit, the novel has fulfilled its writer's original intentions. He has no scruple in laughing men out of their follies and meannesses, for he is a satirist as well as a romancist. But throughout the work he has done nothing contrary to the rules which a great artist is bound to follow. The book is indeed full of overwhelming excellences in this respect of art. Look how each character is painted in ! There is no scamping with the humblest individual honoured by reproduction on the canvas. The same truthfulness to life which we find in the portraits of Mr. Allworthy and Sophia Western we find in the depiction of a maid or a man-servant at an inn. With the enthusiasm which is as necessary to art as is the air we breathe to humanity, the artist labours at the minutest details till he brings all to perfection. Then the story appears rounded and complete, with no patch-work to mar its artistic effect. Dr. Warburton gave expression to our novelist's merits in this regard excellently when he said : 'Monsieur de Marivaux in France, and Mr. Fielding in England, stand the fore-most among those who have given a faithful and chaste copy of life and manners ; and by enriching their romance with the best part of the comic art, may be said to have brought it to perfection.'

M. Taine, whose criticism may too often be described as the sound of 'a rushing mighty wind,' never exhibited his faults and his excellences more strikingly than he does in his observations upon Fielding. Nearly always vigorous, and endowed with a jerky, but oftentimes an admirably epigrammatic, force, the French critic is now and then erratic in his judgments. His eye travels faster than his mind. He perceives, and writes what he perceives before he has given full time for reflection. For instance, he says in describing Fielding : 'You are only aware of the impetuosity of the senses, the up-welling of the blood, the effusion of tenderness, but not of the nervous exaltation and poetic rapture. Man, such as you conceive him, is a good buffalo ; and perhaps he is the hero required by a people which is itself called John Bull.' This is a smart use of a synonym, but one incorrect both as regards what the individual novelist supplies, and what the nation demands. The whole gist of M. Taine's complaint against Fielding is that he wants refinement. 'In this abundant harvest with which you fill your arms, you have forgotten the flowers.' But Fielding is quite as refined as Cervantes, to whom the critic awards the possession of that excellence. Let anyone who wishes to be convinced that Fielding possesses refinement read the chapter in 'Tom Jones' which gives a description of Sophia. There will be found both the poetry and the grace which M. Taine desires. But the critic has misrepresented Fielding in other respects. Not only has he declared the author to be without natural refinement, but he has denied this to all his characters. After the lapse of more than a hundred years, the character of Sophia Western stands forth one of the purest, sweetest, and most attractive in literature. We seem to see the very bloom of health upon her cheek, a bloom only equalled by the perfections of her mind—not so much intellectual perfections simply as those other virtues and charms which make woman the idol of man. Compare this character with those which crowd too many of the novels of the present day. How absurd are the latter as living representations, and stiff as wooden puppets in the hands of their literary parents !

Tinged with false sentiments, lacking in real femininity, they form as great a contrast as could be imagined to the true woman we find depicted in Sophia Western :—

> ' Her pure and eloquent blood
> Spoke in her cheeks, and so distinctly wrought,
> That one might almost say her body thought.'

This dainty conceit of Dr. Donne's exactly expresses the most perfect heroine drawn by Fielding. In Jones himself, too, we may discover some traces of that refinement which lifts a man out of the merely animal category. The namby-pamby element was entirely absent from him, and he was in the habit of calling a spade a spade—a habit much in vogue at the time in which his life was fixed. We should join in the verdict delivered by Mr. Allworthy, after he had carefully studied Jones's character, viz., 'in balancing his faults with his perfections, the latter seemed rather to preponderate.' It must not be forgotten that Fielding never intended to depict a perfect hero ; he would have shuddered at the thought. Whilst he 'would nothing extenuate, or set down aught in malice,' he at the same time never failed to place in full relief—with not a shadow less or more than they deserved—all the characters which he took upon himself to delineate. Remembering this, we feel at once how admirably he fulfilled his task in the picture of

Western, the jolly, rollicking squire. Had he softened in any degree the violence, prejudice, passion, and boisterousness attaching to this man, its value as a faithful picture of a Somersetshire squire would have been utterly destroyed. He is no worse than Falstaff, and why should we yield to the one conception the merit we deny to the other? But the world has within its keeping all characters which have been truly realised, and will not let them die. There is much of the bull in Western's constitution ; and it is meant that there should be, for he is typical. Fielding's power has lain principally in supplying types. Other portraits are drawn in 'Tom Jones' (besides those we have named) with remarkable skill. There is Mr. Allworthy, upon whom the author has laboured with affectionate zeal, and who appears as one of the most finished specimens of his class of humanity. He has the generous heart which prompts to benevolent deeds, and the ready hand to carry out what that heart dictates. He is himself a strong protest against the assertion that Fielding takes no thought of virtue as regards its inculcation upon others, for one instinctively feels that he is purposed by the author to be represented as a being worthy of imitation. Precisely the opposite lesson is intended to be taught by the portrait of Blifil. The villainy of this character is singularly striking, and when the book is closed, the reader will admit that he has followed the fortunes of but few beings who have been rendered more despicable in his eyes. This unredeemed scoundrel, whose meanness is matched only by his cowardice, is flayed alive according to his deserts. And yet the novelist has exercised no prejudice in the matter ; he has simply turned tbe heart inside out, and made its fetid character apparent to the world. There is no artistic bungling, because there has been no attempt to tamper with the character. Fielding has allowed knavery to show itself, just as on the same page he keeps open the way for innocence and virtue.

The genius of Fielding was not strongly developed until the appearance of 'Joseph Andrews,' which, as is well known, preceded the publication of 'Tom Jones.' Before the production of his first novel, the talents of this great wit and humourist seem to have been devoted to the hurried writing of brilliant dramatic and other pieces, which had in them but little positive assurance of a lasting fame. One can well understand, however, what a flutter the launching of 'Joseph Andrews' must have caused in London society. The author's leading idea was to write a story in imitation of the style and manners of Cervantes; and it was his intention therein to set forth the folly of affectation, which he regarded as the only true source of the ridiculous. Great vices, he considered, were the proper objects of detestation, and smaller faults of pity ; but affectation held its own place aloof from both. Referring to the scope of his work, he has the following remarks : ' Perhaps it may be objected to me that I have, against my own rules, introduced vices, and of a very black kind, into this work. To which I shall answer : first, that it is very difficult to pursue a series of human actions, and keep clear from them. Secondly, that the vices to be found here are rather the accidental consequences of some human frailty or foible, than causes habitually existing in the mind. Thirdly, that they are never set forth as the objects of ridicule, but detestation. Fourthly, that they are never the principal figure at that time on the scene ; and, lastly, they never produce the intended evil.' All which is very sound and true, but it availed him nothing; for did not the leading characters of his novel immediately strike people as strong and pronounced caricatures of those in the novel by Richardson which had just been all the rage ? It was in vain for him to assert that he meant to vilify or asperse no one, or to copy characters hitherto conceived, with the addition of considerable burlesque colouring. Richardson himself, on reading through the work, felt what he described as its covert satire keenly, and, it is said, never forgave Fielding for this novel. The closing portion of it was held to put the question of satiric aim beyond doubt, when Fielding makes the lady conduct herself in such a manner that, as one critic observes, 'she enacts the beggar on horseback in a very superior manner.' Yet, making allowance for whatever element of parody there may be in it, 'Joseph Andrews' is a remarkable book for the individuality of its characters. We might search in vain for a more worthy or more vividly-drawn personage than Parson Adams. His natural goodness and simplicity of heart endear him to us beyond measure, and must mitigate our condemnation of his share in certain scenes which are scarcely seemly to the cloth. This character was evidently a favourite of Fielding's, and in his plea on Adams's behalf to his brother-clergymen, for whom, ' when they are worthy of their sacred order, no man can possibly have a greater respect,' the author says : ' They will excuse me, notwithstanding the low adventures in which he is engaged, that I have made him a clergyman ; since no office could have given him so many opportunities of displaying his worthy inclinations.' Of the originality of Parson Adams. there is little to say, for criticism is disarmed ; he is perfect in that respect.

U

Many commentators on Fielding have been unable to
discover a resemblance of even the faintest character
between 'Joseph Andrews' and the immortal work of
Cervantes. But making allowance for the variation in
scenes and incidents, we consider that Fielding's novel
displays a great deal of the breadth of treatment pertaining to the Spanish master. It is somewhat similar in
conception also, being a mock-heroic narrative, and in
it the romance and the apologue are blended in happy
proportions. The spirit of Cervantes has been caught,
while the author has avoided a professed imitation, and
several of the ludicrous catastrophes which occur in the
course of the story give full weight to the assertion that
Fielding had in his mind's eye the author of 'Don
Quixote' when he wrote. The humour of Fielding's
history is rich and yet inoffensive ; it possesses not the
slightest tinge of bitterness, and is distinguished by a
remarkable mellowness. Whatever else the work demonstrated, or failed to demonstrate, one thing was clear—
it predicted the rising of a humourist of the highest
order, and had its authorship been unknown on its first
publication, there was but one man to whom the finger
of society could point as its literary father. Of 'Tom
Jones,' the second novel written by Fielding (taking them
in the order of their appearance), we have already spoken
at length.

The third novel from this master-mind of fiction is one to which a peculiar interest attaches. Whilst it is considered to be, in point of talent, inferior to the others, it is noteworthy as being a transcript of a portion of Fielding's family history. We refer to the story of 'Amelia.' Its fault, as a novel, seems to us to lie in the absence of any supreme interest in the several characters individually. They are not boldly drawn : and the fact that the gold was not of so rich a quality as that previously dug from the same soil, immediately induced the detractors of Fielding to rejoice over the supposed decay of his powers. They forgot, in their spite, that Shakspeare only produced one 'Hamlet,' and that if Fielding had written no other work but his crowning novel, that alone had ensured him his place amongst the gods. But, in truth, while 'Amelia' is not by any means equal to its predecessors, it exhibits many graces of style, and its pathos is deep and true. The style is not so strong nor the humour so ceaseless, so abundant ; but there are frequent genuine touches of passion in it, and some scenes of truthful domestic painting. Captain Booth is a strange mixture of weakness and fidelity : his character is supposed, and truly, to bear some resemblance to Fielding's own ; there was the same readiness in both to fall a victim to their own passions, and the same deep

tenderness when they had recovered themselves. Booth
is trustful and devoted, and worships the woman of his
love. 'If I had the world,' he says, 'I was ready to lay
it at my Amelia's feet ; and so, Heaven knows, I would
ten thousand worlds.' He is not the man to inspire
admiration so much as to provoke an affectionate
interest. Herein is one of the failures of the novel : the
hero is not strong enough to occupy the centre. We
expect to do something more with a hero than condole,
laugh, or shed with him an occasional tear. He must
appeal to wider sympathies. He must be greater than
ourselves in some way, no matter what ; but never
beneath or even on a level with us. The same trait of
devotion is very conspicuous in Booth's wife Amelia, who
is supposed to be the representation of Fielding's first
wife. We can partially agree with M. Taine in his
criticism of this character when he says that Amelia is
'a perfect English wife, an excellent cook,' so devoted
as to pardon her husband for his numerous failings, and
'always looking forward to the accoucheur.' This may
be accepted as true with regard to a great number of the
English wives of that period, though there were many of
a superior *calibre*, such as we could imagine Sophia
Western might make. Amelia is happy because she is
typical—typical of a portion of English wives, but not by

any means a universal type. The novel in which these two amiable beings appear may be beautiful, but it lacks the pith which stronger characters would have given to it. We have to travel away from these to a subordinate individual in the story to discover a genuine point of interest—which is a great transgression of one of the cardinal principles of novel writing. Fielding, nevertheless, did not prove by this story that he had written himself out. It is neither so brilliant nor so incisive as his other novels, and has no concentration of force or continuity of plot, and for these reasons it cannot be expected to take so worthy a position ; but it is without doubt far above mediocrity.

Incensed by the adulation paid to successful villainy, Fielding wrote the history of 'Jonathan Wild the Great.' In his day, more than in our own, perhaps, the world worshipped at the shrine of success—certainly of a lower order of success—nor stayed to enquire too closely into the cause of any rapid rise of fortune, however disreputably acquired. It is our general rule not to measure a man by the inherent qualities of good which he possesses, or by the claim which his genuine acts of benevolence establish upon us, but by the figure he is able to make in society, even though that gilded exterior be a covering for much that is base and contemptible.

An income of ten thousand a year will always cover a
multitude of sins.   Virtue itself has a terrible struggle to
maintain its own against it.   And this insane feeling of
adulation of material success was, as we have observed,
carried still further and still lower in Fielding's day.   It
went so far as to shed a halo round the head of the man
whose natural place was the felon's cell, provided he
were clever enough to evade the grasp of justice, and
preserve a bold and brilliant outward appearance.   This
hollowness in the conditions of society annoyed Fielding
deeply ; he was moved to his innermost depths of
contempt by it ; and in his apology for treating the
subject of the great criminal, Jonathan Wild, he explains
the motives which led to the production of this extraordinary piece of satirical writing.   'Without considering
Newgate,' he remarks, 'as no other than human nature
with its mask off, which some very shameful writers have
done—a thought which no price should purchase me to
entertain—I think we may be excused for suspecting that
the splendid palaces of the great are often no other than
Newgate with the mask on.   Nor do I know anything
which can raise an honest man's indignation higher than
that the same morals should be in one place attended
with all imaginary misery and infamy, and in the other
with the highest luxury and honour.   Let any impartial

man in his senses be asked for which of these two places a composition of cruelty, lust, avarice, rapine, insolence, hypocrisy, fraud, and treachery, was best fitted, surely his answer must be certain and immediate. And yet I am afraid all these ingredients, glossed over with wealth and a title, have been treated with the highest respect and veneration in the one, while one or two of them have been condemned to the gallows in the other.' This, of course, is the fault of society, which rarely estimates a man for his intrinsic worth, whatever groove he moves in. He may be as gigantic a fraud as was ever palmed off upon the human race, but if he only manages to dazzle the eyes of those who are beneath him on the ladder, nothing will be whispered about his peccadilloes. Let him make one slip, however, and lose his hold, and a thousand gazers will rejoice in his fall, declaring that they always knew it would come. It was to help in destroying, therefore, the bombastic greatness of society, that Fielding wrote his 'Jonathan Wild.' It is marked by a singular perception of motives, and a careful dissection of those unworthy passions which attain so great a sway over men. He invariably keeps one leading point in view, viz., the proper distribution of strict justice amongst his various characters. The hero, who flourishes in apparent security before our eyes through the course of the narrative, cannot escape his just doom at the last. On the gallows he fulfils the proper ends of his being, which was corrupt and unreformable. Fielding's position as magistrate undoubtedly furnished him with many ideas for this history, which he failed not to make the most of, though as a composition, regarded in its entirety, it is somewhat deficient. It was written for a special purpose; it fulfilled that purpose admirably; but beyond that fact, and that it contains much of its author's sarcastic genius, the fragment is not in any other aspect very noticeable.

Little has been said at any time of Fielding as a writer of verse, and yet he appears to have penned a considerable amount of rhyme in his day. But his verse is much inferior to his prose, his strength seeming to evaporate under the influence of rhyme. He has not the polish or the strength of Swift in this respect; but he might have made some figure as a rhymester had he adhered to the Muse. What he has left behind him is necessarily completely dwarfed by his excellence as a writer of fiction. It will not be without interest, notwithstanding, if we glance slightly at his attempts in verse. In a poem on 'Liberty' he gives vent to a noble exordium upon the good which she has accomplished for the human race, and for the progress in arts which we owe chiefly to her. Then comes the following apostrophe :—

> ' Hail, Liberty ! boon worthy of the skies,
> Like fabled Venus fair, like Pallas wise.
> Through thee the citizen braves war's alarms,
> Though neither bred to fight, nor paid for arms ;
> Through thee the laurel crowned the victor's brow,
> Who served before his country at the plough ;
> Through thee (what most must to thy praise appear)
> Proud senates scorn'd not to seek Virtue there. '

In form and conception the poem reminds us something of Goldsmith, being, however, in parts less pastoral than he, but having more force. The whole concludes with the following lines, which will stir an echoing sentiment probably in the mind of every reader :—

> ' But thou, great Liberty, keep Britain free,
> Nor let men use us as we use the bee ;
> Let not base drones upon our honey thrive,
> And suffocate the maker in his hive.'

Other poetical effusions by Fielding, while not exhibiting the strength and width of view which we gain in this poem, show considerable tenderness of feeling and delicacy of treatment. He has a set of verses ' To Celia,' supposed to be addressed to the lady whom he afterwards married, and which he closes thus happily, after descanting upon the hollowness of the world and

the sickness of heart which the knowledge of it has produced in him :—

> ' Ask you then, Celia, if there be
> The thing I love ?   My charmer, thee :
> Thee more than life, than light adore,
> Thou dearest, sweetest creature, more
> Than wildest raptures can express,
> Than I can tell, or thou canst guess.
> Then though I bear a gentle mind,
> Let not my hatred of mankind
> Wonder within my Celia move,
> Since she possesses *all* I love.'

Other poems could be cited which betray a lively
fancy ; and as a specimen in another vein we may reproduce his lines for Butler's Monument. Fielding was
moved to great indignation at the treatment of Butler
by an ungrateful court, and his sarcasm took the following form :—

> ' What though alive, neglected and undone,
> O let thy spirit triumph in this stone !
> No greater honour could men pay thy parts,
> For when they give a stone they give their hearts.'

In contrast to Fielding's poems in the didactic and
sentimental vein, we may turn, lastly, to a specimen of
the humourous.   When labouring under pecuniary
embarrassments, he addressed an appeal to Sir Robert
Walpole, in which, under a playful guise, he administered

a rebuke to that great minister for his neglect. In this
rhyming missive the following stanzas occur :—

> ' Great sir, as on each levée day
> I still attend you—still you say—
> " I'm busy now, to-morrow come ; "
> To-morrow, sir, you're not at home ;
> So says your porter, and dare I
> Give such a man as he the lie ?
> In imitation, sir, of you
> I keep a mighty levée too :
> Where my attendants, to their sorrow,
> Are bid to come again to-morrow.
> To-morrow they return no doubt,
> And then, like you, sir, I'm gone out.'

In other verses the poet presses Walpole to assign
him some appointment ; he is not particular what, as will
be gathered from the following cosmopolitan choice
which he gives to the Minister :—

> ' Suppose a Secretary o' this Isle,
> Just to be doing with for a while ;
> Admiral, gen'ral, judge, or bishop ;
> Or I can foreign treaties dish up.
> If the good genius of the nation
> Should call me to negotiation,
> Tuscan and French are in my head,
> Latin I write, and Greek—I read.
> If you should ask, what pleases best ?
> To get the most, and do the least.
> What fittest for ?—You know, I'm sure,
> I'm fittest for—a sine-cure.'

Of Fielding as a dramatist, there is, perhaps, no necessity to say much; and what must be said is not of the most flattering character. His comedies are not so suggestively indecent as those of Wycherley, but there is a good deal of actual impurity in them. The license of the stage, to a large extent, has been pandered to, while the literary talent displayed is not of so high an order as that which shines through his novels. One point should be remembered in connection with these comedies and farces—that they were written under great pressure, their production having been a matter of urgency with the author. A good deal of the wit of Fielding is encountered, but altogether they are not equal to his fine intellect. Smart sayings flash from the page now and then, as in ' Don Quixote in England,' where he remarks that 'Every woman is a beauty if you will believe her own glass: and few if you will believe her neighbours'.' Again: 'All men cannot do all things; one man gets an estate by what gets another man a halter;' which is a very acute remark upon the disjointed conditions of English life. In 'The Modern Husband,' a comedy whose general scope must be condemned as being worthy of the worst period of the Restoration, the following reflection occurs: ' Never fear your reputation while you are rich, for gold in this world covers as many sins as charity in the next : so that, get a great deal and give away a little, and you secure your happiness in both.' A remark made by Sir Positive Trap in one of Fielding's comedies seems to have anticipated the conduct of society in the nineteenth century, or if not of the whole of our present society, of more of it than we like to admit, if whispers from its sacred circle are to be believed : 'I hope to see the time,' said the worthy knight, 'when a man may carry his daughter to market with the same lawful authority as any other of his cattle.' Of all Fielding's dramatic pieces 'Pasquin' seems deserving of the highest praise, and it touches pretty freely upon the political corruptions of the times. Considered in the light of a satire alone it may be pronounced very successful, showing its author as usual at his best in the unsparing use of the lash. It is of course difficult to say where the line should be drawn upon the stage in regard to satire. The power of the press is not so strong as that of personal ridicule, and it is on record that the great Chancellor Hyde was ruined at court by the absurd manner in which he was mimicked in farces and comedies, an end which never would have happened to him by mere abstract criticism. Fielding was, upon occasion, exceedingly free in his use of this weapon of ridicule ; and however deficient his comedies may be in those qualities which are admitted to sustain the drama upon the boards, there are many passages in them of unquestioned brilliancy and power. His strong capacity for parodying the great is demonstrated in more than one of the comedies ; and it is but just to add the observation that what is good and virtuous in itself is always exempt from ridicule. He perceived the moral fitness of things so clearly that he never transgressed propriety in this respect. Shocked we may occasionally be when he reproduces too faithfully the follies and vices of his period, but never through the whole of his works do we remember a single sneer at what is good, honest, or noble.

In 'A Journey from this World to the Next' Fielding has been the forerunner of a host of works of our own day, of which the reading public has become unconscionably weary. Undoubtedly the best of these modern efforts to describe another world is 'Erewhon;' but it is singular to find Fielding, upwards of a hundred years ago, describing what took place in another sphere, after the death of the supposed writer of the narrative. It shows what little originality there is in the matter of great bold outlines of thought in the world; and doubtless many things which we consider new and of great merit in our own day have been done in ages past, and in much superior style. We do not mean to imply in any way that the work we have named and other similar works which followed it resemble in detail Fielding's ' Journey,' but simply desire to point out how early the author of ' Tom Jones' was in the field in this very idea of describing another world, for which there appears at present to be an unreasonable mania. His work is both curious and interesting, and forms excellent occupation for a quiet hour's literary relaxation.

Authors are measured in various ways; some are fitted for the great mass of ordinary readers alone ; others find their devotees in a few choice intellectual spirits ; but of few can it be said that they are favourites of both. When we are able to affirm that this last is the true position of a writer we have paid him the highest tribute it is in our power to offer. It means that we are speaking of lofty genius ; for that is really great which can satisfy the philosopher and the peasant at the same moment. ' Hamlet' is the product of such a mind ; so is the ' Pilgrim's Progress,' and to these books must indubitably be added the masterpiece of Fielding. It possesses that salt of genius which will arrest dissolution. Years roll on and only add to the imperishable character of all such works. What novelist has delighted a greater number of individuals than Fielding, or satisfied more with his exquisite delineations of human nature? We

know what his influence has been over millions of un-
distinguished men ; but look for a moment at the estima-
tion in which he is held by the conspicuous descendants
of his own craft. Dickens always had the most unfeigned
admiration for him, and has described the keen relish
with which he devoured his works as a boy. This love
grew as he grew, and there was no novelist for whom
Dickens cherished such a feeling of respect for his singular power as Fielding. It is said that he took him for
his model; but if so he has failed in catching his spirit,
notwithstanding his profound admiration ; for in truth to
us the two methods—those of Fielding and Dickens—
seem to differ most widely. That is a question, however,
which cannot be discussed here, and we pass it by with
the observation that Fielding's power over Dickens was
unquestionably immense. The same remark applies to
Thackeray, whose genius, far more than that of Dickens,
resembled Fielding's own. ' What,' said the author of
' Vanity Fair,' when speaking of his great predecessor in
fiction, ' an admirable gift of nature it was by which the
author of these tales was endowed, and which enabled
him to fix our interests, to waken our sympathy, to seize
upon our credulity, so that we believe in his people.
What a genius, what a vigour ! What a bright-eyed in-
telligence and observation ! What a wholesome hatred

for meanness and knavery! What a vast sympathy; what a cheerfulness; what a manly relish of life! What a love of human kind! What a poet is here, watching, meditating, brooding, creating! What multitudes of truths has the man left behind him! What generations he has taught to laugh wisely and fairly!' And again, speaking of his works as a whole—'Time and shower have very little damaged those. The fashion and ornaments are, perhaps, of the architecture of that age; but the building remains strong and lofty, and of admirable proportions—masterpieces of genius and monuments of workmanlike skill.' Who is there who cannot subscribe to this exalted opinion of our author, first given utterance to in its full boldness and generosity by Gibbon, and perpetuated by Thackeray? Whether we regard Fielding in the light of an observer of human nature or as a humourist, he has but few rivals. In the matter of the combination of both these excellences in the garb of fiction, we fearlessly reassert that he is entitled to the position assigned him in the outset. He is at the head of his race. Other novelists may show a particular aptitude, he is the one being who has no aptitudes, for his art is universal. The temple he has reared has no dwarfed or stunted columns; it is perfect and symmetri-

x

cal, and of towering and magnificent dimensions. Years have not defaced its beauty or shaken its foundations.

Another tribute to those already paid to this great king of fiction—more ephemeral, perhaps, than some, but as sincere as any—is now laid at his feet. Henry Fielding might have been a better man, but it is impossible not to love him, and to recognise shining through him that glorious light of genius which grows not dim with Time, but whose luminous presence is ever with us to cheer, to reprove, to delight, and to elevate.

ROBERT BUCHANAN

[CONTEMPORARY REVIEW]

THAT the present age is unfavourable to the production
of the highest and most permanent forms of poetry, is an
observation which has now become almost trite ; yet it
may be doubted whether, in making it, we have ever
grasped its full weight and significance. What is the
nature, and what the extent, of the opposition offered
by an age of progress to the development of the dramatic and epic genius ? In the first place, rapid general
progress means that we exist in an essentially middle-
class era, which is detrimental to any thought that goes
deeper than the slight intellectual operations necessary
to procure material success ; and in the second place,
progress means restless activity, and an utter inability to
secure that calm essential to the conception and comple-
tion of works destined to survive the lapse of centuries.
Such are the positions generally assumed, we believe, in
this matter, and on the first blush they appear to have
very plausible support. Yet upon careful consideration
they must be pronounced untenable. The imperiousness

of genius will set both at defiance, for in this respect of times and seasons genius knows no law. It is like the wind of Heaven ; 'it bloweth where it listeth,' and neither man nor circumstance can arrest its advancement to ripeness and perfectibility. The facts of history, also, are against the propositions we are combating. The times signalised by the greatest achievements in arts and commerce have been those in which we have beheld the great luminaries of thought, stretching away down from the flourishing of the oldest poets to the Elizabethan age. What century in the world's history was not a century of progress ? and why should we, because the progress differs in degree and somewhat in kind, arrive at the hasty conclusion that the decay of genius is in accord with the ratio of progress ? Further, observe to what this idea commits us. It implies, so far as England is concerned, that the days of her intellectual supremacy are over. The shopkeeper has come and the poet must depart. And what is our prospect for the future ? For it must be remembered that we are but regarded as on the threshold of progress ; and if the present period is so unfavourable to the exercise of the poetic faculty in its sublimest forms, what can we look for in the next, and the next ? We cannot believe it impossible that even now that repose could be attained which should leave the Seer calm and unmoved amidst the thunder and the roar of contemporary life.

Whether or not the nineteenth century has produced a poet of the very first rank may be an open question, to be judged differently by different minds ; but there can be no doubt that they are wrong who disparage it in comparison with the two preceding centuries. Given the brilliant Pope, the stately Dryden, and the gentle Cowper, the eighteenth century is still far behind our own, which has produced its Wordsworth, its Byron, and its Shelley, not to mention our principal living poets. Neither can Milton, solitary in his grandeur, weigh down this latter list of names, and bear off the palm from us in favour of the seventeenth century. Alone, he is far greater than any of them—Wordsworth most nearly approaching his altitude perhaps—but he shone in the firmament 'a lonely star.' We have to go back still another century to come to that age which not only eclipses the present but every other in the world's annals for the splendour of its imaginative literature.

The mode of criticism in vogue tends to discourage rather than assist the higher development of the poetic faculty. And in this, to a great extent, criticism but follows the thought of the age, which is sharp and shallow, not broad and deep. That which cannot be

grasped by the nineteenth-century intellect without many
throes of labour, is to be thrown on one side as unsuitable, and missing the tendencies of the time.   Literature
must be a relaxation, not a study ; the palate must be
tickled, not the whole body made strong.   We are in the
transition period.   We have had our Shakspeare, and
do not want another; what readers desiderate now is
mosaic-work which shall attract attention and admiration
by its finish.   We do not know, but we should imagine
that even the Poet-Laureate must have at times felt
depressed by the inattentiveness, and almost positive
dislike, of the age to what is loftiest in his vocation.   Insensibly, too, all our authors gradually bow to the influences of the period, which prove too strong for their
individual feelings and convictions in matters of art in
poetry.   It is with the hope of recalling the attention of
our best writers to the fact that if we proceed in the
same degree of decline which the past thirty years have
witnessed, our poetic literature will have been emasculated,
that we have ventured to offer these somewhat general,
but we believe necessary, observations.   Mr. Matthew
Arnold asks, in one of his poems—

> ' What shelter to grow ripe is ours ?
> What leisure to grow wise ?'

And then, further on in the same poem, he declares
that —

> ' Too fast we live, too much are tried,
>   Too harass'd to attain
> Wordsworth's sweet calm, or Goethe's wide
>   And luminous view to gain.'

This is another reiteration of the idea we are desiring to
demolish. It is, in reality, a fallacy. If ever there was
an age when the opportunity was given to write epic
poems this is the one. Since the time that the last
great epic was penned there have been some half-dozen
events, or series of events, in civilised Europe, which
afford scope for the most inspired Seer who could arise.
These events must naturally suggest themselves to any
person who indulges the most cursory thought as to
the rapid growths and tremendous convulsions which
have occurred in continental empires. And indepen-
dently of this, there is one period of English history
a'one—the period of the sublime Milton—which seems
to us to contain within it the sources of dramatic and
epic poetry such as can scarcely be found in any other
cycle of this kingdom's existence. Napoleon Buona-
parte, again—the great Napoleon—will undoubtedly at
some time or other, perhaps two centuries hence, attract
the first genius of the time, who will be enthralled by the

immensity of his theme in this respect, that it as clearly marks off the age of the man by his own absorbing and diastrous eminence as does the life of any other unit of humanity such past age as may have been overshadowed by the splendour of his name.   There are considerations which always prevent an immediately contemporary topic from being made available for epic or dramatic poetry. But why need this disconcert our living poets, who can find so many other subjects, not quite contemporary, which are more suitable for their pens ?   Criticism would not be altogether in vain if it could rouse the race of our professed Seers from their lethargy.   An opportunity is within their grasp such as seldom falls to the lot of genius.   Partly with a view to estimate the work which has already been accomplished by one of our English poets, and partly to indicate what he is capable of attaining, we have selected for some comments the collective works of one of the youngest of our present-day singers.

Robert Buchanan has himself given us a sketch of his own life, and has supplemented that by a paper on what he calls 'My own Tentatives,' which is in reality one of that most interesting class of articles which poets can give us—viz., a view of the inner life—inadequate, it may be, but still a recital of the moving springs of

their endeavours and ambitions. Mr. Buchanan is
egotistical; but till we can find a poet who is not,
there is no necessity to be severe upon him for that.
Egotism is not a crime; neither is it a blunder till it
becomes offensive in its manifestation, and it certainly
cannot be said to be so in the present case. The poet
is one of the few men whom we can bear to hear speak of
themselves: so much of the success of his work depends
upon the thermometer of his own feeling. The eagerness
which every person displays to learn something of the
actual life of our great writers cannot be founded altogether in a morbid sensationalism. What would we give,
for instance, for the details relative to the *personnel* of
Homer and Shakspeare, if written by themselves? And
the same feeling, chastened only in degree, we cherish
towards all whose works have enlightened and elevated mankind. It is the tribute which ordinary humanity pays to genius—to that quality which stands
between them and the Almighty, elucidating the mysteries
of the latter, and gathering up for presentation to the
Unseen the woes and the hopes of man. We are dis·
posed, then, always to forgive the poet any tendency he
may exhibit towards a personal garrulity, assured that
the offence will be a thousand times condoned by the
riches he has to communicate. It is not proposed to

make further reference to Mr. Buchanan's life (as concurrently related in his charming sketch of poor David Gray) than is absolutely necessary for the exposition of his manner in his earlier poems. But undoubtedly, we imagine, his life had a considerable influence in moulding the character of his works. When Gray was but a boy, it appears that he made the acquaintance of Robert Buchanan at Glasgow, and that the two spent some years in dreaming and thinking together. At a very early period Gray seems to have contracted a morbidly exaggerated opinion of himself, affirming that the dream of his life would not be realised unless his fame were ultimately to equal that of Wordsworth ; and he had even dared to set up as models, which he had some hope of rivalling, two still greater men—Shakspeare and Goethe. The danger which attended these floating ideas, if they should assume the substantial form of disease, was quickly perceived by Mr. Buchanan. But he was helpless. Another was to solve the difficulty, and the interposition of Death averted the great trial which would have resulted when Gray awoke from his brilliant dreams, to find his gorgeous castle dismantled. Early in 1860 the two young men were brought face to face with a necessity which, according to the temper and grit of a man, either makes him the slave or the master of the world. Poets being

amenable to the ordinary laws of nature, they discovered
that to live they must work. One day Gray said to his
companion, ' Bob, I'm off to London.' ' Have you funds?'
asked Buchanan. ' Enough for one, not enough for
two,' was the response. ' If you can get the money any-
how, we'll go together.' The journey was arranged, but
owing to a mistake they travelled separately, though they
arrived in London about the same time. Now began
the bitterness of existence. The sensitive Scotchman
Gray found that in the hurry of London life there were
none who turned aside to regard him as a great Seer, or
even as one who promised to become such. Accordingly,
though he received many individual kindnesses from one
or two friends, we find him writing, ' What brought me
here? God knows, for I don't. *Alone* in such a place
is a horrible thing. People don't seem to understand
me. Westminster Abbey ; I was there all day yesterday.
If I live I shall be buried there—so help me God!'
The strife went on—bitter indeed, as only those can
testify whose experience has been of a similar character.
The forecasting of the future, which ought to have preceded their advent, now became an absolute necessity
when it seemed of little use. There were, of course,
many positions open, but nobody willing to induct them
into possession, and after severe vicissitudes we find one

of them becoming a supernumerary at a theatre. It is impossible to follow the melancholy story in all its details ; suffice it to state, that, after numberless trials and buffetings, the disease of consumption, which had been latent in Gray, rapidly developed itself, and he was carried off in his twenty-fourth year. After his decease, one of the most beautiful epitaphs ever written was found amongst his papers, penned by himself in view of his dissolution. Mr. Buchanan appears to have cherished for his friend one of those attachments which are an honour to human nature, and which cannot fail to have effect in the growth of character. In verse which deserves to live (viz., in the poem ' To David in Heaven '), the survivor of these two friends endeavoured to set forth the virtues of the dead, and at the same time to embalm him with the spices of remembrance and affection. The rest of Mr. Buchanan's life as regards his work is sufficiently known to the public. He early gained its ear, and has steadily maintained himself in its favour, ripening, as poets should do, with personal experience and observation of the world.

One result of strenuous labour and of material deprivation is to deepen the pathos of life. And when the individual is a poet the experience is doubly valuable to him. A poet without pathos—either natural or acquired

—seems to us one who will utterly fail in reaching the
highest ends of his being. It was anguish which sublimated the genius of Dante and led to what is grandest
in his divine compositions. His was an example of what
we should call acquired pathos—that is, the pathos
begotten in the spirit through suffering. An example of
natural pathos is to be found in Wordsworth, whose life
was singularly free from the ordinary sadnesses of humanity, but who yet possessed, as it has been so beautifully
expressed, and he might have claimed for himself—

'Thoughts that do often lie too deep for tears.'

Take the choicest spirits in our poetic record, the most
mirthful, unembarrassed, and careless of their species,
and there will be found running through all their natures
this subtle yet sweet chord of sadness, which makes
them so tender to the race, and sympathetic withal. The
poet is commissioned to feel for humanity, and without
pathos he would surely have no more to communicate
than other men. It is his real voice, and that which
makes him the sweet singer of creation.

Many years have now elapsed since Mr. George
Henry Lewes—no mean judge in these and cognate
matters—affirmed that Mr. Buchanan was a genuine
poet. At the time, those who guarded the gates of

literature were divided in opinion, though by far the greater bulk of the critics—and that the most competent portion of them—welcomed the new-comer as a true singer, one who had something new to communicate. In looking to the volume which evoked the varied opinions now, 'Idylls and Legends of Inverburn,' one is struck with this thought—the courage of the man who should dare to challenge the world on subjects which in themselves appeared to possess but few of the elements of poetry, and whose treatment in the hands of most must certainly result in disastrous failure ! But the fact alone that the author was so successful in investing the simplest themes with an interest which could not be gainsaid appeared to us, and does now after the lapse of many years, an undoubted proof of genius. There was not placed before the critics a volume of verse on heroic or old-world subjects—subjects which of themselves are instinct with the poetic feeling—treated with all the glow and fancy which could be thrown about them. The facts were simple in the extreme. A youth whose heart was large—large in the sense of active poetic sympathy—and whose imagination was quick, took from the lives of certain characters which had crossed his path, or with whose inner experience he was somewhat acquainted, incidents which had apparently no special significance whatever for other men, and said to himself that he could draw from thence what should be a delight and profit to the world. And he succeeded, notwithstanding the fact that he worked in a style which had hitherto been unappreciated, and which was remarkable for its simplicity. The world had been accustomed to regard poetry as a trimmed garden, discovering colour, beauty, symmetry—it seemed to have forgotten that it might also be a forest, or an irregular hill-side, with naked rocks and the majesty of trees. These Idylls have little in them to recommend them to those who regard poetry simply as the art of turning melodious periods; but they possess the higher qualities of imagination and the music of natural emotion. Above all, they exhibit the first requirement in a poet—viz., insight, that faculty which is the initial point in his isolation from the rest of the species. The poems are not great in themselves, but they undoubtedly exhibit those qualities which, rightly fostered, develop into greatness. The thing which was of most importance to the writer to secure he was successful in accomplishing; he caused the reader to reflect, after the reading of the poems, upon the gifts which had been exhibited in their production. Let us look for a moment at one or two of these Idylls. Take the story of Willie Baird, narrated by the schoolmaster of Inverburn. Told

in the simplest of blank verse, there is yet a grip about it
which enrols its author at once amongst the players on
the harp of the human heart.   The old man tells of the
influence of little Willie upon his spirit, chastening and
refining it.   He imagines that he has seen the face somewhere before in the beauteous life of the north ; and then
he says as the result—

> ' Alone at nights,
> I read my Bible more and Euclid less.
> For, mind you, like my betters, I had been
> Half-scoffer, half-believer ; on the whole,
> I thought the life beyond a useless dream
> Best left alone.'

Then the boy's philosophy came on, and one day he
puzzled the old schoolmaster by asking, as he clasped
his white hands round the neck of the collie Donald, ' Do
doggies gang to Heaven ? ' a question to be repeated in-
definitely without answer.   It is interesting to note the
gradual return of the old man to a well-grounded faith,
engendered so beautifully, and almost consummated by
the death of Willie.   The language in which the history
is unfolded is sustained, and abounds in imagery which,
if not so lofty as we find in some of Mr. Buchanan's other
works, is true and appropriate.   Of a higher stamp, however, is the poem ' Poet Andrew,' which depicts the
short sad life of young Gray.   The story is told by the

father of Andrew, a simple-hearted weaver, who does not
understand the gift wherewith his son is dowered. The
character of the father is drawn with great power and
individuality, and the whole poem, shining with the
tenderness which springs from a loving heart, is full of
the deepest human interest. Andrew's parents endeavoured to teach him common-sense, and when they were
reproached for having a poet in the house, exclaimed,
' A poet? God forbid ! ' somewhat dubious as to the full
meaning and import of their terrible possession. But at
length they discovered Andrew's printed poems, with

> ' Words pottle-bellied, meaningless, and strange,
> That strutted up and down the printed page,
> Like Bailies, made to bluster and look big '—

a graphic description of what was doubtless a source of
terror to the old man, who had never been guilty of such
a heinous offence as writing a line in his life. The youth
was grumbled at in vain for his tendencies to ruin, and
at length he left his home and went up to the great City,
where he was followed by a mother's deep love and a
father's solicitude, in spite of his apparent wrongheaded-
ness. But the dark shadow drew near—the trouble that
was deeper than all others. The poet came home to die,
and the scene is depicted with a pathos which has rarely

been excelled for calm and yet strong simplicity. Thus
speaks the broken-hearted father :—

> ' One Sabbath day—
> The last of winter, for the caller air
> Was drawing sweetness from the barks of trees—
> When down the lane, I saw to my surprise
> A snowdrop blooming underneath a birk,
> And gladly plucked the flower to carry home
> To Andrew.
>
> *   *   *   *   *
>
> Saying nought,
> Into his hand I put the year's first flower,
> And turn'd awa' to hide my face ; and he—
> He smiled—and at the smile, I knew not why,
> It swam upon us, in a frosty pain,
> The end was come at last, at last, and Death
> Was creeping ben, his shadow on our hearts.
> We gazed on Andrew, call'd him by his name
> And touch'd him softly—and he lay awhile,
> His een upon the snow, in a dark dream,
> Yet neither heard nor saw ; but suddenly,
> He shook awa' the vision wi' a smile,
> Raised lustrous een, still smiling, to the sky,
> Next upon us, then dropt them to the flower
> That trembled in his hand, and murmured low,
> Like one that gladly murmurs to himsel'—
> " Out of the Snow, the Snowdrop—out of Death
> Comes Life ; " then closed his eyes and made a moan,
> And never spake another word again.'

It will be admitted, we think, by the most exacting, that
an exquisiteness and also an emotional fervour dwell

about this description which are so precisely suited to the subject as to raise it to a very lofty rank of poetry. It would scarcely be possible to find language and thought more happily wedded than they are here. The 'Widow Mysie,' in the same volume, betrays qualities of quite another stamp, exhibiting principally a strange, quaint humour which seems to dimple every page into laughter.

Another poem, in this same volume as originally published, but one since suppressed by Mr. Buchanan on artistic grounds, contained imagery of the choicest description. It was entitled 'Hugh Sutherland's Pansies,' and described the troubled life and pathetic death of the youth who gave name to the poem. It is a pity that the author could not have preserved by some means the final scene, for it exhibited beauty of description of a rare order. The following passage combines both a tenderness and a truth in the imagery which give finish to the poetry, and leave nothing to be desired in the way of idyllic excellence :—

> ' By slow degrees he grew
> Cheerful and meek as dying man could be,
> And as I spoke there came from far-away
> The faint sweet melody of Sabbath bells.
> And, "Hugh," I said, " if God the Gardener
> Neglected those he rears as you have done
> Your pansies and your Pansy, it were ill

For we who blossom in His garden.   Night
And morning He is busy at His work.
He smiles to give us sunshine, and we live :
He stoops to pluck us softly, and our hearts
Tremble to see the darkness, knowing not
It is the shadow He, in stooping, casts.
He pluckt your Pansy so, and it was well.
But, Hugh, though some be beautiful and grand,
Some sickly, like yourself, and mean, and poor,
He loves them all, the Gardener loves them all ! "
Then later, when no longer he could sit
Out on the threshold, and the end was near,
We set a plate of pansies by his bed
To cheer him.   " He is coming near," I said,
" Great is the garden, but the Gardener
Is coming to the corner where you bloom
So sickly ! "   And he smiled and moaned, " I hear ! "
And sank upon his pillow wearily.
His hollow eyes no longer bore the light,
The darkness gather'd round him as I said,
" The Gardener is standing at your side,
His shade is on you and you cannot see :
O Lord, that lovest both the strong and weak,
Pluck him and wear him ! "   Even as I prayed,
I felt the shadow there and hid my face :
But when I look'd again the flower was pluck'd,
The shadow gone : the sunshine thro' the blind
Gleam'd faintly, and the widow'd woman wept.'

We are unable to point to a more distinctly poetical idea
than the one embodied in the three lines marked in
italics, and in truth there is a great suffusion of poetry

through the entire passage. The whole volume is not, of course, written with this wealth of imagery and power of delineation. There are many pages here and there which are scarcely, if at all, lifted out of the level of commonplace; but enough has been shown to demonstrate that those critics were right who thought that a new poet had come who had the real ring about him, and whose further fortunes were worthy of being watched with considerable interest.

Before offering some general remarks on the peculiarities or characteristics of Mr. Buchanan's genius, we will first glance very briefly at the various works which he has written. There was a volume entitled 'Undertones' which preceded in publication the one we have just dealt with. With the notable exception of the introductory poem, it deals almost exclusively with classical subjects. While it could not appeal directly to the feelings of so many people as its predecessor, there is stamped upon it the same realistic power. There was quite enough in the volume to cause the lovers of poetry to wonder at the new writer, who lavishly threw about undoubted riches in every poem. One of the best features of the book is its workmanship, which is eminently satisfactory,—in truth, leaving little to be desired. For those who wish to see what could be done by one

who was just entering upon a literary career, let them
turn to the poem ' Proteus,' and note the description of
the death of Pan.   He dies because of the birth of the
infant of Bethlehem.   The idea is fine, and finely
worked out.   The world was again renewed with the
presence of Christ, and, as it is well expressed,—

> ' Gladden'd by the glory of the child,
>   Dawn gleam'd from pole to pole.'

Then, the lines which follow are exceedingly striking.
In other poems the old-world subject is again and again
made to live in modern modes and thought. ' The
Syren ' is full of music, its rhythm being superior to that
of any other of its fellows, and the spirit is taken away
from its enclosure to the scene which the poet is endeavouring to depict.   The gifts of the writer are here
put to excellent uses, and he is as successful, imagina-
tively, as he is in attaining his leading purpose.   Of
' Pygmalion the Sculptor,' and one or two other efforts,
something might be said, but inasmuch as the volume
was one of probation chiefly, there is perhaps no necessity to delay here further.   What other references should
be made to the volume can be made, either directly or
inferentially, at another juncture.

The work, however, which left no doubt in the public

mind that its author had no ordinary career before him, was 'London Poems.' It clearly shows that the poet was possessed of this definite idea—viz., to get free from the flash and glitter which encrusted the writings of other authors, and, in too many cases it is to be feared, blinded their readers to the poverty of thought which lay beneath. Mr. Buchanan's desire was to understand and interpret humanity. That he was singularly successful in those views of it which he has given us—restricted though they were in scope—there is no possibility of denying. Each poem is impregnated with a local truth that is truly astonishing, and the setting is the only one adapted to the subjects. Had he essayed to tell these stories of the poor in the loftiest style, the probability is we should have lost the depth of effect in the dazzle of outward show. Their strength is proved in the very fact that they affect us so deeply when they are cast in the very simplest mould. The style is, indeed, sometimes bald to simplicity. But altogether it may be conceded that the result has justified the author's method. It was made a reproach to Mr. Buchanan by one of his own craft that he had chosen such humble subjects ; but surely the man or the poet who forgets the poor forgets the paths in which the Godhead most frequently walks ! Where can the divinity of endurance be found so nobly developed as in those very beings whose touch is contamination to the curled darlings of society? Instead of contempt, that man is deserving of gratitude who boldly goes into the lowest strata of society, and dares to show to the higher world the streaks of goodness and nobility of character which are to be traced there. Turn to the sister art of painting, and note where the finest pathos is to be met with. Is it in the great historical pieces to which we are sometimes treated, or in the fashionable nonentities who, in various guise, cover the walls of the Royal Academy in such wondrous profusion—or, lastly, is it not rather in such pictures as Faed's 'Mitherless Bairn'? Everyone admits at once that what is emotional is strongest in its influence. With some such feeling as this, coupled with the desire to demonstrate that art was not restricted in its treatment, Mr. Buchanan probably produced 'London Poems.' One admirable result of his artistic skill is this—that in reading the poems the poet is absent from our thoughts, and we are able to concentrate our attention upon the objects presented to us. The style, as we have before remarked, is such as not to destroy, by superior force, the effect of the work. For real music and the gift of embodying simple ideas in a form which gives pleasure to the soul—the lyric at the same time being infused with the true spirit of humour—

'The Starling' deserves high commendation : it is thoroughly novel, clever, and original.

In the same volume we are discussing there are poems which for strength and grasp of passion are most graphic and remarkable, in particular ' Liz,' and ' Edward Crowhurst.' In the first, a wretched, unfortunate girl tells the story of her life to the parson. She is bad and wants to die ; fine ladies are missed from the world when they go, but not such beings as she. With terrible truth she assures her visitor that men have the best of the world in many ways, whilst women suffer and are beaten down.

> ' If they grow hard, go wrong, from bad to badder,
>   Why, Parson, dear, they're happier being blind :
>   They get no thanks for being good and kind—
>   The better that they are, they feel the sadder ! '

A world of miserable but unimpeachable philosophy lives in these lines, which have been always true in the history of the race. Woman must bear the degradation, while man goes free. A pathetic relation is that where poor Liz tells the parson how she once went into the country hoping to live there, and earn her bread. The air was so clear, 'it seemed a sin to breathe it,' and she was glad to leave it and come back to the black streets of London, fittest for such as she.

' I would not stay out yonder if I could,
   For one feels dead, and all looks pure and good—
I could not bear a life so bright and still.
All that I want is sleep,
Under the flags and stones, so deep, so deep !
God won't be hard on one so mean, but He,
   Perhaps, will let a tired girl slumber sound
   There in the deep cold darkness underground ;
And I shall waken up in time, may be,
Better and stronger, not afraid to see
   The great, still Light that folds Him round and round.'

Surely such writing as this is better than the thousand
meaningless eccentricities and tricks of style which so
often pass current as poetry. This is substantial ; it has a
living power about it which satisfies both the brain and
heart. The same remark would apply to other idylls in
the volume. ' Edward Crowhurst ' is a poem bearing a
considerable resemblance to the one on David Gray in
treatment. It is told in blank verse, and has many
masterly touches upon it. ' Attorney Sneak ' reminds
one in its rough humour and form of execution of some
of the poems of Browning; whilst 'Nell' exhibits a terrible
realism rarely equalled amongst modern lyrics. Of
polish in the volume there is not enough ; what is done
is done in a broad, rough manner, as though the artist
feared he would lose the effect of his strong manipulation
if he devoted himself too much to refinement. Doubt-

less there is some truth in this. At any rate, for effec-
tiveness only, this batch of poems stands almost by itself
amongst Mr. Buchanan's works.

But the work which showed the deepest insight into
the human life around him was that entitled ' North
Coast, and other Poems,' and in this volume there is one
poem which chiefly challenges attention. By ' Meg
Blane,' our author not only sustained his previous claim
to the attention of the public, but deepened his hold as
the translator of the tragic elements of modern existence
into the common language of humanity. There is a
strange mingling of weirdness and reality about the ballad
which is both fascinating and appalling. Edgar Allan
Poe has given us a thrilling picture of despair in the form
of a monologue, and though we are bound to admit that
on the score of musical effect the American poet has the
advantage, yet there are other points in which the verdict
must be decidedly in favour of the English one. In the
first place, the elements which compose the poem, while
of the plainest kind, are also more really tragic in themselves than those of ''The Raven '; and in the second
place, the story is capable of appealing to a far greater
number of persons. Poe has certainly more elaboration,
more finish ; in fact, it would be impossible for the most
fastidious workman to alter his poem with advantage ;

but in this later effort the narrative (though not the solitary idea, it should be borne in mind) is more realisable. Meg Blanc, the heroine of the story or ballad, is a fisherwoman on the north coast of Scotland. She lives in one of the usual huts by the seashore, and has an idiot son of some twenty years. Meg is a brave creature, and is always ready with the lifeboat on the roughest night to weather the storm, and go to the assistance of a crew in danger of sinking. And yet this woman, who possessed a heroic nobility of spirit, was not what the world would call pure. She was not a wedded wife, but had left the way of the just. However, she had repented sincerely, and was no longer afraid of looking into the eyes of those whom she met. Delicacy and strength, these were her personal characteristics ; the former remained with her, because her soul had recovered its uprightness before God ; as for her strength and daring, these had been abundantly proved by deeds which would have made many a man turn pale. Yet when alone in the midnight hours the real travail of her soul was manifested. She often awoke naming an unknown name, and became white as death on missing the object of her quest. One of those northern storms, so majestic in their force, is depicted in the first part of the poem, and during its raging, Meg had gripped the helm and gone out to sea. As the result of her grand courage she saved a human life ; but now mark the terrible pathos of the story. The life she saved was the one which had wronged her own in years gone by ; the being she had yearned for through days and nights of agony was given to her again; but too late ! He was no longer hers ; deeming her dead his life had been given to another. The stony despair of the shattered woman, her haggard aspect, that feeling of sorrow almost too sublime to be realised by the soul of any other mortal, are here sought to be rendered, in lines instinct with pathos :—

> ' With her wild arms around him, he looked stern,
> With an unwelcome burden ill at ease,
> While her full heart flow'd out in words like these—
> " At last ! at last ! O Angus, let me greet ![1]
> God's good ! I ever hoped that we should meet !
> Lang, lang hae I been waiting by the sea,
> Waiting and waiting, praying on my knee ;
> And God *said* I should look again on you,
> And, tho' I scarce believed, God's word comes true,
> And He hath put an end to my distress ! "—
>
> *   *   *   *   *   *   *
>
> But he was dumb, and with a pallid frown,
> Twitching his fingers quick, was looking down.
> " What ails thee, Angus ? " cried the woman, reading
> His face with one sharp look of interceding ;

[1] To greet ; *Anglicè*, to weep.

Then looking downward too, she paused apart,
With blood like water slipping through her heart,
Because she thought, " Alas, if it should be
That Angus cares no more for mine and me,
Since I am old and worn with sharp distress,
And men like pretty looks and daintiness ;
And since we parted twenty years have past,
And that is long for a man's love to last ! "
But, agonised with looking at her woe,
And bent to end her hope with one sharp blow,
The troubled man, uplifting hands, spake thus,
In rapid accents, sharp and tremulous :
" Too late, Meg Blane ! seven years ago I wed
Another woman, deeming you were dead,—
And I have bairns ! "   And there he paused for fear.
    As when, with ghostly voices in her ear,
While in her soul, as in a little well
The silver moonlight of the Glamour fell,
She had been wont to hark of nights alone,
So she stood now, not stirring, still as stone,
While in her soul, with desolate refrain,
The words " Too late ! " rang o'er and o'er again ;
Into his face she gazed with ghastly stare ;
Then raising her wild arms into the air,
Pinching her face together in sharp fear,
She quivered to the ground without a tear,
And put her face into her hands, and thrust
Her hair between her teeth, and spat it forth like dust.'

Twenty years have passed away since her sin, and
the penalty is re-exacted. If the object of tragic poetry
be to concentrate the attention of the reader upon its

subject, it was never better attained than in the whole
division of the poem of which this is an extract, and in
the succeeding passages. The portrait of Angus Blane,
the fisherwoman's son, is also drawn in vigorous lines,
and the gradual torpor which overcame Meg's spirit is
followed with truthful delineation till the death. In the
reaping time she lay a-bed making her own shroud, and
this is the refrain she murmured night and day :—

> ' " O bairn, when I am dead,
>   How shall ye keep frae harm?
>   What hand will gie ye bread?
>   What fire will keep ye warm ?
> How shall ye dwell on earth awa' frae me ?"—
>   " O Mither, dinna dee !"
>
> " O bairn, by night or day,
>   I hear nae sounds ava,
>   But voices of winds that blaw,
>   And the voices of sprites that say,
>   ' Come awa ! come awa !'
> The Lord, that made the Wind and made the Sea,
>   Is sore on my son and me,
> And I melt in His breath like snaw."—
>   " O Mither, dinna dee !"
>
> " O bairn, it is but closing up the een,
>   And lying down, never to rise again.
>   Many a strong man's sleeping hae I seen,—
>   There is nae pain !

z

I'm weary, weary, and I scarce ken why ;
    My summer has gone by,
And sweet were sleep, but for the sake o' thee."—
    "O Mither, dinna dee ! "'

Now the power of this poem, of which we are only
able to afford the barest idea, consists in its isolation or
individualisation of character in the first instance, and
further in the helming into one compact and indivisible
whole both the individuals and the circumstances. And
this has been achieved with materials which in themselves
seemed unpromising. It is for this reason that Mr.
Buchanan might almost take his stand on this one poem
alone, and challenge the world upon his general capacity
as a poet. There breathes through it something of that
old vital force which has handed down to us the work
of long-past ages. It is such things as this which are
able to defy Time in its power to wreck mundane
achievements. We wish to speak with no exaggeration ;
the best criticism is that which is felt to be the most
truthful summing-up of the feeling of the greatest number,
but in this matter in hand we firmly believe that all who,
calmly and without bias, sit down to consider the poem
which we have been examining, in its high and noble
aspects towards humanity, will arrive at similar conclusions to those which have been expressed. We talk
of inspiration in poetry ; to us it seems there are two

kinds—the inspiration of intuition, and the inspiration
of interpretation. A better example of the second form
could not be found than in ' Meg Blane.' The author
does not profess therein to have discovered any new
truths ; his poem may rather be described as a canvas
on which the inner life of his heroine is depicted, and its
emotions exposed. The titles of ' The Ballad of Judas
Iscariot' and 'The Dead Mother' can only be indicated, but the reader, on turning to the ballads, will
discover that they are full of singular power and weirdness.

Of ' The Drama of Kings,' the bulkiest and at the
same time the most ambitious of Mr. Buchanan's works,
we cannot, as to construction, speak in terms of such
high praise, that is, as an entirety ; but there are isolated
passages which will vie with anything he has written, and
which ought not to be allowed to die. If we can read the
genius of its author rightly, it is rather epic than dramatic
in character, and a careful perusal of his most elaborate
work only tends further to support this view. The poet
would be more successful in grasping the *import* of the
lives of the individuals of whom he writes than he
would in grasping the intricacies of the characters themselves. For this reason he would be more successful
in subduing the individualities to his own grand lead-

ing purpose than he would in placing his personages upon
the stage and allowing them to work out their own
destinies, as is required in the drama. Then, again,
whatever may be said to the contrary, in this dramatic
work the events which form its basis are of too contemporary a character to be satisfactorily dealt with.[1] We do
not say this for the purpose of following in the wake of
any criticisms which may already have been passed upon
it, but it was the honest impression left upon the mind
after twice carefully reading the whole work. If Mr.
Buchanan has failed, he has only failed where no other
living author could have succeeded : even Mr. Browning
could not have hoped to have achieved a happy result
in this chosen field. Some events might possibly be
dealt with by contemporary writers, but the series of
circumstances chosen in this drama are not of that
character. And for that reason, probably, a proper meed
of justice has not been dealt to ' The Drama of Kings.'
There are parts of it, as already stated, which must not
be allowed to fall out of existence : the author has had
prescience to discover this, and in future his readers will
not be deprived of what is really valuable therein.
The subject had a great fascination for Mr. Buchanan,

[1] Since the above appeared, Mr. Buchanan himself has admitted
the force of this objection.

and gave him an excellent opportunity of exhibiting those
two qualities which he has always been endeavouring to
combine in his writings with more or less success—viz.,
earthliness and spirituality—those two qualities which
find interpretation best perhaps in the formulas—'I
live' and 'I love.' He is perfectly right, too, in his
opinion that the man who can see no poetry in his own
time must be very unimaginative. Our difference with
him would not be on that score. The point is, the form
of the reproduction of that poetry for the benefit of his
species. It has been said that Mr. Tennyson, of all the
poets of his time, is the one who best grapples with the intellectual doubts of the age. Perfectly agreeing with that
sentiment, the Poet Laureate is yet by no means uniformly successful in overcoming those doubts. But what
is his method? The union of contemporary thought with
a form of expression and choice of subject not necessarily
contemporary. His Arthurian poems find half their
strength in their power to appeal to the intellect and the
spirit of a century so remote as the nineteenth. 'The
Drama of Kings' may be successful in accomplishing its
author's purpose of making people feel the events it
describes as he never felt them before, but it does not
make them feel in precisely the *same* way as they ought
to feel. The genius exhibited in the volume is great

undoubtedly, but we do not know that if Shakspeare
himself were alive he could give us portraits of Prince
Bismarck and Napoleon which would be perfectly satisfactory from the inner-life point of view. In our judgment, the man does not live at the same time with these
men who would be able to do it. We do not believe
in the absence of intellectual and spiritual bias to the
extent necessary for dramatic purposes. So that it
should be well understood that it is not Mr. Buchanan's
poetry which is at fault in this volume. It is his subject,
and his method in the treatment of it. He says that
the same method is adopted as he used in the characters
of 'Nell' and 'Meg Blane.' Granted : but the result
is different. Could Mr. Buchanan have as thoroughly
grasped Napoleon and Bismarck as he has those two
humble beings just named, he would have possessed
one element of success. But we deny that that is possible. Yet, supposing it had been done, there is then
the difficulty of his mode of presenting the characters.
The indirect, instead of the direct, dramatic mode of representation would have best suited the quality of his genius.

And this remark naturally leads to that volume which
we regard as not only the most successful, but the most
valuable of all, and indicating the groove in which he
ought to work. 'The Book of Orm,' partly for what it

yields in itself, and more still for the promise which it holds forth, is, in the majority of aspects, the greatest piece of work which Mr. Buchanan has accomplished. It is, as he himself describes it, the spiritual key to all that he has written. When we understand it, we understand what the poet means—what is the task which he has set himself. It is a mystical poem, but with a strictly modern application. To describe it as a study in the Ossianic manner, and to pass it over as a poem with no reference to ourselves, but as the diversion of a man who loves to play at mysticism, seems to us a foolish and preposterous method of treating this volume. The fact indeed is that it unfolds the ripening of a purpose which had been foreshadowed in the very earliest writings of the author. The same idea observable here had run through his earlier poems, and through 'The Drama of Kings,' though the mysticism was not so pronounced in those previous works. But he evidently wishes to combine the realism of human life with the insight of the mystic. He believes that there is no contradiction and no incompatibility between the two. And it is a noticeable point, and one which should not be passed over at the present moment, that some of the most realistic of men—for example, Swedenborg—have also been the purest mystics. There is no reason whatever why the

mystic should be regarded as a being far removed from
ordinary life, and with no part nor lot in the strivings and
throes of humanity.   His clear eye has been in times
past, and may be again to an extent immeasurable,
serviceable in glancing into the heart of things and
discovering for us the solution of many problems which
harass and vex the spirit.   It may seem to interfere with
preconceived notions that this should be the case ; but
as this is pre-eminently an age for the reversal of hereditary errors, this need not give us any alarm.   The race
of the Celts is one of the most mystical of the species ;
but the glamour of the spirit does not involve the exclusion of sympathy with the actual volitions and passions
of the human unit.

'The Book of Orm' takes for its motto a sentence from
Bacon which well explains the author's intentions in the
construction of his poem.   It is from the prayer of the
student who begs 'that Human things may not prejudice
such as are Divine, neither that from the unlocking of
the Gates of Sense, and the kindling of a greater Natural
Light, anything of incredulity or intellectual night may
arise in our minds towards Divine Mysteries.'   The book
is in nine divisions, and the whole scope of the poem
most daring and stupendous.   The author has essayed a
style of poetry in which previously he had no rival, and

notwithstanding small faults of style, he has succeeded. We
do not know whether we always catch the poet's meaning,
there is so much of cloud as well as substantiality about
his song, but his speculations are grand in the extreme,
and the final result is a feeling of awe, the creation of
which would satisfy the mystic himself. 'The First Song
of the Veil' treats of the dark film which envelopes
Nature, and prevents man from seeing God's face behind
it. The Wise Men are called and asked if they can
penetrate the darkness, but they can discern no more
than others. ''Twere better not to be,' they reply, for
'there is no God!' Then comes the weird poem introducing 'The Man and the Shadow,' the shadow intrud-
ing itself wherever the wanderer moves, and presaging
doom. The Rainbow appears in the Heavens, but the
Vision has no real consolation. He asks—

'Is it indeed
A Bridge whereon fair spirits come and go?
O Brother, didst thou glide to peace that way?
Silent—all silent—dimmer, dimmer yet,
Hue by hue dying, creeping back to heaven—
O let me too pass by it up to God!
Too late—it fadeth, faint and far away!'

That hope for solution of the great life-problems is lost.
The mystery deepens with the 'Songs of Corruption.'
The poet tries to picture the world without death.

Humanity has cried out against Death for six thousand years ; but in a sublime picture it is shown that Earth would be worse than the deepest Hell but for the power of Death.   In the world without death there was no happy (if bitter) parting, no farewell in hope of reunion.

' There was no putting tokens under pillows,
   There was no dreadful beauty slowly fading—
   Fading like moonlight softly into darkness.

   There were no churchyard paths to walk on, thinking
   How near the well-beloved ones are lying.
   There were no sweet green graves to sit and muse on,

   Till grief should grow a summer meditation,
   The shadow of the passing of an angel,
   And sleeping should seem easy, and not cruel.

   Nothing but wondrous parting and a blankness.'

So that the abolition of Death could afford no help to the distressed spirit. 'The Soul and the Dwelling' is, too, a beautifully wrought division, and enlarges still further on the awful mystery, and the hardihood of man in desiring to see God's face when he has never looked on the poorest soul's face in this world full of windows with no light.   The theology of many will receive a rude shock when it is brought face to face with the 'Songs of Seeking.'   The same amount of boldness of thought was never, perhaps, witnessed in a seeker before, and the stanzas on Doom give utterance to a thought which is

rapidly becoming prevalent, that God is not God if there
be ultimate condemnation for one soul in this wide universe. The dream of the lifting of the Veil is most
poetically treated ; but of all the divisions in the volume
that which is loftiest in thought and grandest in expression is the one entitled 'Coruiskeen Sonnets.' Mr.
Buchanan, in several of these Coruiskeen poems, has
reached a great height. What could be finer, for example,
than the following ?—

'Come to green under-glooms,—and in your hair
   Weave nightshade, foxglove red, and rank wolfsbane,
   And slumber and forget Him ; if in vain
Ye try to slumber off your sorrow there,
Arise once more and openly repair
   To busy haunts where men and women sigh,
And if all things but echo back your care,
   Cry out aloud, " There is no God !" and die.
But if upon a day when all is dark,
Thou, stooping in the public ways, shalt mark
   Strange luminous footprints as of feet that shine—
Follow them ! follow them ! O soul bereaven !
God had a Son—He pass'd that way to heaven ;
   Follow, and look upon the Face divine !'

Wordsworth himself could scarcely have manipulated
the thought better than it is done there. The following,
also, is a magnificent sonnet, though there is not the same
ease of construction about it that we mark in the previous

one: observe, however, in the lines in question, how they
touch a large part of the ground occupied by ' In Memoriam '—the same thoughts must have been coursing
through the two minds : the music of Tennyson is more
bewitching, but there is a strong under-current of pathos
in these finely-measured tones :—

> ' But He, the only One of mortal birth
>   Who raised the Veil and saw the Face behind,
> While yet He wandered footsore on the earth,
>   Beheld His Father's eyes,—that they were kind ;
>   Here in the dark I grope, confused, purblind,
> I have not seen the glory and the peace,
>   But on the darken'd mirror of the mind
> Strange glimmers fall, and shake me till they cease—
> Then, wondering, dazzled, on Thy name I call,
>   And, like a child, reach empty hands and moan,
> And broken accents from my wild lips fall,
>   And I implore Thee in this human tone ;—
>   If such as I can follow Him at all
>   Into Thy presence, 'tis by love alone.'

The capacity for high conception is best illustrated in
the final division of the volume, ' The Vision of the Man
Accurst.' It is not often that we meet with so much
clearness and daring combined. Neither the thought nor
the imagination has been trammelled. Mr. Buchanan
shows us the world after the Great Judgment, when all have
been redeemed save one man—the man accurst. The
wretched spirit mocks at the Almighty from the lonely

deep. His shrieks, his revilings, his laughter, disturb the harmony of the universe. The Lord asks if there is anyone who will share the exile of this loathsome being, and two respond affirmatively :—

> 'The woman who bore him and the wife he wed—
> The one he slew in anger, the other he stript,
> With ravenous claws, of raiment and of food.'

They went forth and conquered ; they kissed the fearful thing's bloody hands, and the man wept. The Lord said, 'The man is saved ; let the man enter in.' Such is the end of what is indubitably a lofty effort of the imagination. Mr. Buchanan says this poem is but the prelude to an epic. If the epic be at all of the same character, there is no difficulty in deciding that it will assume one of the highest positions in contemporary poetry. All the qualities which are admirable in poetic art find a lodgment to a greater or less degree in 'The Book of Orm.' It has simplicity, grandeur; beauty, sublimity; sweetness, pathos. The word-painting—to adopt a phrase for which we have no special liking, but which is very expressive—is wonderful ; whilst we witness also a felicitous handling of all kinds of rhythm and rhyme. A surface reading of such a volume as this is a great injustice ; it is to be read many times, and never without a new and singular light being thrown upon passages which seemed hazy and meaningless before. There is also to be discerned, beneath much that is tempestuous, and apparently the tossings of a wild and rebellious spirit, the firm purpose of a soul which has not slipped its anchor.

A year or two ago a remarkable poem, entitled ' St. Abe and his Seven Wives,' was published anonymously. Although first issued in this country, the reviewers were unanimous in ascribing it to an American poet, part assigning the authorship to Lowell and part to Bret Harte. It was a picture of Salt Lake life, as its title implied, and the local colouring was so strong that any suspicions one might cherish that the author was an Englishman were almost imperatively laid to sleep. Yet portions of the poem were cast in a form which led the reader to associate with it the name of Robert Browning, of whose hand much that had place in it was not unworthy. The humour was of excellent quality, and the sense of delicacy, even with so dangerous a subject, rarely, or indeed never outraged. It is not our intention to go over this poem now, which will be more operative as an exposure of the evils of Mormondom than any more serious or pretentious book ; but we refer to it because it has been succeeded by a work from the same hand which betrays, we think, the author beyond the power of contradiction. We refer to ' White Rose and

Red,' one of the most remarkable poems issued for a considerable period. It has all the gorgeous colour of Titian, with the breadth of Rembrandt. Anonymous though it be, its author might stake his fame upon that poem as lifting him to a very high place amongst his brethren. Though an American story—and all the singular local truthfulness has been attained which distinguished the previous poem—there are signs about the later work which, as already observed, unmistakably fix the authorship. It is a work which would command attention from its total dissimilarity in style to all the poetry of the time. With a development of powers of satire and feeling of no mean order, there is the seizure and portrayal of nineteenth-century life in the most realistic manner. The various metres in which the divisions of the poem are composed add to the general effect and value of the work, whilst art of a high order is exhibited in the construction. The story follows the adventures of two heroines who furnish the title for the book—one belonging to the dusky Indian race, and the other to the New England whites. Red Rose is the type of all that is luxuriantly beautiful and graceful, with a semi-wildness of nature. This is a portrait of her as she rests coiled on her warm forest couch,—

'Around her brow a circlet of pure gold,
  With antique letters scrolled,

Burns in the sun-ray, and with gold also
 Her wrists and ankles glow ;
Around her neck the threaded wild cat's teeth
 Hang white as pearl, beneath
Her bosoms heave, and in the space between,
 Duskly tattooed, is seen
A figure small as of a pine-bark brand
 Held blazing in a hand.
Her skirt of azure, wrought with braid and thread
 In quaint signs yellow and red,
Scarce reaches to her dark and dimpled knee,
 Leaving it bare and free.
Below, moccasins red as blood are wound,
 With gold and purple bound ;—
So that red-footed like the stork she lies,
 With softly shrouded eyes,
Whose brightness seems with heavy lustrous dew
 To pierce the dark lids through.
Her eyelids closed, her poppied lips apart,
 And her quick eager heart
Stirring her warm frame, as a bird unseen
 Stirs the warm lilac-sheen,
She slumbers,—and of all beneath the skies
 Seemeth the last to rise.'

Is not this a finer description than any pencil could accomplish, touching, as it does, character as well as bodily outlines? Another portrait, equally well drawn, is presented to us in Eureka Hart, the gigantic white man of the State of Maine. Red Rose comes upon him in the woods, falls in love with him on the spot, thinking

she never beheld anything more beauteous, and he is
taken captive by a number of her tribe. The captivity,
however, which binds him stronger than the hold of the
tribe is the captivity of love. He is just an easy-going,
handsome animal, and becomes hopelessly enchained by
the beauty of Red Rose. The nuptial rites are such, we
regret to state, as would not make the marriage legitimate
in any well-regulated, civilised country, but the two
seem none the less happy in spite thereof. The passages
which immediately follow this incident betray so much of
Mr. Buchanan's spirit and manner that we wonder his
name never suggested itself as the author, to any of the
numerous critics of the poem. Eureka Hart at length
grew weary of his lot, and in proportion to the evapo-
ration of his passion grew vividly the remembrance of his
relatives far away. He persuaded Red Rose ultimately
to consent to a brief visit to his native place, just to bid
a final farewell to those he loved. He departed, leaving
behind him a paper with the writing (in his blood)
' Eureka Hart, Drowsietown, State of Maine.' The
little paper lies for ever on the woman's heart to soothe the
sad pain of parting. The Sixth Canto of the Second Part
bears, we think, almost irresistible evidence of having
been written by the author of ' London Poems,' allowing
that the style has ripened in the interim. Did not space

fail we should desire to reproduce some of the charming
passages which so truthfully depict Drowsietown, the
abode of the Harts.   When Eureka arrives and settles
down there, it is not without some twinge of conscience
with regard to the splendid, impulsive creature he has
left behind.   But these thoughts become fainter and
fainter as he is bewitched by Phœbe, the White Rose,
who presents a marked contrast in every particular to his
former love.   Dainty, mild, and prudish, she is meant to
be a happy mother, very sober-mooded and very faithful.
The upshot is that Eureka finds himself shortly at the
altar with Phœbe, who is united to him in holy matri-
mony by Parson Pendon.   And now begins the really
grand and tragical part of the story.   We have had
spring, summer, and autumn painted by the poets again
and again, but winter very seldom.   Let anyone who
wishes for a perfect description of the season turn to the
book devoted to the Great Snow.   Never was anything
more beautifully and accurately realised, and as we read
we are sensible of the fact that there is more after all in
the cold, calm, white season than we have hitherto
imagined.   During the great snowstorm Phœbe is at
home wondering what keeps Eureka in the town.   Meanwhile, there is a foot on the snow, drawing nearer and
nearer.   A low murmur is at last heard, and something

taps at the window. The door is opened, and in
staggers a woman—the Red Rose—with an infant at her
breast. She has been wearied with the absence of her
lover, and affection has guided her steps right away from
the haunts of her tribe to Drowsietown. Phœbe finds the
paper bearing her husband's name upon the wanderer,
but in the midst of her conflicting emotions the door
opens, and Eureka Hart walks in. The poem from this
point is full of force and pathos. The loving heart of
Phœbe conquers her anger when she beholds the death-
touch upon Red Rose, and in pitying she forgives. Her
rival dies in the arms of the conscience-stricken Eureka,
still regarding him as her godlike chief. This is the
final glimpse of her :—

> 'See ! her hand points upward slowly,
>   With an awful grace and holy,
>   And her eyes are saying clearly,
>   " Master, lord, beloved so dearly,
>   We shall meet, with souls grown fonder,
>   In God's happy prairies yonder ;
>   Where no snow falls ; where, for ever,
>   Flows the shining Milky River,
>   On whose banks, divinely glowing,
>   Shapes like ours are coming, going,
>   In the happy star-dew moving,
>   Silent, smiling, loved, and loving !
>   Fare thee well, till then, my Master ! "
>   Hark, her breath comes fainter, faster,

> While, in love man cannot measure,
>   Kissing her white warrior's hand,
> She sinks, with one great smile of pleasure—
>   Last flash upon the blackening brand !'

Now, although in an artistic sense some would consider this poem to fail because of its ending, we cannot so regard it. The author has obviously meant to exhibit to us the fragmentary character, and utterly disappointing nature, of human life. To say that he does not manifest art because his work closes with a feeling of melancholy, seems to us most inefficient criticism. The work ends tragically, exactly as the author had intended it should end from the first inception of the story ; though of course the most prominent impression left on the mind is that the poem was conceived mostly for the purpose of developing the passion of the Red Rose. The very realism to which the poet is devoted would be defeated had he attempted to reconcile ideas and facts which are seen to be in positive discord. If the poem be inartistic, certainly one half of our pathetic literature—both in prose and verse—must bear it company. But its genius is too true to permit of such a false conclusion. The poem is great—great in truthfulness, in conception, and in elaboration. The matter, however, in which we are most concerned is, that though its authorship has not been acknowledged, there are traces of workmanship about it which point to Mr. Buchanan as its author. It exhibits, in the first place, an amplification of one of his strongest personal canons in poetry—that the writer should be perfectly disinterested, and free himself completely from faulty systems of ethics which are too often accepted without due consideration. Then, again, several of the situations in the poem, which would have been rejected by other living poets, of sufficient standing capable of writing it, as vulgar, have been deliberately chosen, and successfully handled. In short, as Mr. Buchanan desired it to be distinctly understood by his ' London Poems ' and ' Meg Blane,' we have conventionalities set aside, and the human heart inverted, with all its passions, so that the remainder of the world, as well as the poet, might be able to witness its subtle workings. Between Nell and Red Rose we perceive a great amount of approximation. In both we have an out-of-the-way creation, but from him who gave us the first it would not be difficult to predicate the gift of the latter. Character has been preserved in both cases, and the truth spiritualised in precisely the same mode. There is no more vulgarity in one portrait than in the other. Neither does the poet profess to explain everything : enough for him to dare to be true. The personal chord running through this poem, ' White Rose and Red,' we should have considered sufficient to identify it. Besides Tennyson and Browning, there is no other person except Mr. Buchanan whose work we could consider it to be, and there are insuperable aspects which would immediately forbid us associating the authorship with the Poet Laureate, or the writer of ' Pippa Passes.' We shall at some future day probably receive confirmation of the views just expressed from the (at present) unknown author of the work.[1]

Upon the prose works of Mr. Buchanan there is no room left to enlarge, nor perhaps is there any great necessity for doing so. They exhibit to a large extent the same qualities as his labours in verse. There is the same absolute truthfulness to the scenes he professes to describe, with a strong power of words. In the 'Land of Lorne' we have more than one passage which for eloquence can vie with anything accomplished in the measures of song. The author has found himself amongst the beauties and the wonders of Nature in which his soul delights, and his fancy has been allowed to wander free and unrestrained. The crudity which distinguished his essays has completely disappeared, and he writes almost

[1] The authorship of the poem in question has now been admitted by Mr. Buchanan.

as freely as in his more natural element. The attractiveness and grandeur of Scotch scenery were but a shadow
and a name to us till we read his glowing descriptions,
but now we feel as though we also had been subject to
the terrors of the Gulf of Corryvrechan, and had beheld
the gloom and the mystery brooding over Loch Corruisk.

In making some final observations upon Mr. Buchanan as one of the prominent poets of the time, there is
an excellent sign visible in his works which is most hopeful for the future. He is not an echo of any other poet.
Whatever may be thought of his song, or whatever position may be assigned to it, it is perfectly original and
spontaneous. He has not sung because he has been
moved to imitation by the graces of other poets, nor for
any other reason, except the one which should always
determine the poet—viz., because song was in his heart.
That is an election whose end is always inevitable—more
commanding and imperious than Fate. As well try to
eliminate music from the bird as suppress the volitions
and the manifestations of the poet. It is his life to sing.
There may be false singers who for the moment contrive
to attract the public ear, but their influence is fleeting.
They can no more satisfy the world than could the sounds
which would proceed from an automaton being. The
moment it is discovered that a singer is unnatural and

that his music is a forced growth, that moment will his power begin to decline. It is something, then, that our author is of sufficient calibre to be able to be perfectly independent of any of his species. He has studied deeply at many imaginative springs, but his own well of song is unmixed with their waters. His utterance is growing clearer and more distinct every year. But in addition to this originality, there is the merit of endeavouring to assist in the formation of a superior school of poetry to that which generally attracts singers of a lower order. So far from regarding the subjects which he has chosen as unworthy of the poet's pen, we think it redounds to his credit that he has thus probed the depths of society. All his graphic, dramatic force would have been a mere shadow, nay lost altogether, if he had missed the realism which is impressed on everything he has written. The art which delineates the career of a poor coster-girl may be as fine and correct as that which conceives a Hamlet : false art lies not in the subject, but in the manner of treatment. Essential service is ren-dered to humanity when any life is so presented to it as to beget sympathy for the object, whilst Vice is left un-toyed with, and appears in all its naked hideousness. In such a way as was never before accomplished, we believe, Mr. Buchanan has, in his London lyrics, come between society and the degraded beings who have been the objects of its contempt and disgust, and has acted as an interpreter. It is poetry of this description which will succeed in retaining its hold upon humanity. Whatever else may die, song which is impressed with a true and profound human interest is imperishable.[1]

Again, his genius and pathos are not local. Man the unit being mortal, but man the species being immortal,

---

[1] Many of the observations in this paragraph would apply to two other poets of the day, who seem scarcely to have received sufficient credit for the work which they have achieved. I refer to the Hon. Roden Noel and the Hon. Leicester Warren. With regard to the former, his 'Red Flag, and other Poems,' and more recently 'Livingstone,' would bear out my assertions. In the volume of the 'Red Flag' we find the poet take up topics which have intense interest to men around us, and they are dealt with in a vigorous and poetical manner. I was struck greatly by the strength and originality of many of the poems in this volume. Occasionally the metre is rough, but the work is infused with a fine spirit, and Mr. Noel, like Mr. Buchanan, is no imitator. Again, his 'Livingstone' is an admirable attempt at dealing with a contemporary subject, and the natural scenery of Africa is glowingly depicted. Mr. Warren has, perhaps, caught more of the true classical spirit than any other of our poets. though not to the exclusion of that of the age in which he lives. His 'Searching the Net, and other Verses' exhibits a keen sympathy between the writer and the subject and circumstances which he endeavours to depict. I think that in the case of both these writers, their poetry appeals to what is best and purest, both as regards the intellect and the spirit. We have not so many genuine poets that we can afford to pass by, with the barest recognition merely, those whom we do possess.

that which has its foundation in the essential lot of humanity—joy and suffering—must also pass on from age to age, gathering strength and vitality. But how is the pathos of a life to be seized? It cannot be done in the attempted revivification of beings long dead, without the aid of the finest qualities of the great poet—insight, emotion, sincerity. Given these qualities, and witness their exercise upon contemporary subjects, and we have at once poetry which is not only true to-day, but must be immortally so. When we read Mr. Buchanan's 'London Poems' we felt that they were great, if even from their courage alone. Nothing was wanting save those finishing touches to the marble which are no essential part of the portrait, but which leave unoffended the eye of the mind. The spiritualisation was complete. His ethology, too, was accurate; there was no contradiction between persons individualised and their actions —owing to the perfect disinterestedness of the poet we had the beings themselves, and not beings partially deprived of their identity by the plastic influence of the artist. What our author lacked in his earlier work he has been gradually assimilating since, and has now succeeded in getting his language and his art under the fullest control.

In the great power, then, of appealing to universal

humanity lies Mr. Buchanan's security. 'The Book of Orm' is an assurance that we shall yet receive from him a loftier poem. The full richness of his genius only began to unfold itself clearly in his latest work. A wide field in which laurels are to be won lies before him; and his future is within his own making. Competent critics have assured him that he has already added to English literature much which ought not to perish; and in this verdict we unhesitatingly agree. The light of Nature has been his guide, and the human heart his study. With these still as his greatest incentives he must unquestionably attain an exalted position amongst the poets of the nineteenth century. His doubts, his interrogatories, do not alarm us. In a poet they are healthy signs, and prevent stagnation or deterioration. They beget hope that Light will be seen at last. To the Seer belongs the power of elevating the human soul, of unravelling life's mysteries, and of piercing through many of those folds which prevent man from apprehending God. This power, or this glamour, or whatever it be, is indubitably upon Mr. Buchanan. Let him be faithful to himself and to his gifts, and in an age which does not promise to be rich in lofty poetry, he will produce works which cannot fail to be accepted as incontestably great, and worthy of the world's preservation.

ENGLISH FUGITIVE POETS

[EDINBURGH REVIEW]

In poetry and creative art the ancient world left little or no room in which the modern could demonstrate its superiority. Science has multiplied the appliances for the diffusion of knowledge, and invention has achieved many and extraordinary triumphs, but the individual mind has not shown itself capable of higher flights of imagination than those of the old bards. In these later centuries we have seen but one poet capable of sustaining the mantle of Homer. And the superiority of the ancients is equally undoubted when we consider those slighter efforts in verse which are confessedly of a somewhat ephemeral character, and meant principally to embody only the feelings of the age in which they are written. Horace was the best writer of light lyrical verse the world has seen, while, at the same time, he was something much greater and higher. But regarding him in this passing reference mainly as a poet of society, what higher compliment can we pay to a poet of our own time than to say that he is truly Horatian in spirit, or

writes with the Horatian pen? But Horace himself was
not the father of this fugitive poetry. The Roman poet
acknowledges that Anacreon was its originator; but
whether that be so or no, the Anthology is full of excellent examples of it, and the earliest known specimens
now in existence were left by the Greeks.

> ' Nec, si quid olim lusit Anacreon,
>   Delevit ætas ; spirat adhuc amor,
>   Vivuntque commissi calores
>   Æoliæ fidibus puellæ.'

Great proficiency was attained in all forms of song, the
amatory, the didactic, the literary and artistic, the witty
and satirical, and others. The poems themselves have
occupied the leisure of men of eminence in the modern
world, and were 'favourite objects of study with Eras-
mus and his friend Sir Thomas More.' Chesterfield, it
is true, denounced the Greek epigrams in his Letters to
his son, but against his solitary testimony—which in
this matter is of no particular weight—is to be set that of
Cowper, Johnson, and many other men of equally opposite temperaments, to whom they were a solace and
a delight. Lord Neaves (himself no mean proficient in
the art of gay and gaillard rhymes) observes, in his
very graceful little volume, that 'from the time of Martial
the epigram came to be characterised generally by that

peculiar point or sting, which we now look for in a
French or English epigram, and the want of this in the
old Greek compositions doubtless led some minds to
think them tame and tasteless. The true or the best
form of the early Greek epigram does not aim at wit or
seek to produce surprise. Its purpose is to set forth
in the shortest, simplest, and plainest language, but yet
with perfect purity and even elegance of diction, some
fact or feeling of such interest as would prompt the real
or supposed speaker to record it in the form of an
epigram ; though it is true that, particularly in the later
period of epigrammatic writing, these compositions, even
among the Greeks, assumed a greater variety of aspect,
and were employed as the vehicle of satire or ridicule,
as a means of producing hilarity and mirth.' It would
be tedious to trace the gradual developments and
changes in this kind of verse from the days of the first
Greek writers to the time of Horace. The latter, however, seems to have conserved many of its best elements,
and to have added others which gave him so distinctive
a place that, even more than his predecessors in the art,
he has become a type for modern poets. His imitators
for the most part serve but to denote the painful difference there is between the founder of a style and he
who attempts to copy it. Our purpose is not to institute

a comparison between the Roman poet's work and that of his successors, but to glance at the songs of those English writers who, taking him to a great extent as their model, have written the verse of passing moods and emotions, and have not attempted that higher branch of poetry which secures the loftiest renown from posterity.

What do we mean by *vers de société* if, with Mr. Locker, we must use a French phrase to denote a thing as old as the English language? They are the expression of common sentiment and common feeling in graceful but familiar rhyme. Poetry of this kind excites in us no wonder, no unwonted excitement; but it pleases us because, apparently without effort, it has translated into verse the ordinary sensations of humanity, those which change with the hour, which are again and again renewed, and which are the property of almost every nature. For instance, when a writer of *vers de société* gives us his impressions of female beauty, they are usually drawn from those points of view which belong to common æsthetics, and not from that hidden deeper spring of beauty which has in it something of the spiritual, and which requires the soul of the true poet rightly to apprehend. The arch smile, the dress, the peach-like bloom of the cheek—these are the things which arrest the eye of the poet of society just as they are the things which strike the vast majority of men.

He who writes of the world must mingle with the world. The most successful and the most brilliant of the school of authors to which we are referring have been those who have lived largely in society; who have studied its movements, its caprices, and its spirit. They have generally been men of ease and observation, and yet men of no settled purpose as regards the expression of their thoughts. They have not so much sought the muse as left the muse to come to them; when she has given them an *àpropos* inspiration they have written. The pen has served as a medium to turn a compliment, to secure a fleeting idea, or to enshrine a random reflection. Such an end may seem trivial, but the result in the bulk of these verses has been most valuable. What a glance at contemporary history we obtain from the time of Raleigh down to our own day through the aid of our minor English poetry! It is as trustworthy as a book of costume, with the addition of a living human interest.

Writers of fugitive verses hang, as it were, upon the skirts of the greater poets of their own time, and all that they do takes a tinge from them. Accordingly, we find that the minor verse of the Elizabethan period possesses a nobler expression and a greater sweetness than that of

the nineteenth century, from the fact that it was an echo
of that sublime period in English literature. The satel-
lites of Shakspeare, Spenser, and Jonson were likely to
emit a stronger radiance than those of Wordsworth,
Byron, or Tennyson. The grace of the first writers of
this humbler poesy has never been surpassed. With
every century there has been a corresponding change
between the two kinds of verse, though the age must also
be counted as a factor in the production of such general
result.

The writing of this poetry, simple as it appears, requires special gifts. In the first place, terseness is an
especial requisite. To be verbose in verse which, as it
were, flies with the wind, is to fail in the first principle of
the art. The best writer of society verse is always
happiest when he is concentrated. Light verse written
in cantos—unless it took the form of a humourous or
satirical narrative like 'Don Juan'—would fatigue the
reader. It is not the highest kind of genius which de-
votes itself to this work, and the verbosity which we
could tolerate, if we could not always enjoy, in the
greater writer becomes insufferable in the lesser. The
man who writes *vers de société* must have as decided a gift
in his own form of expression and conception as the
artist who takes a higher rank. To quote the words of

Isaac D'Israeli :—' It must not be supposed that because these productions are concise they have, therefore, the more facility ; we must not consider the genius of a poet diminutive because his pieces are so, nor must we call them, as a sonnet has been called, a difficult trifle. A circle may be very small, yet it may be as mathematically beautiful and perfect as a larger one. To such compositions we may apply the observation of an ancient critic, that though a little thing gives perfection, yet perfection is not a little thing. The poet to succeed in these hazardous pieces must be alike polished by an intercourse with the world as with the studies of taste, to whom labour is negligence, refinement a science, and art a nature. Genius will not always be sufficient to impart that grace of amenity which seems peculiar to those who are accustomed to elegant society. . . . These productions are more the effusions of taste than genius, and it is not sufficient that the poet is inspired by the Muse, he must also suffer his concise pages to be polished by the hand of the Graces.'

Steele, who himself regarded Sappho, Anacreon, and Horace as the completest models in this range of verse, was the author of a charming paper in his ' Guardian,' which really exhausts the subject. ' These little things,' he says, ' do not require an elevation of thought, nor any extraordinary capacity, nor an extensive knowledge ; but then they demand great regularity and the utmost nicety; an exact purity of style, with the most easy and flowing numbers ; an elegant and unaffected turn of wit, with one uniform and simple design. Greater works cannot well be without some inequalities and oversights, and they are in them pardonable ; but a song loses all its lustre if it be not polished with the greatest accuracy. The smallest blemish in it, like a flaw in a jewel, takes off the whole value of it. A song is, as it were, a little image in enamel, that requires all the nice touches of the pencil, a gloss, and a smoothness, with those delicate finishing strokes which would be superfluous and thrown away upon larger figures, where the strength and boldness of a masterly hand give all the grace.' This description of what a song should be is extremely felicitous, and covers the ground which we are desirous to include within the scope of our observations. Steele considers the ancient writers whom he names great in the art because they pursue a single thought, whereas the moderns cram too much into one song. Waller occasionally commits this error, while Cowley is defective through a redundancy of wit. The reader is dazzled by the starting of so many trains of thought, whereas a song should be constructed as we would construct an epigram.

The limitation to which we have committed ourselves will forbid an examination of the claims of those who on the Continent first cultivated the art of light versification. But even were the scope widened it would be practically impossible to touch upon the French and Italian writers from the time of the Troubadours and of Ronsard downwards who have attained great proficiency in spontaneous and courtly verse. The two countries named were more prolific in a single age, perhaps, than England has been in the course of three centuries in the production of these writers. But besides their excellency in the construction of songs and lyrics, the Italians perfected another style which finds an admirable exponent in Boiardo, the author of the ' Orlando Innamorato,' and in Berni, who is remembered principally for his Rifacimento of that celebrated work. This style is full of episode and description, and although the element of lightness may be often discovered in it, it is scarcely germane to our subject Boiardo's style was first imitated in this country within the present century by Hookham Frere in ' Whistlecraft,' and afterwards by Byron in ' Beppo' and ' Don Juan.' But comic epic, or mock heroic poetry, notwithstanding that it possesses the one feature of familiarity common also to lighter verse, is removed from the true subject of this enquiry. In the one we have many trains of ideas

started ; in the other we have the bending of the energies
to the complete grasping and setting forth of one leading
thought.   So in familiar poetry : 'Don Juan' presents us
with a series of pictures, but real fugitive verse expends
itself in the perfection of one.   The power of improvisa-
tion, which was so remarkable a feature of the Italian
poetic genius generally, and of the French at certain
spasmodic periods, has been almost wholly absent in
England.   We have no parallel to the court of King
René, which swarmed with singers of no mean order, and
musicians of a sweet and delicate if not powerful melody.
We are a heavy and practical, in distinction from a light
and sunny race ; and our accomplishments in fugitive
verse cannot for grace and elegance be ranged in comparison with those of France and Italy.   Such as we are,
we are, however ; and we shall doubtless discover that in
other important respects our writers have the superiority
over Continental poets.

Arriving now at a consideration of some of the riches
of English literature as regards this attractive class of
poetry, let us first devote a brief space to those writers
who flourished before the time of Waller.   Much of the
best verse issued from the versifiers of the sixteenth century and the earlier portion of the seventeenth.   In the
lyrics of that period we are struck with the especial beauty

and sweetness of many whose authorship is unknown. It speaks well for the popular taste, notwithstanding, that though the authors have long since crumbled into dust, their work has been preserved and handed down from generation to generation. What could be more exquisite, for instance, than the following verses, which seem to combine all the requisites for *vers de société*, and the writer of which is still and must always remain unknown?—

> 'Since first I saw your face I resolved
>   To honour and renown you ;
> If now I be disdained, I wish
>   My heart had ne'er known you.
> What? I that loved, and you that liked—
>   Shall we begin to wrangle ?
> No, no, no, my heart is fast,
>   And cannot disentangle !
>
> If I admire or praise too much,
>   That fault you may forgive me ;
> Or if my hands had strayed to touch,
>   Then justly might you leave me.
> I asked you leave, you bade me love,
>   Is't now a time to chide me ?
> No, no, no, I'll love you still,
>   What future e'er betide me.
>
> The sun, whose beams most glorious are,
>   Rejecteth no beholder ;
> And thy sweet beauty, past compare,
>   Made my poor eyes the bolder.

> Where beauty moves, and wit delights,
>   And signs of kindness bind me,
> There, oh ! there, where'er I go,
>   I leave my heart behind me.'

Most of these old poems touch upon the passion of love, and in none has the thought been better conveyed than in Ben Jonson's address to Celia, which, familiar as it is, can never be read without delight :—

> ' Drink to me only with thine eyes,
>   And I will pledge with mine ;
> Or leave a kiss but in the cup
>   And I'll not look for wine.
>
> The thirst that from the soul doth rise
>   Doth ask a drink divine ;
> But might I of Jove's nectar sup,
>   I would not change for thine.'

A lightness and an intensity are combined here so perfectly as to make the gem complete. The language is of the simplest, is free and unrestrained, and the idea exceedingly pretty. Now and then in these earlier days we light upon verses in which the feeling of melancholy predominates, as in those soft and somewhat sad lines by Carew, which would seem to have been penned after a rebuff sustained at the hands of the cruel fair one :—

'He that loves a rosy cheek
　Or a coral lip admires,
Or from star-like eyes doth seek
　Fuel to maintain his fires ;
As old Time makes these decay,
So his flames must waste away.

But a smooth and steadfast mind,
　Gentle thoughts, and calm desires,—
Hearts with equal love combined,
　Kindle never-dying fires ;
Where these are not, I despise
Lovely cheeks, or lips, or eyes.'

It would be a task to scrutinise at length the varied
lyrical treasures of the Elizabethan era, as we have
received them from the pens of Wither, Sir Henry
Wotton, Donne, Cowley, Sir Philip Sidney, Sir Robert
Ayton, Sir Walter Raleigh, and others. Raleigh was
a master in the art of verse, though his superiority in
other respects has somewhat detracted from his fame in
this. Everybody, however, remembers his reply to
Marlowe's song of the ' Passionate Shepherd to his Love,'
beginning—

'If all the world and love were young
And truth in every shepherd's tongue,
These pretty pleasures might me move
To live with thee and be thy love.'

Raleigh's poetical pieces are especially marked by conceits—often rivalling Donne in that respect. Neither were they without strength, as indeed might well be predicated when we consider the man. It is a question, however, whether they have as yet been rated at their full value. Stately and vigorous is his language, bearing the impress of an unbending will, a will that did not quail when the block even was in view. Many poems which were once associated with his name have been discovered not to be his workmanship, but those which remain, and which have been unquestionably authenticated, bear witness to the variety of his gifts. He was certainly a writer of *vers de société*, but being naturally a man of a grave and strong spirit, rather than a laughing and volatile one, his verse is now and again heavy and sententious.

In the course of reading through the earlier English poems it is interesting to note how the ideas of a later day are but simply the refurbishing of those of the older men. In a set of verses supposed to be by the dramatist John Heywood, entitled ' A Description of a most Noble Lady,' and written before 1557, we discover the thought which Byron gave utterance to in his monody on Sheridan. The passage will be remembered when we quote Heywood's lines :—

> ' I think Nature hath lost the mould
>   Where she her shape did take ;
> Or else I doubt if Nature could
>   So fair a creature make.'

Beyond all dispute, the best of the early lyric poets is Robert Herrick, whose verses are flushed with a joyous and tender spirit. He may be styled the Burns of his time, and was imbued with something of the reckless soul of the great north-countryman. Herrick was born in Cheapside in the year 1591, and educated at Cambridge. In 1629 he became vicar of Dean Prior, in Devonshire. The time of the Civil War, however, found him living at Westminster, where he resided also during the Commonwealth. After the Restoration he came into his vicarage again, but by this time he was an old man, and none the better for his devotion to the convivial company to be found in the London taverns, where he was ever one of the gayest of the gay. He died in 1674, having left behind him some of the sweetest word-music that we possess. Nothing could be more delightful than these verses on the Daffodils :—

> 'Fair Daffodils, we weep to see
>   You haste away so soon :
> As yet the early rising sun
>   Has not attained his noon.

                    Stay, stay,
                Until the hasting day
                    Has run
                But to the even-song ;
                And having prayed together, we
                    Will go with you along.

                We have short time to stay, as you,
                    We have as short a spring ;
                As quick a growth to meet decay
                    As you, or anything.
                        We die,
                    As your hours do, and dry
                        Away
                Like to the summer's rain ;
                Or as the pearls of morning dew,
                    Ne'er to be found again.'

Besides the grace that is inseparable from all Herrick's compositions, we have here that sympathy with Nature which made good his claim to the title of poet. Flowers, music, woman, all these had their intense and several charms for him, and, strangely enough for a middle-aged clergyman, he was clearly an amorous and erotic poet. There is a tinge of sensuousness about all that he does, which sometimes exceeds the limits of a later age. But all his poems to Julia are singular for their beauty. Take the Night Piece addressed to her :—

            ' Her eyes the glowworm lend thee,
              The shooting stars attend thee,

And the elves also,
Whose little eyes glow
Like the sparks of fire, befriend thee.

No Will-o'-th'-wisp mislight thee;
Nor snake or slow-worm bite thee;
   But on, on thy way,
   Not making a stay,
Since ghost there's none to affright thee.

Let not the dark thee cumber;
What though the moon does slumber?
   The stars of the night,
   Will lend thee their light
Like tapers clear, without number.

Then, Julia, let me woo thee,
Thus, thus to come unto me,
   And when I shall meet
   Thy silvery feet,
My soul I'll pour into thee.'

The age in which Herrick lived, and in which he wrote such verses as these, was distinguished for its poetic excellence, and its indulgence in fancy and conceit. Another writer to whom slight reference has been made, George Wither, was of the same school as Herrick, and almost his equal in tenderness and delicacy of treatment. Sir John Suckling was also a great master in the art, though he is frequently robbed of his true honours. His Ballad upon a Wedding is one of the most naturally-expressed poems in the language. How these stanzas make us realise the charming being whom he describes !—

> ' Her feet beneath her petticoat,
>   Like little mice, stole in and out,
>   As if they feared the light :
>   But O ! she dances such a way !
>   No sun upon an Easter-day
>   Is half so fine a sight.
>
>   Her cheeks, so rare a white was on,
>   No daisy makes comparison ;
>   Who sees them is undone ;
>   For streaks of red were mingled there,
>   Such as are on a Cath'rine pear,
>   The side that's next the sun.
>
>   Her lips were red ; and one was thin,
>   Compared to that was next her chin,
>   Some bee had stung it newly ;
>   But, Dick, her eyes so guard her face,
>   I durst no more upon them gaze,
>   Than on the sun in July.'

We have now glanced sufficiently at this early poetry to apprehend its character by the aid of the examples given. Its great feature is its naturalness. All its similes and its reflections are drawn from outward objects. The close breath of cities does not seem to have tainted the souls of the poets, who revel in flowers, and woods, and meads, which are the springs of laughter, joy, and pathos to them.

Advancing a stage, we arrive at the minor poets of the Restoration. While not missing a great portion of the sweetness which belonged to their earlier brethren, we find that their prevailing characteristic is sentiment, sometimes degenerating into exaggeration. The age of Charles II. being famous for its gallantry, the courtly poets fill their pages with an extravagant homage to the women of the day. Now and then the adulatory amatory poetry of Lovelace, Montrose, Rochester, and their *confrères* affects the reader as being what the Americans would describe as 'high falutin',' and the point of a compliment is often made absurd by its prodigious unsuitability and extravagance ; but in the verse of this period there still remains the genuine ring of song. The cavalier hangs his heart upon his sleeve, and talks loudly enough about it, it is true. He is more than Cupid's follower ; he is the little god's very humble slave. There is a certain lightness of touch in Lovelace's ballads that we rarely meet with elsewhere, and his lines written to Althea from prison are 'familiar in our mouths as household words.' He reaches a loftier strain when he serenely asserts in immortal lines that though immured between stone walls he is nevertheless free. Sedley, justly famous for his songs, and as justly infamous for his dissolute character, is the author of the charming lyric, 'Phillis is my only Joy.' Buckingham was a man of a lower order of talent than these, and yet—through the adventitious aid derived from his position at Court—his pieces spread far and wide, though nobody cares for them now. There is no power in them, though there is sometimes a facile execution. Dryden, it will be remembered, described Buckingham in the character of Zimri as one who

'In the course of one revolving moon
Was chemist, fiddler, statesman, and buffoon.'

He wrote the fashionable verses of his time from an overweening conceit which would not suffer him to be behind his contemporaries, and never stayed to ask himself whether he possessed the necessary gifts. The Earl of Rochester had a more genuine vein ; but one cannot avoid the impression that most of the singers of his time had simply a parrot-like title to fame. Sackville, Earl of Dorset, was stronger than any of those just named, and his stirring ballad, 'To all you Ladies now on Land,' written the night before an engagement with the Dutch, is as widely known as any of Dibdin's songs. Even in the navy debates of the House of Commons during the last year some of its admirable lines were quoted. The effeminacy which so strongly marked the poetry of the time is completely eliminated from this ballad, which possesses both a fine swing and epigrammatic force.

But a poet who lived slightly anterior to those we mentioned, the brilliant Marquis of Montrose—who was even still readier with the sword—appears to have excelled them all, with the exception of Lovelace—that is, in the poetry of love. He has almost dropped out of recollection now, but the whole of the ballad from which the following verses are extracted is of equal merit :—

> ' My dear and only love, I pray
>   That little world of thee
> Be governed by no other sway
>   Than purest monarchy ;
> For if confusion have a part,
>   Which virtuous souls abhor,
> And hold a synod in thine heart,
>   I'll never love thee more.
>
> As Alexander I will reign,
>   And I will reign alone ;
> My thoughts did evermore disdain
>   A rival on my throne.
> He either fears his fate too much,
>   Or his deserts are small,
> Who dares not put it to the touch,
>   To gain or lose it all.

*   *   *   *

But if thou wilt prove faithful, then,
    And constant of thy word,
I'll make thee glorious by my pen,
    And famous by my sword ;
I'll serve thee in such noble ways
    Was never heard before ;
I'll crown and deck thee all with bays,
    And love thee more and more.'

Edmund Waller, however, has left behind him a name more durable in connection with this class of poetry than any other man of his century. It is to be hoped he was more constant in his friendships than he was in his politics. Having twanged the lyre, and beautifully too, in praise of Cromwell, he afterwards poured forth congratulatory strains for Charles II. There was no element of greatness in his compositions ; possessing as much sweetness as Milton, he yet was a perfect contrast to him in all other respects. Compared with the grand old blind poet, he was a rose beside an oak. There was fragrance, but no stability, and he rapidly fell to pieces. Yet even from the dried leaves of the rose, which have been preserved, we can extract pleasant odours. His imagination was not of a striking order, and his verse is more distinguished for its finish than for any other quality ; indeed in this respect he has scarcely had an equal since. His 'Go, lovely Rose,' which we have already had occasion to mention, and 'Lines on a Girdle,' are the best specimens we possess of his writing, but these are matchless in their way. Had he owned a larger and more sincere nature we might have had in him a great poet.

We can hardly assign a place amongst these canary-birds to the satanic muse of Swift. He was a bird of prey in comparison with them, and threw too much of passion and hatred into the most playful of his verses to be ranked with such singers. But what force and command of language, of metre, and of rhyme! what a mastery of all he touched! We prefer for our present purpose to take him in his gentlest mood, and to transcribe a few lines to Stella, which might have been written by a man who had not betrayed another woman.

> 'Stella, say, what evil tongue
> Reports you are no longer young;
> That Time sits with his scythe to mow
> Where erst sat Cupid with his bow;
> That half your locks are turned to grey?
> I'll ne'er believe a word they say.
> 'Tis true, but let it not be known,
> My eyes are somewhat dimmish grown:
> For Nature, always in the right,
> To your decay adapts my sight:
> And wrinkles undistinguish'd pass,
> For I'm ashamed to use a glass;

And till I see them with these eyes,
Whoever says you have them, lies.
No length of time can make you quit
Honour and virtue, sense and wit ;
Thus you may still be young to me,
While I can better hear than see.
O ne'er may Fortune show her spite,
To make me deaf, and mend my sight.'

One other name amongst the earlier minor poets
must arrest our attention before we come to those of the
nineteenth century. In alluding to Matthew Prior, we
cannot do better than quote Cowper's words upon our
whole subject. 'Every man conversant with verse-
making knows, and knows by painful experience, that
the familiar style is of all styles the most difficult to
succeed in. To make verse speak the language of prose,
without being prosaic, to marshal the words of it in such
an order as they might naturally take in falling from the
lips of an extemporary speaker, yet without meanness,
harmoniously, elegantly, and without seeming to displace
a syllable for the sake of the rhyme, is one of the most
arduous tasks a poet can undertake. He that could
accomplish this task was Prior. Many have imitated his
excellence in this particular, but the best copies have
fallen short of the original.' This is a generous tribute,
coming as it does from one who was himself no mean

adept in the same art. Cowper, though he has much sense and humour, is no match for Prior in this unpretending kind of poetry. The French are more exquisite than ourselves in drawing-room verses, and there is a decided smack of their quality in Prior. It has been remarked of him that he 'drank Burgundy in its own vineyard.' But he was a sad, rollicking dog, this author of 'Solomon,' and exactly after his patron, the Earl of Dorset's, own heart. Prior rose from the humblest rank of life to occupy a position of some importance in the State. He was born at Abbot Street, in Dorsetshire, but early removed to London with his father, who kept a tavern called the 'Rummer Inn,' at Charing Cross, and it was here in the garb of a waiter that Lord Dorset one day discovered the future poet reading Horace. Acting the part of a generous patron, Dorset sent the youth to St. John's, Cambridge, of which College he afterwards became a Fellow. After leaving the university, Prior, in conjunction with Montagu, wrote 'The Town and Country Mouse,' which opened a path for him to the diplomatic service. Promotion was only a question of time, and accordingly we find that during his somewhat chequered existence he filled the offices of Secretary at the Hague, and at the Court of Versailles, and Commissioner of Trade. His life was a singular

mixture of noble feeling and dissoluteness. Fickle in
the extreme, and an easy prey to the wiles of the
other sex, he was frequently reduced to the very depths
of degradation and poverty. As a writer his longer
poems have not many claims to a lasting remembrance ;
but his shorter pieces justly deserve all the fame they
have acquired. They come barely short of perfection ;
Prior strives hard after obtaining a classic grace and
just misses it. As a specimen of the finished character
of his verses we cite one of his short odes :—

' The merchant, to secure his treasure,
    Conveys it in a borrowed name :
Euphelia serves to grace my measure,
    But Chloe is my real flame.

My softest verse, my darling lyre,
    Upon Euphelia's toilet lay—
When Chloe noted her desire
    That I should sing, that I should play.

My lyre I tune, my voice I raise,
    But with my numbers mix my sighs ;
And whilst I sing Euphelia's praise,
    I fix my soul on Chloe's eyes.

Fair Chloe blushed : Euphelia frowned :
    I sang, and gazed ; I played and trembled ;
And Venus to the Loves around
    Remarked how ill we all dissembled.'

And thus the poet spent his time between his Chloes and Euphelias, constant to none, but writing charmingly of each. All his poetry has a devil-may-care air about it; it gives the impression that it was written by a man who found himself in a world where there was much that ministers to pleasure, and who meant to suck its sweets to the uttermost. The complete absence of consciousness that life had in it something nobler than animal pleasure deprived his poetry of the high tone which should give a flavour even to light and unpretentious verse. Whenever Bacchus and Venus are the poet's gods we may look for enervation in his intellectual offspring. That taint of scepticism in his nature of which an eminent French critic writes—and which he declares was transferred to Voltaire, and was not of the latter's own originating—is apparent in Prior's lines to his soul :—

'Poor little, pretty, fluttering thing,
    Must we no longer live together?
And dost thou prune thy trembling wing,
    To take thy flight thou know'st not whither?

Thy humourous vein, thy pleasing folly,
    Lie all neglected, all forgot :
And pensive, wavering, melancholy
    Thou dread'st and hop'st thou know'st not what.'

Occasionally he had a satirical touch which was very

pointed if not great. If he could not stab with the
rapier he could prick with the needle. He describes in
one of his effusions a remedy that is worse than the
disease :—

> ' I sent for Ratcliffe ; was so ill,
>   That other doctors gave me over :
> He felt my pulse, prescribed his pill,
>   And I was likely to recover.
>
> But when the wit began to wheeze,
>   And wine had warm'd the politician,
> Cured yesterday of my disease,
>   I died last night of my physician.'

Mat. Prior was held in high esteem by the most competent of his contemporaries, with whom he lived on
excellent terms. But the judgment upon him must be
that he faithfully represented in himself the follies of his
time. His verse is flexible, sparkling, and flowing ; at
times, but very seldom, it merits higher praise ; yet there
was no one in his own day who wrote such verse so well.
His views of woman, society, life, and pleasure were
those almost of the lowest stratum, though his power
over his art was so great that he could frequently counter-
feit sentiments of a higher order.

As we approach our own times, Winthrop Mackworth
Praed may be said to enjoy the distinction of having hit

upon a new vein of poetry, and of having been himself
its happiest explorer. Without possessing the highest
gifts of the poet, his smoothness and elegance have
earned for him his reputation.   It is not a little singular
that his great ambition should have been to distinguish
himself in a very different field from that with which his
name is principally associated. He became a subordinate member of Sir Robert Peel's first administration,
and an effective speaker in the House of Commons.
His career was cut short by his death from consumption,
at a moment when he was beginning to put forth broader
and more sympathetic views than those which animated
the great bulk of the Conservative party.   His spirit was
keen and eager, and the great incentive to all he did
was the desire to excel. This passion mastered his
whole being ; and the momentary earnestness he
threw into every successive undertaking was probably
instrumental in undermining his constitution.   Praed
takes us into another atmosphere altogether from that
in which Swift and Prior moved.   Even satire had
become good-natured and love decorous. We discover
no single line which could not be read aloud in the
most fastidious circle. Praed has the sweetness of a
summer's night, and his wit represents the twinkling of
the stars. Yet, in the midst of all his gaiety, in some of

his poems a tinge of melancholy seems to indicate a premature weariness of life :—

> ' I think that very few have sighed
>   When Fate at last has found them,
> Though bitter foes were by their side,
>   And barren moss around them ;
> I think that some have died of drought,
>   And some have died of drinking ;
> I think that nought is worth a thought—
>   And I'm a fool for thinking !'

But, again, he resumes in a more sprightly and hopeful tone :—

> ' I think that friars and their hoods,
>   Their doctrines and their maggots,
> Have lighted up too many feuds,
>   And far too many faggots ;
> I think, while zealots fast and frown,
>   And fight for two or seven,
> That there are fifty roads to Town,
>   And rather more to Heaven.'

The satire of Praed always conveys the impression that it is veiled. The poet is so vivacious, and so longs for all men to be blithe, that he strikes rather with the back of his sword than with its edge. There is the flash of the blade in air, but something arrests its descent—some sudden second impulse in the spirit of him who wields it. From a very early period in life Praed gave himself up to

the writing of light and amusing verse, and the magazine
he edited at Eton contained much that was choice and
sparkling. Macaulay had already shown that these
amusements were not unworthy of a man of genius, and
his Valentine to Lady Mary Stanhope, written after his
return from India, is a capital illustration of the style of
verse written by literary men in leisure hours. The
stately verse of the Whig historian, as we find it in the
' Lays of Ancient Rome,' is far in advance of any serious
poetry written by Praed; but, on the other hand, the
latter excelled his distinguished collaborateur in the
poetry of the drawing-room. His work is all executed
with a care and minuteness which are very admirable.
He knew exactly the precise amount of seriousness to
infuse into his lines, and we are never wearied with too
much sermonising. Could there be anything better of
its kind than his portrait of ' Quince,' who stands out in
bold relief, in pure flesh and blood, with his last words
on bidding farewell to the world ?—

> ' My debts are paid—but Nature's debt
> Almost escaped my recollection ;
> Tom! we shall meet again, and yet
> I cannot leave you my direction ! '

And with what fluency and whimsicality of expression he
describes his Vicar !—

'His talk was like a stream which runs
　　With rapid change from rock to roses ;
It slipped from politics to puns ;
　　It passed from Mahomet to Moses :
Beginning with the laws that keep
　　The planets in their radiant courses,
And ending with some precept deep
　　For dressing eels or shoeing horses.

　　*　　　*　　　*　　　*　　　*

He did not think all mischief fair,
　　Although he had a knack of joking ;
He did not make himself a bear,
　　Although he had a taste for smoking :
And when religious sects ran mad,
　　He held, in spite of all his learning,
That if a man's belief is bad,
　　It will not be improved by burning.

And he was kind, and loved to sit
　　In the low hut or garnished cottage,
And praise the farmer's homely wit,
　　And share the widow's homelier pottage :
At his approach complaint grew mild,
　　And when his hand unbarred the shutter,
The clammy lips of fever smiled
　　The welcome which they could not utter.'

This is not poetry to move the world ; there is no vehe-
mence of passion in it, but it is true drawing in quiet lines,
and more powerful than the mere form of it will suffer to
appear.   The emotional element was not over-developed
in the author or he would sometimes have been able to

give to his sketches just that complementary strength which would have made several of them great. If he has not the highest command over the pathetic, however, in a certain flow of humour he is unapproachable. A specimen of this is found in his reminiscences of the old school-days at Eton, where he describes the school and his school-fellows. He could throw round attachments of this kind an indescribable charm. Another character entitled 'The Belle of the Ball-room,' though not so clever and clearly cut in every line, is more humourous than 'The Vicar.' Even his love verses took a semi-humourous form :—

'Our love was like most other loves ;
   A little glow, a little shiver,
A rose-bud, and a pair of gloves,
   And "Fly not yet" upon the river :
Some jealousy of some one's heir,
   Some hopes of dying broken-hearted,
A miniature, a lock of hair,
   The usual vows—and then we parted.

We parted ; months and years rolled by ;
   We met again four summers after :
Our parting was all sob and sigh ;
   Our meeting was all mirth and laughter ;
For in my heart's most secret cell
   There had been many other lodgers ;
And she was not the ball-room's belle,
   But only—Mrs. Something Rogers.'

Although Praed's more pretentious poems exhibit considerable taste and the same wonderful facility for rhyming, they are evidently not penned in his most natural vein. Not equal to the music of higher poets they pale still further, and are somewhat dull and heavy reading, when compared with stanzas such as those we have been quoting, and which have in them the sparkle and the fizz of champagne. His serious work has a reminiscence of the same flavour, but the spirit has fled. We are dealing with him only as a writer of fugitive verse, for he is one of the men who will be remembered longer for the trifles in which he succeeded than for the greater undertakings in which he failed. Racy, graphic, witty, and brilliant, he was just such a poet as the society in which he moved demanded : and, as he had a decided scintillation of genius, he was able to endow his fancies with more permanence than it is usual for such verse to attain.

But Praed must not blind us to the merits of other writers contemporary with him who are in danger of passing from recollection. Peacock the novelist, author of ' Headlong Hall ' and many other remarkable works, had a decided gift in verse, though he seldom made use of it. His poem of ' Love and Age ' is amongst the best of its kind, and may well entitle him to mention here. Now and then his contempt for preconceived notions, and the

bitterness of his soul, oozed out, as when he wrote upon
the rich and poor :—

> ' The poor man's sins are glaring ;
>   In the face of ghostly warning
>   He is caught in the fact
>   Of an overt act—
>   Buying greens on Sunday morning.
>
>   The rich man has a cellar,
>   And a ready butler by him ;
>   The poor must steer
>   For his pint of beer
>   Where the Saint can't choose but spy him.
>
>   The rich man is invisible
>   In the crowd of his gay society ;
>   But the poor man's delight
>   Is a sore in the sight,
>   And a stench in the nose of piety.'

Yet Peacock's nature was too caustic for a writer of light
verse.   A much better man in this respect was Luttrell,
whose social talents were of a high order.   He had not
the genius of a Praed, but at times nevertheless showed
much happiness in expression.   One could scarcely
imagine, for instance, a better or more perfect epigram
than this on the distinguished singer, Miss Tree :—

> ' On this Tree, if a nightingale settles and sings,
>   The Tree will return her as good as she brings.'

Luttrell wrote a lengthy poem styled 'Advice to Julia,' which contains many witty descriptions of life in the upper classes of society, and a most amusing description of London fog and smoke. His 'Ampthill Park' shows that he possessed no mean powers of poetical description. Of various things which he wrote may be mentioned his verses to Lady Granville, his epigram on Moore's verses being translated into Persian and sung in the streets of Ispahan, and the lines still inscribed in Rogers's arbour at Holland House. On this same arbour it will be remembered Lord Holland penned the pretty conceit—

> 'Here Rogers sat, and here for ever dwell,
>   To me, those " Pleasures " that he sang so well.'

One of Luttrell's efforts was a *tour de force* in rhyming on 'Burnham Beeches.' Some of the stanzas run as follows :—

> 'What though my tributary lines
>   Be less like Pope's than Creech's,
> The theme, if not the poet, shines,
>   So bright are Burnham Beeches.
>
> O'er many a dell and upland walk,
>   Their sylvan beauty reaches ;
> Of Birnam-Wood let Scotland talk,
>   While we've our Burnham Beeches.
>
> If sermons be in stones, I'll bet
>   Our vicar, when he preaches,

He'd find it easier far to get
  A hint from Burnham Beeches.

*   *   *   *   *   *

Here bards have mused, here lovers true
  Have dealt in softest speeches,
While suns declined, and, parting, threw
  Their gold o'er Burnham Beeches.

O ne'er may woodman's axe resound,
  Nor tempest, making breaches
In the sweet shade that cools the ground
  Beneath our Burnham Beeches.

Hold ! though I'd fain be jingling on,
  My power no further reaches—
Again that rhyme ? enough—I've done :
  Farewell to Burnham Beeches.'

It would be idle to recapitulate what Moore has accomplished in the way of light lyrical verse, seeing that his songs are almost as widely known as the language itself. Other poets must be passed over who do not depend upon their lighter achievements for fame—as Pope, Cowper, Mrs. Browning, Lord Byron, Campbell, Coleridge, Hood, Sheridan, and Rogers. Two names, nevertheless, warrant a slight pause—those of Thackeray and Walter Savage Landor. The former has bequeathed to us two or three pieces of light verse, exquisite of their kind. One is 'The Cane-bottomed Chair,' whose simple description and pathos must have touched all who have read it. Easy, natural, and flowing, it is as good as anything that Praed ever wrote, and has glimpses of endowments which he did not possess. With all his wonderful finish there was not the same width in Praed as in Thackeray; and had he not achieved one of the highest reputations as a novelist, the latter would have gained no inconsiderable place as a singer of every-day life. Imagination was absent in him; but humour, satire, playfulness, tenderness, were abundant. 'The Ballad of Bouillabaisse' might serve as a model of most of these qualities. Its writer shows here, as in other poems, the wonderful attachment he felt for old things, old places, and old faces. His riper genius loved to dwell on characters which were simple-hearted, and through the medium of his verse he talks to us in a pleasanter vein than in his novels. His 'Peg of Lima-vaddy' has been a thousand times spoken of for its light dancing music, in which it is unapproachable except by Father Prout's 'Bells of Shandon;' and it has the manifest advantage over the latter in that it possesses a human interest, whilst Prout's lines are simply musical—almost nonsensical—and nothing more. But of all Thackeray's lyrics commend us to the one 'At the Church Gate,' for simplicity, beauty, and sweetness :—

'Although I enter not,
Yet round about the spot
   Ofttimes I hover !
And near the Sacred Gate
With longing eyes I wait,
   Expectant of her.

    *   *   *   *

My lady comes at last,
Timid, and stepping fast,
   And hastening hither
With modest eyes downcast :
She comes—she's here—she's past—
   May Heav'n go with her.

Kneel undisturb'd, fair Saint ;
Pour out your praise or plaint
   Meekly and duly :
I will not enter there,
To sully your pure prayer
   With thoughts unruly.

But suffer me to pace
Round the forbidden place,
   Lingering a minute,
Like outcast spirits who wait
And see through Heaven's gate
   Angels within it.'

In a somewhat similar vein of refined feeling, and with
a genuine classical grace, Walter Savage Landor wrote:—

   'The maid I love ne'er thought of me
      Amid the scenes of gaiety ;

But when her heart or mine sank low,
Ah, then it was no longer so.

From the slant palm she raised her head,
And kissed the cheek whence youth had fled.
Angels! some future day for this,
Give her as sweet and pure a kiss.'

There is something glowing, soft, and Oriental about Landor's genius. He stands alone in his gifts as clearly as any poet. Some of his minor works are worthy of a place in the Greek anthology.

Lord Houghton is another poet who has translated into graceful verse the impressions gained from society; but he possesses a stronger and a fresher air than belong to the poets of society generally. Music and thought are what he gives us rather than point and dashing description. In his quiet strains we come sometimes upon reflections of considerable depth, and the shadow of the literary devotee always falls athwart his pages. We like his utter freedom from artificiality; his range of poetic powers is not of the highest order, but there is scarcely a poet who could be named who has done so uniformly well in all themes selected for treatment. Those who attach no merit to dealing with ordinary and every-day subjects, might attempt to detract from Lord Houghton's praise by affirming that he too often recurs to such

topics : but it ought to be recognised fully by this time that
it requires no ordinary gift to treat of homely things in
a successful manner. And he has the especial merit of
looking beneath the surface of things and touching the
springs of life and thought which are in the heart. On one
occasion he sings of

> 'A sense of an earnest will,
> To help the lowly living,
> And a terrible heart-thrill
> If you have no power of giving :
> An arm of aid to the weak,
> A friendly hand to the friendless,
> Kind words, so short to speak,
> But whose echo is endless.'

Everyone is acquainted with the song 'I wandered
by the Brook Side,' which is a happy specimen of the
minor lyric; but many others could be cited of equal
value, including the pretty pastoral verses commencing
'When long upon the scales of Fate.'

Amongst the best living writers of this kind of verse
must indisputably be placed Mr. Frederick Locker; and
for this reason it will be well to give his work a somewhat closer inspection. There are two distinct sides to
his talent, both of which find adequate representation in
his 'London Lyrics.' In a note appended to these
lyrics, which is one of the cleverest pieces of writing in
the volume, the author has given a faithful summary of

the requirements of that branch of the poetic art to which he is devoted. He says—and his words will help to find the clue for understanding his own claims upon us— ' Light lyrical verse should be short, elegant, refined, and fanciful, not seldom distinguished by chastened sentiment, and often playful. The tone should not be pitched high, and it should be idiomatic, the rhythm crisp and sparkling, the rhyme frequent and never forced, while the entire poem should be marked by tasteful moderation, high finish, and completeness ; for however trivial the subject matter may be, indeed rather in proportion to its triviality, subordination to the rules of composition, and perfection of execution should be strictly enforced. Each piece cannot be expected to exhibit all these characteristics, but the qualities of brevity and buoyancy are essential.' But he concludes these remarks by a confession that his volume may contain a few pieces which ' ought to have been consigned to the dustbin of immediate oblivion.' That is possible ; we cannot commend all alike. The writer of these trifles is in constant danger of falling into triviality or childishness. But if he amuses us we are not disposed to put butterflies on the rack, or to ask of him more than he aspires to give. Mr. Locker is not quite so elegant, perhaps, as his forerunner Praed ; but he is more sprightly and humourous. Liveliness, and what we should call the humour of surprise, are two of his distinguishing features. These qualities shine in the verses entitled ' Episode in the Story of a Muff.' The reader is kept on the tiptoe of expectation till the very last line, and the revulsion of feeling then experienced is due to a very unexpected stroke of drollery.

' She's jealous ! Am I sorry ? No !
I like to see my Mabel so,
   Carina mia !
Poor Puss ? That now and then she draws
Conclusions, not without a cause,
   Is my idea.

We love ; and I'm prepared to prove
That jealousy is kin to love
   In constant women.
My jealous Pussy cut up rough
The day before I bought her muff
   With sable trimming.

These tearful darlings think to quell us
By being so divinely jealous ;
   But I know better.
Hillo ! Who's that ? A damsel ! come,
I'll follow ; no, I can't, for some
   One else has met her.

What fun ! He looks a lad of grace !
She holds her muff to hide her face ;
   They kiss,—the sly Puss !
Hillo ! Her muff—it's trimmed with sable !
It's like the muff I gave to Mabel ! . . .
   Good Lord, she's MY *Puss !* '

A similar surprise, though not of so humourous a nature, follows the reading of ' The Old Cradle,' which is amongst the lyrics that have deservedly become general favourites. Mr. Locker sees the emptiness of life, and pursues like every poet the unattainable ideal, and yet is able to extract a modicum of enjoyment in the pursuit. The knowledge that things ' are not (exactly) what they seem ' is not to be suffered to make him miserable. It cannot, for instance, stop his song—

> ' If life an empty bubble be,
>   How sad for those who cannot see
>   The rainbow in the bubble !'

Whatever may be the case with society in the nineteenth century, or a large portion of it, at any rate there is no *blasé* air in Mr. Locker's verses. To read them makes one cheerful, and causes us to lose the sensation of selfishness and isolation which the individual course of life is apt to create. To write with ease and simplicity strains which shall touch the peasant and the peer is no small achievement, and when the poet attains to that he needs no other *raison d'être.* Some writers have not that airy quicksilver spirit which catches momentary impressions of grace and beauty ; they are too cold and too severe, and hence their works are not adapted to any mood or any person. The true writer of occasional verse has the

advantage of his stronger intellectual brother in this
respect. He never comes amiss; his music is ever
welcome and refreshing. We do not require him to fill
us with awe, to dilate on the grandeur of nature, and to
discuss the great problems of life and mind. We ask
him to speak to us as a brother, to laugh with us as in
the family circle, and, if need be, to mourn with us as a
friend. But this poet of society does not always sing
with the cap and bells on. Now and then, though very
seldom, he must draw from the fount of tears. He will
do it tenderly, but it must be done, for life is not made
up entirely of either the grave or the gay. He knows
that every man has his ' skeleton in the cupboard,' and
there is nothing to be gained in blinking the fact.
Having, therefore, an unpleasant subject to encounter,
but also a most pressing one, this is how he must deal
with it :—

' We hug this phantom we detest,
    We rarely let it cross our portals :
It is a most exacting guest—
    Now, are we not afflicted mortals ?

Your neighbour, Gay, that jovial wight,
    As Dives rich, and brave as Hector—
Poor Gay steals twenty times a night,
    On shaking knees, to see his spectre.

*   *   *   *   *

Ah me, the world ! How fast it spins !
  The beldames dance, the caldron bubbles;
They shriek, and stir it for our sins,
  And we must drain it for our troubles.

We toil, we groan ; the cry for love
  Mounts upwards from the seething city,
And yet I know we have above
  A Father, infinite in pity.'

And thus our poet, in his quiet and unobtrusive manner, becomes a moral teacher. The verses we have just quoted are from Mr. Locker's serious poems, and may serve to correct a very prevalent but erroneous notion respecting his poetry. He has acquired so conspicuous a position as a writer of *vers de société* that people are in the habit of speaking of him as though he never wrote anything else. True, if the scope of this class of verse be vastly widened, and in the manner we have indicated, all he has written would come under the definition. But if the narrow, restricted meaning be taken, then there is a side of Mr. Locker's work which has been completely misapprehended. He manifests a lode of much richer quality than is ever witnessed in mere fugitive verse. Thus in ' The Widow's Mite' there is a vein of genuine pathos :—

    ' A widow—she had only one !
    A puny and decrepit son ;

But, day and night,
Though fretful oft, and weak and small,
A loving child, he was her all—
    The Widow's Mite.

The Widow's Mite—ay, so sustain'd,
She battled onward, nor complain'd
    Though friends were fewer :
And while she toil'd for daily fare
A little crutch upon the stair
    Was music to her.

I saw her then,—and now I see
That, though resign'd and cheerful, she
    Has sorrowed much :
She has, He gave it tenderly,
Much faith ; and carefully laid by,
    A little crutch.'

One other copy of verses we must quote from Mr.
Locker before quitting this portion of his writings. 'The
unrealised Ideal' seems to us not only to be full of a
sweet naturalness, but to catch the very echo of regret
It is not unworthy of Schiller or of Heine :—

'My only love is always near,—
    In country or in town
I see her twinkling feet, I hear
    The whisper of her gown.

She foots it ever fair and young,
    Her locks are tied in haste,
And one is o'er her shoulder flung,
    And hangs below her waist.

She ran before me in the meads ;
　And down this world-worn track
She leads me on ; but while she leads
　She never gazes back.

And yet her voice is in my dreams,
　To witch me more and more ;
That wooing voice ! Ah me, it seems
　Less near me than of yore.

Lightly I sped when hope was high,
　And youth beguil'd the chase,—
I follow, follow still ; but I
　Shall never see her face.'

There is not much visible sign of deterioration in the
public taste when these and similar true and melodious
strains remain popular.　In other respects Mr. Locker
has one of the best gifts which the writer of this class of
verse ought to possess—viz., spontaneity.　We do not
remember any of his pieces which it was in the least
tedious to read.　It does not follow, however, that
verses which have apparently so spontaneous an air have
been written with ease ; on the contrary, they are often
produced with the greatest care, and very seldom given
forth to the world till they have undergone a long process
of elaboration and finish.　The most exquisite lyrics of
the Poet Laureate, those which from their sweet flow
and naturalness seem to have been most readily com-

posed, are really the productions of intense and constant effort.

Of Mr. Locker's humour we have as yet said little, and some reference to it is almost imperative, seeing that it permeates more than three-fourths of what he has written. More than any writer almost he interweaves it with some serious threads, as in the lines on 'A Human Skull'—of which lines, it may be noted, Thackeray had a very exalted opinion :—

'A human skull ! I bought it passing cheap !
   Indeed 'twas dearer to its first employer !
I thought mortality did well to keep
   Some mute memento of the Old Destroyer.

Time was, some may have prized its blooming skin ;
   Her lips were woo'd, perhaps, in transport tender ;
Some may have chuck'd what was a dimpled chin,
   And never had my doubt about its gender !

Did she live yesterday, or ages back ?
   What colour were the eyes when bright and waking ?
And were your ringlets fair, or brown, or black,
   Poor little head ! that long has done with aching ?

It may have held (to shoot some random shots)
   Thy brains, Eliza Fry, or Baron Byron's ;
The wits of Nelly Gwynne, or Doctor Watts—
   Two quoted bards ! two philanthropic sirens ?

But this I trust is clearly understood,
   If man or woman ; if adored or hated ;
Whoever own'd this skull was not so good,
   Not quite so bad as many may have stated.

Who love can need no special type of Death ;
　　He bares his awful face too soon, too often ;
Immortelles bloom in beauty's bridal wreath,
　　And does not yon green elm contain a coffin ?

O true-love mine, what lines of care are these ?
　　The heart still lingers with its golden hours,
But fading tints are on the chestnut trees,
　　And where is all that lavish wealth of flowers ?

The end is near.　Life lacks what once it gave,
　　Yet death has promises that call for praises ;
A very worthless rogue may dig the grave,
　　But hands unseen will dress the turf with daisies.'

Thus we get beaten out for us pure and noble thoughts when the skilled hand turns over the old skull. These verses are worthy of all the praise that has been bestowed upon them, and betoken the possession of a power of secret analysis and comparison. Mark, also, how the writer has contrived, not to suppress the humourous thoughts which divided his brain with those more purely reflective, but simply to veil the humour, so that we see it shining through the sombre substance of the verses.

In a more sprightly vein Mr. Locker sings :—

'　The world's a sorry wench, akin
　　To all that's frail and frightful :
The world's as ugly, ay, as Sin—
　　And almost as delightful !

The world's a merry world (*pro tem.*)
And some are gay, and therefore
It pleases them, but some condemn
The world they do not care for.

The world's an ugly world. Offend
Good people, how they wrangle !
The manners that they never mend,
The characters they mangle !
They eat and drink, and scheme, and plod,
And go to church on Sunday ;
And many are afraid of God—
And more of Mrs. Grundy.'

To Mr. Locker, then, pertain the general excellences of extreme naturalness, simplicity, and fine human feeling, the last of which saturates all his poetry. Praed had more wit and fancy, but Mr. Locker has far more humour and pathos ; and if Praed drew some of his inspiration from Byron and Moore, his successor has been imbued with the sweeter and finer spirit of Wordsworth and Charles Lamb. We consequently get more of the poet's heart in his verse.

Mr. Locker's talent is in harmony with the spirit of the time. He lives so in the age and belongs so much to what is best in its society that he may fairly be remembered and quoted hereafter as a representative of the period. His earnestness and sincerity are very marked characteristics, and the genuineness of his song will

provide against its extinction.   His fancy is chaste and
selective, his wit delicate, his style polished and graceful,
and it is possible that some of his light fabrics may
outlive more stately and solid edifices.

A word remains to be said of other living writers of
this class, but there is little that merits a lengthened
detention.   Just as a passing reference must suffice for
second-rate writers in generations which have recently
expired—Haynes Bayly, the Hon. W. R. Spencer,
Maginn, and others—so must a few sentences suffice for
their successors.   Yet, as we pass them by, we must
reserve a place for the songs of Mrs. Arkwright, whose
exquisite voice still vibrates in the ear, whilst some
couplets of her composition linger in the memory.
The following lines of hers may be new to many
readers :—

> ' I used to love the Winter cold,
>   And when my daily task was done
> To roll the snowy ball, and hold
>   My crystal daggers in the sun.
> How beautiful, how bright !
> How soon they melt away,
> Till drop by drop they vanish quite—
>   Ah ! well a day !
>
> And then the Spring, the smiling Spring,
>   The flowers, the fruit, the murmuring rill !

To chase the shadows o'er the hill
And dance within the fairy ring.
Ye flowers so bright and gay
Within the garden wall,
Ye'll meet again all smiling, all—
  Ah ! well a day !

Untir'd the Summer's heat to bear,
Beneath the flow'ry load to bend,
The mimic banquet to prepare,
And share it with some joyous friend !
How soon the day is done—
The longest summer day !
'Tis morn—'tis noon—'tis set of sun—
  Ah ! well a day !'

The most promising of the younger writers of minor verse is Mr. Austin Dobson, whose 'Vignettes in Rhyme' betoken considerable poetic fancy, though his wit is far inferior to that of Mr. Locker.[1] The succeeding stanzas, which are a fair example of Mr. Dobson's style, are taken from his poem suggested by a chapter in Mr. Theodore Martin's ' Horace : '—

[1] It is but fair to Mr. Dobson to say that I regard him as something more than a writer simply of fugitive verse. There is a distinct poetic vein in his work which should lead to something more ambitious than he has yet accomplished. He is not profound, but graceful. His more serious verses are the best of those which he has yet done, and should suggest to him his *métier*. He may yet prove a sweet and genial, though not a lofty and impassioned, singer.

'" HORATIUS FLACCUS, B.C. 8,"
    There's not a doubt about the date,—
        You're dead and buried :
    As you remarked, the seasons roll ;
    And 'cross the Styx full many a soul
        Has Charon ferried,
    Since, mourned of men and Muses nine,
    They laid you on the Esquiline.

            *   *   *   *   *

    Ours is so far-advanced an age !
    Sensation tales, a classic stage,
        Commodious villas !
    We boast high art, an Albert Hall,
    Australian meat, and men who call
        Their sires gorillas !
    We have a thousand things, you see,
    Not dreamt in your philosophy.

            *   *   *   *   *

    Science proceeds, and man stands still ;
    Our " world " to-day's as good or ill,—
        As cultured (nearly),
    As yours was, Horace ! You alone,
    Unmatched, unmet, we have not known.'

The author of the ' Carols of Cockayne' is deserving of
mention for his humour and observation—he also ought to
have given us more good work than he has done ; but
the clever writer of 'The Bab Ballads' scarcely comes
under our category ; his effusions partake too much of
the character of broad farce. Mr. Calverley, again,

whose parodies are very close and really brilliant, belongs
to that school whose best exponents were James and
Horace Smith, the incomparable authors of ' Rejected
Addresses.' Mr. Mortimer Collins is a much nearer
approach to what we require, but he has by no means
done such good work as was expected of him. Lord
Lytton's ' Fables in Song ' deserve to occupy a higher
rank in poetry than such lyrics as form the basis of our
reflections. They are full of thought—sometimes over-
burdened with it ; but they have a graceful facility of
versification which entitles their author to rank with many
of our cultivated poets.

The question may be asked, of what use is this
Horatian poetry ? but we apprehend it will be its own
justification in the eyes of most lovers of the poetic art.
The brooklet is not so imposing as the mighty river to
which it is tributary, but its music may be as sweet and
true. Men cannot always be climbing the magnificent
passes of the Alps, but in the absence of sublime scenery
does not the trimly cut and ordered garden present many
points of attraction ? Thus, all singers have their proper
seasons and uses. The minor poets unquestionably
flourish best in seasons of national prosperity, not in
those of stirring events. They are satisfied with what
the world has to offer them, though in the best of them

there is a strain of genuine regret, testifying that this is not sufficient to satisfy the cravings of the soul. In all the excellent writers of Venusian verse whom we have named may be perceived the shade of melancholy, which lends an additional charm to their gaiety. With the deeper questions of the heart they very rarely intermeddle. If they can touch the springs of laughter and emotion in others they receive their reward. These poets, however, have yet something to learn : England has its Shakspeare but not its Horace. To write Horatian verse successfully requires all the earnestness and devotion which the greater poet exhibits in another field. But even these trifles are not without their use and their charm, for they may be accepted by posterity as a faithful commentary upon contemporaneous events, life, and manners. Who knows but that through their aid in some distant era the stranger in our deserted gates may obtain some glimpses of our nineteenth-century civilisation ; just as we now, with Horace or Martial for our friend and guide, may walk through the streets, and converse with the denizens, of ancient Rome ?

LORENZO de' MEDICI, the Magnificent. By ALFRED

VON REUMONT. Translated from the German by ROBERT HARRISON. 2 vols. demy 8vo.

MEMOIRS of CAMILLE DESMOULINS. Translated

from the French. With a Steel Portrait.

The PROSE WORKS of SYDNEY DOBELL. Edited

by JOHN NICHOL, M.A., LL.D., Professor of English Literature in Glasgow University.

HOURS in a LIBRARY. By LESLIE STEPHEN. Crown

8vo. 9s.

'This book contains much acute and thoughtful writing, and not a little of a yet rarer quality—wit.'—*Saturday Review.* 'Good taste, sound judgment, competent knowledge; these literary virtues are evident throughout, and will attract and please the reader.'—*Spectator.* 'Good, plain, solid reasoning.'—*Westminster Review.* 'Very interesting literary studies.'—*John Bull.* 'The author is a true lover of books, and always estimates them, whether new or old, at their genuine value.'—*Standard.*

The BORDERLAND of SCIENCE. By R. A. PROCTOR,

B.A., Author of 'Light Science for Leisure Hours.' Large crown 8vo. with Portrait of the Author, 10s. 6d.

'A really valuable and interesting book.'—*Saturday Review.* 'As a populariser of science, Mr. Proctor deserves to rank with Huxley and Owen.'—*Scotsman.*

RENAISSANCE in ITALY: Age of the Despots. By

JOHN ADDINGTON SYMONDS, M.A., Author of 'Studies of Greek Poets.' Demy 8vo 16s.

'A historical student of the Italian Renaissance must henceforth apply himself to the history which Mr. Symonds has written.'—*Westminster Review.*
'A learned and thoughtful book.'—*Spectator.*

On ACTORS and the ART of ACTING. By GEORGE

HENRY LEWES. Crown 8vo. 7s. 6d.

'A collection of dramatic criticisms by a writer of great and well-deserved reputation.'—*Saturday Review.*
'Under any circumstances, and at any time, the essays would be ready with avidity and will be certain to be found on the shelves of all dramatic libraries.'—*Era.*

Second Edition, crown 8vo. 5s.

A GARDEN of WOMEN. By SARAH TYTLER, Author of

'Citoyenne Jacqueline' &c.

'The stories are told with graphic sprightliness and with a grace and delicacy of touch.'—*Academy.*
'Graceful and pleasant.....Eminently suited for autumn and holiday reading.'
Examiner.

SHAKESPEARE COMMENTARIES. By Dr. G. G.

GERVINUS, Professor at Heidelberg. Translated under the Author's superintendence, by F. E. BUNNÈTT. New and Cheap Edition, thoroughly revised, by the Translator. With a Preface by F. J. FURNIVALL, Esq. Demy 8vo. 14s.

'There is, of course, no necessity to formally recommend such a well-known work. We merely say that Mr. Furnivall's Introduction gives it a new value.'
Westminster Review.
'It is to the pages of the learned Gervinus that the lovers of Shakespeare should go if they want to see an intellectual apotheosis of his genius.'—*Daily Telegraph.*

London: SMITH, ELDER, & CO., 15 Waterloo Place.

www.ingramcontent.com/pod-product-compliance
Lightning Source LLC
Chambersburg PA
CBHW021327110726
47900CB00005B/1379